Budgeting for Women's Rights

Monitoring
Government Budgets
for Compliance with CEDAW

Diane Elson

**Department of Sociology, University of Essex, UK and
Levy Economics Institute, Bard College, USA**

United Nations Development Fund for Women

Acknowledgments

I want in particular to thank Nisreen Alami (UNIFEM, New York), and Meg Satterthwaite and Jayne Huckerby (both of Center for Human Rights and Global Justice, New York University School of Law). Nisreen Alami commissioned this study and gave insightful comments on several drafts, based on her leadership of UNIFEM's programme on gender responsive budgeting. Meg Satterthwaite and Jayne Huckerby gave extensive comments relating to human rights law and procedures, and Jayne Huckerby contributed additional research that greatly strengthened the report.

I would also like to thank Debbie Budlender (Community Agency for Social Inquiry, Cape Town) who provided extensive and valuable comments based on her unparalleled knowledge of Gender Budget Initiatives in developing countries. Thanks also to Elissa Braunstein, Professor of Economics at Colorado State University, for comments on the macroeconomics of the budget.

For their guidance on human rights obligations, I also want to thank Lee Waldorf (UNIFEM, New York) and Margot Salomon (Human Rights Centre, University of Essex). Thanks to Lisa Phillips (Osgoode Hall Law School, York University, Toronto) for comments on tax law.

I also want to thank all the many people engaged in Gender Budget Initiatives in many parts of the world whose work I have drawn on in writing this report, including the UK Women's Budget Group, of which I am a member.

Diane Elson, January 2006

A note on the author

Diane Elson is a professor at the University of Essex, U.K. and Senior Scholar and Co-director of the Levy Economics Institute's program on Gender Equality and the Economy. Her research interests include gender and fiscal policy, and gender and international trade. Elson's recent publications comprise: "The Social Content of Macroeconomic Policies" (with N. Çagatay), World Development, July 2000; Gender Budgets Make Cents (with D. Budlender, G. Hewitt, and T. Mukhopadhyay), Commonwealth Secretariat, London, 2002; Progress of the World's Women 2002 (with H. Keklik), UNIFEM, New York, 2002; "Engendering Government Budgets in the Context of Globalization(s)", International Feminist Journal of Politics, 6(4), 2004.

Diane Elson has been included as one of the 50 key thinkers in a new book edited by David Simon, "Fifty Key Thinkers on Development", Routledge, 2005. Elson was a member of the U.N. Millennium Project Taskforce and the Advisory Committee for UNRISD Policy Report on Gender and Development; and vice-president, International Association for Feminist Economics. From 1998 to 2000, she served as Special Advisor to the Executive Director of UNIFEM. Her academic degrees include a B.A. in philosophy, politics, and economics from the University of Oxford, and a Ph.D. in economics from the University of Manchester.

i

Contents

Boxes

The advocacy work on transparency of budgets and the need for accountability to human rights has changed the way budgeting is carried out. Budgeting is no longer viewed as an exclusive exercise that is carried out by ministries of finance, but rather a process that entails aligning national development plans and goals and human rights commitments with budget policies in a transparent and coherent manner. Budgeting is not only an exercise that seeks to balance income and revenue but one that ought to utilize available resources in an efficient, effective and equitable manner to address needs and achieve aspired development goals.

People's access to services and resources are determined by how budgets are formulated. Discrimination can either be reinforced or eliminated by budget policies. Therefore, budget actors are mandated to situate people's rights at the core of their policies.

Gender responsive budgeting requires a participatory and transparent process, an equitable base and a non-discriminatory rationale. It also requires that women are not regarded as a vulnerable group who are the beneficiaries of government assistance but rather as rights holders, whose governments are under obligation to empower and protect.

This report adds a landmark to our thinking around budgets and women's rights. Political statements and legislation alone will not increase access to services, resources and rights. Progress towards human rights entails monetary investment and a constant scrutiny of economic policies from a rights perspective. Accountability to women's rights needs to be translated into mobilizing the necessary resources to meet the commitments made by the ratification of CEDAW.

This report provides a framework for applying a rights-approach to budgets from a gender perspective that defines the requirements of good budget performance in the planning, formulation and execution stages. It also details the elements that require a critical assessment of budget policy making processes, the appropriateness of budget allocations, and the standard principles for non-discriminatory economic and budgets policies.

This report is timely in the context of discussions on aid effectiveness and new aid modalities. It responds to the challenge of implementation and the need for more concrete measures to be undertaken to increase accountability and ensure the achievement of the MDGs.

Gender equality advocates have increasingly used gender budget analysis tools to identify existing gender gaps and biases in budget allocation, spending and revenue raising measures. The report uses examples of such work to illustrate the relevance of the rights based approach to gender budgeting.

It gives me great pleasure to introduce this publication entitled *"Budgeting for Women's Rights: Monitoring Government Budgets for Compliance with CEDAW"* authored by Professor Diane Elson, a leading feminist economist. By supporting this work, UNIFEM is hoping that it would prove useful to policy makers, gender advocates, human rights advocates and inform the work of the CEDAW Committee as they review country reports

Noeleen Heyzer
Executive Director

Until recently the domains of human rights and government budgets have been treated separately, with separate sets of actors (both state and non-state) dealing with each, each with their different forms of expertise and practice. That is now changing.

There is growing collaboration between civil society groups working on budget analysis and those working on human rights (Schultz, 2002).

Those concerned with the rights of the child have begun to examine government budgets (Creamer, 2002; Gore and Minujin, 2003; Robinson and Biersteker, 1997; Streak and Wehner, 2002).

Some of those involved in Gender Budget Initiatives (GBIs) have framed their work in the context of women's social and economic rights (Budlender, 2003; Hofbauer, 2000; Pearl, 2002; SAGE,1999; Vargas-Valente, 2002).

This report builds on the efforts cited above to develop some ideas that may be useful in monitoring the compliance of government budgets with the Convention on the Elimination of All Forms of Discrimination Against Women (CEDAW) (for the text of this Convention, see Appendix 1). This report covers four dimensions of government budgets:
- expenditure
- revenue
- macroeconomics of the budget
- budget decision-making processes.

This report does not aim to provide separate guidelines for each article of CEDAW. Rather, it discusses the broad implications of the obligation on States Parties to CEDAW and other international human rights treaties to ensure that there is no *de facto* discrimination, as well as no *de jure* discrimination; and to ensure the full development and advancement of women, so that they enjoy 'human rights and fundamental freedoms on a basis of equality with men' (Article 3).

The report aims to clarify:
- how gender budget analysis can help in monitoring compliance with CEDAW;
- how CEDAW can help to set criteria for what constitutes gender equality in budgetary matters and provide guidance for GBIs.

By 2002, in up to 50 countries in all parts of the world, in the North as well as South, there had been some kind of GBI (Budlender and Hewitt, 2002:8). However, some of these amounted to no more than a sensitization workshop, while others were dormant and a few had come to an end. The most effective have produced some institutionalization of gender equality concerns in one or more stages of the budget cycle in one or more Ministries, or resulted in an ongoing public scrutiny of the budget from a gender equality perspective.

Few of these GBIs have been explicitly developed as ways of promoting the realization of CEDAW obligations. Most have primarily been concerned with making gender visible in budgetary polices and processes. Some have implicitly used a rights-based approach, in the sense that they have been concerned with the treatment of women as autonomous citizens, and with the transformation of traditional gender roles so as to achieve substantive equality between women and men. Many have important lessons that are useful for clarifying how gender analysis of government budgets can help in monitoring, and securing compliance, with CEDAW. This report draws on these lessons and goes one step further to set out what it means to take an explicit rights-based approach to government budgets. A rights-based approach to the gender-analysis of budgets enables us to: identify gender inequalities in budget processes, allocations and outcomes; and assess what States are obliged to do to address these inequalities.

UNIFEM is supporting a variety of GBI activities, including initiatives in the following countries:

Latin America: Belize, Brazil, Bolivia, Chile, Ecuador, Mexico, Peru

Sub-Saharan Africa: Kenya, Mozambique, Nigeria, Senegal, United Republic of Tanzania, Uganda

Asia: Afghanistan, India, Nepal, the Philippines, Sri Lanka

North Africa: Egypt, Morocco.

CEDAW requires that the raising and spending of public money be non-discriminatory and consistent with substantive equality between women and men, as autonomous possessors of rights. This implies that a gender perspective on budgets should be primarily concerned with the direct benefits from, and contributions to, government budgets that women and men get as persons in their own right. For instance, women do tend to benefit indirectly from health and education services that go to their sons, husbands and fathers; but that does not justify a smaller share of public expenditure on heath services going directly to women than directly to men.

However, equality does not necessarily imply identical treatment of men and women. Instead, CEDAW recognizes that non-identical treatment is necessary under certain circumstances to address the biological and socially constructed differences between men and women (CEDAW, General Recommendation 25, para. 8). For example, CEDAW provides for:

- General measures to improve the position of women and to guarantee their full enjoyment of economic, social and cultural rights, e.g. the different social roles currently assigned to men and women means that to ensure equal access to services such as housing, sanitation, electricity and water supply and transport and communications (as required by Article 14(g)), services must be designed and delivered with the differing needs of women and men in mind.
- Adoption of temporary special measures to accelerate the achievement of *de facto* (or substantive) equality between women and men (Article 4(1)), e.g. measures to accelerate equal participation in politics by women. Such measures are in place until their desired outcomes are realized and have been sustained for a period of time (CEDAW, General Recommendation 25, para. 20).
- Permanent gender-specific special measures necessitated by biological difference (Art. 4(2)). These measures include maternity health care services (Art. 12(2)). Such measures last until their review is required by the scientific and technological knowledge referred to in Article 11(3) (CEDAW, General Recommendation 25, para. 16).

CEDAW not only requires governments to assess how women compare with men, as beneficiaries of and contributors to government budgets. It also clearly sets out three State obligations that must be central in efforts to eliminate discrimination against women in government budgets (CEDAW, General Recommendations 25, para. 6). These obligations are to ensure:

- relevant laws and policies do not discriminate (directly or indirectly) against women in either form or effect and to provide protection against discrimination;
- improvement of women's *de facto* (or substantive) equality; and
- programmes of which women are beneficiaries and the revenue systems to which they contribute, transform relations and stereotypes that inhibit women's enjoyment of substantive equality.

Other key obligations include the requirement that the government secure women's participation as active citizens in decisions about budgets and their ability to hold governments to account for the way in which public money is raised and spent.

This report is addressed to a broad audience, including:

- members of the CEDAW Committee
- government departments drawing up periodic reports to the CEDAW committee
- NGOs drawing up shadow reports to the CEDAW committee
- gender budget analysts
- members of legislatures, especially those on budget committees
- officials and ministers concerned with budgetary policy
- human rights advocates and analysts concerned about budget analysis under the other major human rights treaties.

The report is divided into nine sections:

Section 1 provides the overall context by setting out some general features of budgetary processes and human rights processes, and some examples of the involvement of human rights treaty bodies with budgetary matters.

Section 2 discusses some examples of analysis of public expenditure from a human rights perspective and draws some conclusions that may be helpful for the application of gender budget analysis to monitoring compliance with CEDAW.

Section 3 sets out the key implications of CEDAW for government budgets and discusses the engagement of the CEDAW reporting mechanism with government budgets.

Section 4 provides a brief guide to GBIs, emphasizing their variety in aims and forms of organization. It draws a distinction between making gender visible in budgets and analysing budgets for compliance with CEDAW.

Section 5 draws upon examples of gender budget analysis to consider how public expenditure might be monitored for compliance with CEDAW.

Section 6 draws upon examples of gender budget analysis to consider how public revenue might be monitored for compliance with CEDAW.

Section 7 draws upon examples of gender budget analysis to consider how the macroeconomics of the budget might be monitored for compliance with CEDAW.

Section 8 draws upon examples of gender budget analysis to consider how budget decision-making might be monitored for compliance with CEDAW.

Section 9 presents the key conclusions and recommendations.

Section 1

Government Budgets and Human Rights:
Some General Considerations

Government Budgets and Human Rights: Some General Considerations

This report brings together two areas of activity that are usually considered separately: government budgets and human rights. This section sets out some key features of both, and considers their interactions.

1.1 Key features of government budgets

Government budgets set out the levels and types of expenditure the government plans to make, and the ways that it plans to finance this expenditure. Expenditure is usually broken down into:
- *debt-servicing charges;* and
- expenditure on government activities.

In poor, highly indebted countries, payment of interest on foreign debt often exceeds expenditure on public services.

The expenditure on government activities is generally presented in a number of ways:
- by *administrative agency*, specifying how much money each Ministry or public sector agency would be allowed to spend in the coming financial year;
- by *economic function*, breaking down total expenditure into a *current account* (e.g. salaries and consumables, such as paper and telephone calls), and a *capital account* (e.g. equipment, such as computers and construction of buildings and other infrastructure);
- by *programme*, specifying the type of activities to be funded (e.g. primary health care, hospitals, medical research); recently, this has been further elaborated in some countries, both rich and poor, to a system of '*performance-oriented budgeting*' in which there are targets and performance indicators for each programme (Sharp, 2003).

The programmes typically include those providing:
- services, such as education
- income transfers, such as child benefits or pensions
- subsidies, such as food subsidies or fertilizer subsidies
- infrastructure, such as roads and water and sanitation systems.

The revenue side of the budget sets out the amount of revenue the government expects to raise from taxation; charges for public services (user fees); sales of public assets (including privatization); and development cooperation grants. Methods of taxation include:
- direct taxes, such as income tax and corporation tax
- indirect taxes, such as Value Added Tax (VAT) and import duties (tariffs).

The flow of revenue does not match the flow of expenditure over time, and so managing the budget always entails governments borrowing, from their own citizens and from overseas investors. This generates an inflow of funds, but entails future expenditure obligations to pay interest and repay debt. Government borrowing is a normal part of fiscal policy. But the appropriate level of government borrowing is a controversial issue. Some economists argue that over the financial year, the government budget should be balanced, with expenditures, including debt service, held to the level of revenue raised. Others argue this is too restrictive and does not allow governments to take action to offset the ups and downs of economic activity. While it is true that a government cannot go on increasing a budget deficit without eventually running into problems like high rates of inflation, there is a variety of views about what the limits to budget deficits should be. This issue is further discussed in Section 7.

The budget process consists of four stages:
- formulation of proposals for financial allocations and revenue raising measures;
- presentation of the budget for approval to elected representatives, followed by legislation to enact the budget;
- implementation, including collection of taxes and other revenues; disbursement of funds and delivery of programmes;
- audit of use of funds and evaluation of performance.

This sequence of decisions is further discussed in Section 8.

Government budgets entail both legal and moral claims and obligations. The budget itself comes into force through the passing of a budget law. The government has an obligation to ensure that the budget law (as with any new law) is consistent with the standards to which the government is legally bound, including human rights law. It is the totality of domestic and international law that enables government to make claims on people and businesses to pay taxes, and to pay charges for use of public services. The budget also provides legally enforceable obligations on governments to pay creditors; to pay pensions to retired government employees; and to meet the costs of programmes to which some sections of the public have a statutory entitlement, such as social insurance schemes.

Budgets also entail moral claims and obligations, resting on social and political norms about willingness to pay taxes, and expectations of what kinds of social protection governments should provide (for instance, universal schemes which involve everyone or targeted schemes that reach only particular social groups). Thus Government budgets rest upon what has been described as a 'fiscal covenant':
> 'the basic socio-political agreement that legitimizes the role of the State and establishes the areas and scope of government responsibility in the economic and social spheres' (ECLAC, 1998:1).

Government budgets affect people in multiple ways: their primary impact is through distributing resources to people via expenditure and claiming resources from them via tax and other measures. They also have secondary impacts via their impacts on job creation, economic growth and inflation. Drawing up a budget entails consideration of how to balance the different claims and obligations; how to balance total expenditure, total revenue and government borrowing, so as to avoid high rates of inflation on the one hand and economic stagnation or recession on the other. This means setting priorities and considering costs; and trying to make the most effective use of resources. It is not possible to meet all the demands that citizens make about revenue and expenditures. Choices have to be made about which ones will be met in any given year. Budgets are always constrained by legal claims and obligations and by the moral claims and obligations inherent in the fiscal covenant.

1.2 Key features of human rights—general

The international human rights law that is legally binding on States comes from two main sources: customary international law and treaties. The focus of this report will be on treaty law.

The main instruments relating to human rights have traditionally been the Universal Declaration of Human Rights (1948) (UDHR) and the two treaties, the International Covenant on Civil and Political Rights (1966) (and its two Optional Protocols), and the International Covenant on Economic, Social and Cultural Rights (1966). However, there are another five key human rights treaties that form international human rights law:
- Convention on the Elimination of All Forms of Racial Discrimination (1966);
- Convention on the Elimination of All Forms of Discrimination against Women (CEDAW) (1979) and the Optional Protocol to the Convention (1999);
- Convention against Torture and Other Forms of Cruel, Inhuman or Degrading Treatment or Punishment (1984);
- Convention on the Rights of the Child (1989) and its two Optional Protocols; and
- Convention on the Protection of the Rights of All Migrant Workers and Their Families (1990).

What are the treaty monitoring bodies?
The treaty monitoring bodies consist of independent experts who monitor the implementation of each of the seven core human rights treaties mentioned above.

What are their functions?
- *Consideration of States Parties' reports* and *issuing Concluding Observations* (or concluding comments in the case of the CEDAW Committee);
- *Consideration of individual complaints or communications* claiming that the State has violated their rights by the Human Rights Committee, the Committee on the Elimination of Racial Discrimination, the CEDAW Committee, the Committee against Torture and *issuing views or decisions*;
- *Conduct of inquiries* by the Committee against Torture and CEDAW Committee if they have received reliable information containing well-founded indications of serious, grave or systematic violations of the conventions;
- *Issuing General Comments or Recommendations* providing guidance on how to interpret the treaty's provisions;
- *Holding days of General Discussion* on particular themes; and
- *Convening meetings of States Parties and meetings with States Parties.*

While the treaty-monitoring bodies do not have the power to enforce their observations when a State fails to comply with their treaty obligations, their recommendations and guidance to States is viewed as authoritative.

Box 1 Treaty-monitoring bodies
(Office of the High Commissioner for Human Rights, Fact Sheet 30.)

Indeed, both the potential uses and limits of the treaties and their monitoring bodies need to be acknowledged. As illustrated in Box 2 (see page 12), the international human rights reporting mechanism provides an invaluable arena for 'naming and shaming' and for identifying good practice but does not have at its disposal sanctions to secure enforcement. The limitations of enforcement mechanisms were recognized at a conference in Mexico in 2002 on using public budgets as tools to advance economic and social rights. Both human rights activists and citizens' budget watchdog groups expressed concern about the limitations of human rights treaties with respect to government budgets. As the conference report puts it:

'the human rights accords … lack sufficient specificity and teeth to force governments to act. Especially in the field of ESC rights and their progressive realization, the field needs more and adequate effective mechanisms to measure progress in a concrete way and to force a response to violations of these rights' (Schultz, 2002:20).

These issues of effective enforcement can be examined more closely by looking to the circumstances in which, and the means by which, human rights constitute legally binding obligations in domestic decision-making.

1.2.2 Circumstances in which human rights are binding legal obligations in domestic decision-making

There are three broad scenarios in which human rights constitute (to varying degrees) legal obligations in domestic budget decision-making: first, where human rights principles (e.g. the prohibition on discrimination) feature in national laws or Constitutions without necessarily being formally derived from what we would describe as international human rights laws or mechanisms; second, where human rights treaties form part of domestic law; and third, where human rights treaties do not constitute part of the domestic legal system.

The National Action Committee on the Status of Women joined together with other Canadian NGOs, such as the Charter Committee on Poverty Issues and the National Anti-Poverty Organisation, to make representations to the ICESCR Committee, requesting that the government of Canada be called to account to explain how the 1995 Budget Implementation Act (BIA) was consistent with the terms of the International Covenant on Economic, Social and Cultural Rights. In a submission in November 1996, the coalition of NGOs stated that:

> '[The BIA] represents, in the opinion of our organizations and many other experts in Canada, the most serious retrogressive measure ever taken in Canada with respect to the legislative protection of the right to an adequate standard of living. On April 1, 1996, Canada was transformed from a country in which the right to adequate financial assistance for persons in need was a legal requirement, enforceable in court by individuals affected, to one in which there is no federal legislation recognizing this right or providing any means of enforcing it.' (Quoted in Day and Brodsky, 1998:114.)

> The Committee on Economic, Social and Cultural Rights did subsequently call upon the government of Canada to provide an account in its third periodic report in 1998. The Concluding Observations of the Committee included the judgment that the BIA, by replacing the Canada Assistance Plan with the Canada Health and Social Transfer 'entails a range of adverse consequences for the enjoyment of covenant rights by disadvantaged groups in Canada' (para. 19) and specifically noted that this had had a particularly harsh impact on women (para. 23). (United Nations, Committee on Economic, Social and Cultural Rights, 1998. UN Doc E/C.12/1Add. 31.)

However, this did not bring about a change of policy in Canada.

Box 2 Human rights and the Canadian Budget Implementation Act 1995

The first scenario is quite straightforward. For example, where a Constitution provides for non-discrimination, this obligation should guide all elements of the budget process and any infringement thereof will provide the basis for a challenge to the budget. Depending on the particularities of the national system, this should enable individuals or groups to sue to hold the government to account for a rights-based approach to decision-making.

In the second scenario (where treaties do form part of the domestic law), the extent to and manner in which treaties can be relied upon will depend on factors such as the relationship between national and international law in that country (Byrnes, 2003).

In the third scenario (cases where international norms do not form part of domestic law) these norms may still have an indirect impact on the domestic decision-making (e.g. to help the exercise of administrative discretion) (Byrnes, 1996).

It is clear from all three of these scenarios that human rights are relevant to budget formation and implementation, no matter how the domestic legal system is set up to incorporate human rights law.

Further, in addition to the legal obligations imposed by human rights, the discourse of human rights also can facilitate a rights-based approach to government budgets, as it enables us to position people who are undervalued, who suffer discrimination, disadvantage and exclusion as active agents, claiming what is rightfully theirs. The worst that an economist can say of a government's budget is that it is 'imprudent', 'unsound', 'unsustainable', 'inefficient', while the human rights advocate can say that it violates human rights; and this may apply even if the budget is 'prudent', 'sound', 'sustainable' and 'efficient'. In this way, the discourse of human rights can make an important contribution to the politics of budgets. Budgets are necessarily political documents, as well as instruments of economic policy (Norton and Elson, 2002). In the words of Pregs Govender, former chair of the South African Parliamentary Committee on the Improvement of the Quality of Life and Status of Women, 'The budget reflects the values of a country—who it values, whose work it values and who it rewards … and who and what and whose work it doesn't' (Budlender, ed, 1996:7). But to have a stronger political impact, such advocacy needs to be backed by detailed analysis of how budget resources are raised and allocated and who benefits from them; by detailed analysis of what it would cost to realize rights that are currently unrealized; and by analysis of how the funding could be found to meet these costs. Three examples of such analysis are discussed in Section 2.

1.2.3 State obligations under international human rights law: Respect, Protect, Fulfill

International human rights law places upon States Parties the duty to respect, protect and fulfill human rights. The duty to respect means that States must not violate those rights themselves; the duty to protect means that States must protect those rights against violation by others; the duty to fulfill means that States must take affirmative steps to ensure full enjoyment of human rights. The obligation to fulfill human rights in turn gives rise to obligations to facilitate, provide and promote human rights. In the context of gender and budgets, the obligation to fulfill can require a State to adopt temporary special measures, gender audits and gender-specific allocation of resources (CESCR, General Comment 16, para. 21).

1.3 General State obligations relating to gender, budgets and resource allocations

1.3.1 Introduction: CEDAW as part of the larger human rights framework

CEDAW clearly sets out a number of general principles (e.g. non-discrimination and equality) that are binding on States in the decisions they make about budgets. The fact that the exact meaning of these principles in specific contexts is not detailed in the Convention does not mean that States are entitled to act without regard to human rights standards. Often human rights conventions are intentionally drafted at a level of generality that excludes specific mention of myriad governmental functions, and inferences should not be drawn from these silences. Instead, the detailed parameters of human rights obligations are often developed through a number of different practices. In this regard, the Committee on the Elimination of Discrimination Against Women has indicated that CEDAW is a 'dynamic' document requiring ongoing efforts to clarify and understand the implications of its provisions (CEDAW, General Recommendation 25, para. 3). What this means in the context of the current report is that the precise implications of CEDAW for budgeting processes is an unfolding area of law and the fact that there are sometimes unanswered questions does not mean that there are no standards binding on the State. For example, CEDAW makes no *specific* reference to the budgetary resources required for its implementation, but it does impose the *general obligation* on States Parties to take 'all appropriate measures' to eliminate discrimination against women. On this basis it is clear that where the failure of the State to allocate appropriate resources is frustrating effective implementation of the Convention, it has failed to comply. Further, despite the absence of a specific reference to resources in the Convention, the Committee has indicated that States have obligations to use budgetary measures to fulfill women's equality. For example, the Committee has explained that the duty to fulfill Article 12 of the Convention (relating to women and health) involves an obligation on States Parties to take, *inter alia*, budgetary measures to the maximum extent of resources to ensure that women realize their right to equality in health care (General Recommendation 24, para. 17).

CEDAW is part of a comprehensive framework for the implementation of human rights. As mentioned above, it contains the guarantees of non-discrimination (Article 2) and equality (Article 3), which apply not only to all of the rights protected by the Convention, but also have broader application. In fact, it is important to note that CEDAW is a *non-discrimination* treaty, meaning that it does not – on its own – create specific substantive rights guarantees. Instead, it sets out clear standards requiring States to pursue women's equality in all spheres. Article 2 applies generically to 'discrimination against women' (Article 2) and Article 3 requires State action to ensure equality in 'all fields, in particular in the political, social, economic and cultural fields' (Article 3). Taken together, these articles impose an obligation on States Parties to ensure equal enjoyment of *all* rights guaranteed by the State – including substantive civil and political, and economic, social and cultural rights set out in the ICCPR and the ICESCR respectively, as well as all the rights guaranteed in a given State's domestic law.

The ICCPR and the ICESCR also contain guarantees of non-discrimination and gender equality. In its recent General Comment 16, the Committee on Economic, Social and Cultural Rights refers to the definition of discrimination provided in Article 1 of CEDAW in interpreting the meaning of the treaty's gender equality provision, and confirms that (like CEDAW) Article 3 of ICESCR requires substantive equality. It also indicates that Articles 2(1) and 3 of the ICESCR are not 'stand-alone' provisions but instead apply to each specific right guaranteed in the Covenant (para. 2). In some instances (especially where CEDAW is less specific than other treaties, and when trying to determine the content of substantive rights binding on a specific State) it is both legitimate and necessary to have resort to other instruments. This is especially true with respect to resource allocation, a subject about which States often seek guidance; the ICESCR is an important source of substantive obligations concerning resource allocation.

Another relevant instrument is the Convention on the Rights of the Child, which covers girls and young women below the age of 18 or a lower age of majority as determined by the State. The CRC explicitly refers to the resources needed for its implementation in Article 4:

'States Parties shall undertake all appropriate legislative, administrative and other measures for the implementation of the rights recognized in the present Convention. With regard to economic, social and cultural rights, States Parties shall undertake such measures to the maximum extent of their available resources, and where needed, within the framework of international cooperation'.

The Committee on the Rights of the Child has frequently commented on budgetary allocations in its responses to States Parties' reports. For example, it has expressed concern at insufficient budgetary allocations; decreases in spending; and the lack of disaggregated data on budgeting allocations for rights-implementation. (See e.g. on Israel, United Nations, Committee on the Rights of the Child, 2002, UN Doc. CRC/C/15/Add.195; and on Sri Lanka, United Nations, Committee on the Rights of the Child, 2003, para. 18, UN Doc. CRC/C/15/Add.207.)

In light of the relationship between CEDAW and the broader human rights framework, the rest of this section briefly identifies the core requirements of non-discrimination and equality under CEDAW; outlines key principles on resource allocation as developed under ICESCR; and considers how the requirements of non-discrimination and equality relate to each of these principles.

1.3.2 Non-discrimination

CEDAW prohibits discrimination against women[1] in all its forms and obligates States to condemn this discrimination and take steps 'by all appropriate means and without delay' to pursue a policy of eliminating this discrimination (Article 2). Article 2 of CEDAW also sets out steps that a State Party must take to eliminate this discrimination, including adopting appropriate legislative and other measures. In terms of budgets, this means, for example, that neither the expenditure nor the revenue side of the budget should discriminate against women in the provision of access to rights. This does not only mean the absence of a discriminatory legal framework, but also means that policies must not be discriminatory in effect. This will be discussed further in Section 3.

1.3.3 Equality

Furthermore, Article 3 of CEDAW imposes the requirement to ensure equality between men and women in relation to all human rights, in particular in the political, social, economic and cultural fields. The full meaning of equality will be explored further in Section 3; however, it suffices at this point to note that CEDAW requires that States achieve both substantive and formal equality and recognizes that formal equality alone is insufficient for a State to meet its affirmative obligation to achieve substantive equality between men and women (CEDAW, General Recommendation 25, para. 8).

---

[1] Defined in Article 1 as follows: 'For the purposes of the present Convention, the term "discrimination against women" shall mean any distinction, exclusion or restriction made on the basis of sex which has the effect or purpose of impairing or nullifying the recognition, enjoyment or exercise by women, irrespective of their marital status, on a basis of equality of men and women, of human rights and fundamental freedoms in the political, economic, social, cultural, civil or any other field'.

1.3.4 'Progressive realization'

The ICESCR specifies that States Parties have the obligation of 'achieving progressively the full realization of the rights recognized in the present Covenant' 'to the maximum of available resources'. This obligation does recognize that the resources at the disposition of a government are not unlimited and that fulfilling economic, social and cultural rights will take time. At the same time the concept of 'progressive realization' is not intended to take away all 'meaningful content' of a State's obligation to realize economic, social and cultural rights (CESCR, General Comment 3, para. 9). Progressive realization imposes a 'specific and continuing' (General Comment 12, para. 44) or 'constant and continuing' (CESCR, General Comment 15, para. 18) duty to move as 'expeditiously and effectively as possible' (CESCR, General Comment 3, para. 9; CESCR, General Comment 12, para. 44; CESCR, General Comment 15, para. 18) towards full realization of rights for men and women.

The 'maximum available resources', which the government should utilize for 'progressive realization' of human rights, depend upon the following factors:
- size and structure of the economy and its rate of growth
- structure of tax rates
- effectiveness of tax administration
- structure of user fees
- effectiveness of administration of user fees
- availability of other sources of revenue
- inflow of foreign aid
- government borrowing
- interest payments for domestic and foreign creditors
- underlying distribution of resources in the society.

The treaty bodies have not elaborated any definitive criteria concerning factors such as how much tax a government should raise and the circumstances in which user charges may be used. There has been more emphasis on the utilization of revenue in a way that is 'deliberate, concrete and targeted'[2] than on the generation of revenue.

1.3.5 Immediate obligations

The Committee on Economic, Social and Cultural Rights has made it clear that the recognition that realization will be 'progressive' does not provide States with an excuse for managing public finance in disregard of human rights. Although human rights law envisages the realization of most economic, social and cultural rights over time, there are two obligations that are of immediate effect for States. The most relevant one in the current context is the obligation to 'guarantee' that there will be no discrimination in the exercise of rights (Article 2(2) of ICESCR) (CESCR, General Comment 3, para. 2; CESCR, General Comment 12, para. 43; CESCR, General Comment 14, para. 31; CESCR, General Comment 15, para. 17). This means that women's equality must always be a priority in the progressive realization of economic, social and cultural rights and that any steps that a State takes to progressively realize such rights must be non-discriminatory in both policy and effect. The second immediate obligation is 'to take steps' (Article 2(1) of ICESCR) (CESCR, General Comment 3, para. 2; CESCR, General Comment 12, para. 43; CESCR, General Comment 14, para. 31; CESCR, General Comment 15, para. 17). These steps towards full realization of rights must be 'taken within a reasonably short time after the Covenant's entry into force for the States concerned' and as mentioned above, such steps should be 'deliberate, concrete and targeted as clearly as possible' in order to meet the obligations of States (CESCR, General Comment 3, para. 2; CESCR, General Comment 12, para. 43; CESCR, General Comment 14, para. 30; CESCR, General Comment 15, para. 17).

---

2 This flows from the requirement that immediate steps towards the full realization of economic, social and cultural rights should be 'deliberate, concrete and targeted as clearly as possible towards meeting the obligations recognized in the Covenant' (CESCR, General Comment 3, para. 2).

1.3.6 Minimum core

States that are parties to the ICESCR are also under a 'minimum core' obligation to ensure the satisfaction of, at the very least, 'minimum essential levels of each of the rights' in the ICESCR. This means that a State Party in which any 'significant number' of persons is 'deprived of essential foodstuffs, of essential primary health care, etc. is *prima facie* failing to meet obligations' under the Covenant (CESCR, General Comment 3, para. 10). The Committee on Economic, Social and Cultural Rights has clarified that:

- This is a continuing obligation, requiring States with inadequate resources to strive to ensure enjoyment of rights (General Comment 3, para. 11).
- However, even in times of severe resource constraints, States must ensure that rights are fulfilled for vulnerable members of society through the adoption of relatively low-cost targeted programmes (General Comment 3, para. 12; General Comment 12, para. 28; General Comment 14, para. 18).
- If lack of resources make it impossible for a State to fully comply with its obligations, it is required to justify its actions. However, a State Party cannot ever justify its non-compliance with core obligations as these obligations are non-derogable (General Comment 14, para. 48; General Comment 15, para. 40).

The Committee on Economic, Social and Cultural Rights has begun to identify the content of the minimum core obligations with respect to the rights to food, education, health and water (General Comments Nos. 11, 13,14 and 15 respectively).

1.3.7 Non-retrogression

There is a strong presumption that retrogressive measures on the part of a State are not permitted. If such retrogressive measures are deliberate, then the State has to show that they have been 'introduced after consideration of all alternatives and are fully justifiable by reference to totality of rights provided for in the Covenant and in context of the full use of the maximum of available resources' (CESCR, General Comment 3, para. 9; CESCR, General Comment 12, para. 45; CESCR, General Comment 14, para. 32; CESCR, General Comment 15, para. 19). In relation to gender and budget processes, it is important to recall that any retrogressive measures that affect the equal right of men and women to the enjoyment of any economic, social and cultural rights violates article 3 of ICESCR (CESCR, General Comment 16, para. 42).

'The principal obligation of result reflected in article 2 (1) [of the ICESCR] is to take steps "with a view to achieving progressively the full realization of the rights recognized" in the Covenant. The term "progressive realization" is often used to describe the intent of this phrase. The concept of progressive realization constitutes a recognition of the fact that full realization of all economic, social and cultural rights will generally not be able to be achieved in a short period of time. In this sense the obligation differs significantly from that contained in article 2 of the International Covenant on Civil and Political Rights which embodies an immediate obligation to respect and ensure all of the relevant rights. Nevertheless, the fact that realization over time, or in other words progressively, is foreseen under the Covenant should not be misinterpreted as depriving the obligation of all meaningful content. It is on the one hand a necessary flexibility device, reflecting the realities of the real world and the difficulties involved for any country in ensuring full realization of economic, social and cultural rights. On the other hand, the phrase must be read in the light of the overall objective, indeed the raison d'être, of the Covenant which is to establish clear obligations for States Parties in respect of the full realization of the rights in question. It thus imposes an obligation to move as expeditiously and effectively as possible towards that goal. Moreover, any deliberately retrogressive measures in that regard would require the most careful consideration and would need to be fully justified by reference to the totality of the rights provided for in the Covenant and in the context of the full use of the maximum available resources.'

Source: United Nations, Committee on Economic, Social and Cultural Rights, General Comment 3, para. 9, 1990, UN Doc. E/1991/23, Annex III.

Box 3 Principles of progressive realization and non-retrogression

1.3.8 Participation

CEDAW and other human rights law require that women be able to participate on equal terms with men in decision-making about the budget. This is provided for in Article 7(a) and (b)[3] which provide respectively for: women to participate in the formulation of government policy and its implementation and to hold public office and perform all public functions (e.g. as Ministers of Finance); and women to participate in nongovernmental organizations and associations which address the State's public and political life (e.g. as members of budget watchdog groups). There are numerous other declarations and conventions that emphasize the importance of the principle of participation of women (see e.g. the list contained in CEDAW, General Recommendation 23 at para. 4). In addition, the Committee on Economic, Social and Cultural Rights has recently indicated that the right of individuals to participate must be an 'integral component' of any policy or practice that seeks to meet the State obligation to ensure the equal right of men and women to the enjoyment of all human rights (General Comment 16, para. 37. (See further General Comment 14, para. 54; General Comment 15, paras. 16(a) and 48). In a statement on Poverty and the ICESCR, the Committee has stated that:

> 'the international human rights normative framework includes the right of those affected by key decisions to participate in the relevant decision-making processes' (United Nations, Committee on Economic, Social and Cultural Rights, 2001, para.12, UN Doc. E/C.12/2001/10).

It has also emphasized that:

> 'rights and obligation demand accountability ... whatever the mechanisms of accountability, they must be accessible, transparent and effective' (United Nations, Committee on Economic, Social and Cultural Rights, 2001, para. 14. UN Doc. E/C.12.2001/10).

This clearly has applicability to budget processes. The principle of participation is further addressed in Section 8.5.

1.3.9 Procedural obligations under treaties

The General Guidelines for the periodic reports that States Parties have to make to the Committee on the Rights of the Child (adopted in 1996) specifically mention government budgets (see Box 4).

This concern of the Committee on the Rights of the Child with the budget was strengthened in 2003 with the issuing of General Comment 5 on general measures of implementation for the Convention on the Rights of the Child, which called for children to be made visible in budgets (see Box 5). This Comment also called for a link between national strategies for realizing children's rights, specific goals, adequate resources and targeted implementation measures.

1.4 Relationship between human rights and budgets

Irrespective of how human rights obligations are interpreted in detail, the State requires a budget to carry them out. The amount of resources required will vary according to the right to be implemented. The challenge in thinking about government budgets and human rights is how to reconcile the different kinds of claims, obligations and constraints that characterize the two domains. Our starting point is twofold. First, to recognize that the government budget is subject to human rights not only because it is one state activity among many, but also because it is the financial framework for all government activities. Second, human rights principles must take precedence, because human rights are an end in themselves, while budgets are merely a means to other ends. This does not mean ignoring financial prudence. It means that financial objectives must not be achieved in ways that violate human rights or that fail to fulfill them.

These requirements (i.e. that a State both promote rights and refrain from their violation) are often referred to as the 'positive' and 'negative' aspects of State obligations. In the budget process, governments often fall short of meeting either of these obligations. While governments in general do not make calculations of how much public money may be saved by violating human rights, on the other hand, they generally make no systematic attempt to ensure that the budget does not violate human rights or to ensure that the budget facilitates their promotion

---

[3] See further CEDAW, General Recommendation No. 23.

In relation to reporting on general measures of implementation, the Guidelines state:
'Using indicators or target figures where necessary, please indicate the measures undertaken to ensure the implementation at the national, regional and local levels, and where relevant at the federal and provincial levels, of the economic, social and cultural rights of children to the maximum extent of available resources, including:

- the steps undertaken to ensure co-ordination between economic and social policies;
- the proportion of the budget devoted to social expenditures for children, including health, welfare and education, at the central, regional and local levels, and where appropriate at the federal and provincial levels;
- the budget trends over the period covered by the report;
- arrangements for budgetary analysis enabling the amount and proportion spent on children to be clearly identified;
- the steps taken to ensure that all competent national, regional and local authorities are guided by the best interests of the child in their budgetary decisions and evaluate the priority given to children in their policy-making;
- the measures taken to ensure that disparities between different regions and groups of children are bridged in relation to the provision of social services;
- the measures taken to ensure that children, particularly those belonging to the most disadvantaged groups, are protected against the adverse effects of economic policies, including the reduction of budgetary allocations in the social sector'.

(United Nations, Committee on the Rights of the Child, 1996, para. 20, Un Doc. CRC/C/58)

In relation to reporting on measures to implement specific articles, the Guidelines call for information on budgetary allocations in a number of cases, including rights of disabled children (article 23); children's rights to health (article 6 and 24); children's rights to social security and childcare services (article 26); children's right to an adequate standard of living (article 27); children's rights to education (article 28); children's rights to leisure, recreation and cultural activities (article 31).

Box 4 General guidelines for periodic reports to the Committee on the Rights of the Child

and realization. Budgetary calculations are usually confined to checks on the consistency of the budget with macroeconomic stability (ECLAC, 1998:177). However, these acts of omission are culpable as well as acts of commission. For instance, the 1997 Maastricht Guidelines on Violations of Economic, Social and Cultural Rights state that:

'A violation occurs when a State pursues, by action or omission, a practice or policy which deliberately contravenes or ignores obligations of the covenant, or fails to achieve the required standard of conduct or result' (*Human Rights Quarterly,* 20, 1998:695).

However, as will be clear from the next section, the principle that human rights take precedence over budgetary considerations does not mean that there is an open-ended obligation upon governments to spend public money.

As well as human rights principles having implications for budgetary practices, budgetary principles also have implications for human rights practices. In particular, they mean that attention has to be paid to costs, that priorities have to be set and resource constraints have to be recognized. Sometimes human right activists worry that this breaches the principle of the indivisibility of human rights. (The principle was reaffirmed at the 1993 UN World Conference on Human Rights in the statement 'all human rights are universal, indivisible and interdependent and interrelated'.)

General Comment 5 (United Nations, Committee on the Rights of the Child, 2003, UN Doc. CRC/GC/2003/5) calls for 'Making Children visible in budgets':

'If a government as a whole and at all levels is to promote and respect the rights of the child, it needs to work on the basis of a unifying, comprehensive and rights-based national strategy, rooted in the convention' (para. 28).

'The comprehensive national strategy may be elaborated in sectoral national plans of action—for example for education and health—setting out specific goals, targeted implementation measures and allocation of financial and human resources. The strategy will inevitably set priorities, but it must not neglect or dilute in any way the detailed obligations which States Parties have accepted under the Convention. The strategy needs to be adequately resources, in human and financial terms' (para. 32).

'In its reporting guidelines and in examination of States Parties reports, the Committee has paid much attention to the identification and analysis of resources for children in national and other budgets. No State can tell whether it is fulfilling children's economic, social and cultural rights "to the maximum extent of ... available resources", as it is required to do under Article 4, unless it can identify the proportion of national and other budgets devoted to the social sector and within that, to children, both directly and indirectly. Some States have claimed it is not possible to analyse national budgets in this way. But others have done it and publish annual "children's budgets". The Committee needs to know what steps are taken at all levels of government to ensure that economic and social planning and decision-making and budgetary decisions are made with the best interests of children as a primary consideration and that children, including in particular marginalized and disadvantaged groups of children, are protected from adverse effects of economic policies or financial downturns' (para. 51).

Box 5 Making children visible in budgets

This issue was raised at the International Budget Project conference in 2000 by Dominique Ayine of the Centre for Public Interest Law in Ghana:

'... [W]hen rights are seen in terms of budgetary allocation we are forced to prioritize, as funds are not unlimited in our countries. This raises more difficult questions, which challenge the very concept of human rights, and is perhaps where the intersection of rights and budgets weakens'. (www.internationalbudget.org/cdrom/sessions/expenditure/humanrights.htm)

However, Mary Robinson, the former UN High Commissioner for Human Rights, makes a distinction between prioritizing rights and prioritizing resources:

'Civil and political rights, on the one hand, and economic, social and cultural rights, on the other, must be treated equally. Neither set has priority over the other. Although every country must set priorities for the use of its resources at any given time, this is not the same as choosing between specific rights'. (UNDP, 2000:113)

The emphasis on the indivisibility of human rights can thus be seen as a way of ruling out attempts to realize one right in ways that violate other rights. It emphasizes that the ultimate goal must be realization of all human rights. However, it does not seem reasonable to interpret it as meaning that progress in realizing human rights has to proceed at the same rate for all rights, and that resources have to be allocated according to this principle. The Committee on the Rights of the Child explicitly recognized the need to set priorities, in General Comment 5 (see Box 5) but required that this be done in a way that 'does not neglect or dilute in any way the detailed obligations ... under the Convention'.

Section 2

Analysing Government Expenditure
from a Human Rights Perspective:
Selected Examples

Analysing Government Expenditure from a Human Rights Perspective: Selected Examples

This section discusses the use of international benchmarks to evaluate expenditure in relation to the International Covenant on Economic, Social and Cultural Rights; an evaluation of the health budget in Mexico in relation to the right to health; and an evaluation of the budget for the child support grant in South Africa in relation to children's rights as specified in the South African Constitution.

2.1 Prioritizing expenditure for economic and social rights: the Human Development Expenditure Ratios

Maria Diokno, Secretary General of the Free Legal Assistance group of the Philippines, has suggested that the fulfilment of the obligations of states under the Covenant on Economic, Social and Cultural Rights) can be evaluated using some benchmarks put forward by the UNDP *Human Development Report 1991* (Diokno, 1999). The norms focus on the share of expenditure that goes to services which are argued on *a priori* grounds to be important for poor people (see Box 6).

- *Public expenditure ratio* (share of national income that goes to public expenditure)
  25% of GNP
- *Social allocation ratio* (share of public expenditure that goes to social services, including health, education, welfare, social security, water, sanitation, housing and amenities)
  40% of public expenditure
- *Social priority ratio* (share of human priority concerns within social services; which for poor countries will be basic education, primary health care and basic water)
  At least 50% of social sector expenditure
- *Human expenditure ratio* (share of national income that goes to expenditure on human priority concerns, which for poor countries are specified as basic education, primary health care, basic water)
  5% of GNP

Box 6 The Human Development Report 1991 public expenditure benchmarks

The Human Development Report does not specify the rationale for these particular ratios, simply stating that they are the 'preferred option' (UNDP, 1991:40). They have been quite widely used in national human development reports; and they were used in the gender budget audit of Nepal (Acharya, 2003:31-32). These benchmarks are useful indicators of the *allocation* of expenditure but they say nothing about the *impact* of public expenditure. They are indicators of the *priority* given to services likely to be important to poor people.

An attempt to increase the priority given to basic social services was made through the 20/20 initiative agreed at the World Summit on Social Development in 1995. Governments of developing countries agreed to increase spending on basic social services until it amounted to 20% of public expenditure, while government of countries giving development aid agreed to increase aid to basic social services so that it amounted to 20% of official development assistance (UNDP, UNESCO, UNFPA, UNICEF, WHO and World Bank, 1998).

Calculating these ratios often requires quite a lot of sifting through different data. Governments do not present their budgets in formats that make it easy to see what their priorities are, and how resources are being distributed and used. The primary purpose of budget documents is to authorize expenditure and to provide a standard against which actual expenditures can be audited to see whether money has been spent as authorized or has been mis-appropriated. Expenditures in budget documents are thus presented in a number of administrative formats showing allocations:

- to different government agencies and programmes;
- to current and capital expenditure; and
- to purchase of different kinds of inputs (staff, equipment, etc.).

Allocation by agency and programme is the one that corresponds most nearly to the classifications used in the Human Development expenditure ratios and the 20/20 initiative. But this classification rarely fits exactly the classifications used in the ratios. It is thus often difficult to ascertain how much a government has been spending on *primary* health care, or *basic* water services (Mehrotra and Delamonica, forthcoming).

The presence of multiple tiers of government often makes it difficult to analyse public expenditure. Lower tiers of government generally fund a high proportion of their expenditure from financial transfers from higher tiers of government. Clarifying how much has been spent on what is particularly difficult in countries with a federal system, and in countries where a great deal of public expenditure has been decentralized to the local level. There is a danger of underestimating expenditure by counting only central government expenditure; and of overestimating expenditure by double counting through including inter-governmental transfers in the expenditure of both the transferring and the receiving government agency. A further complication is that actual expenditure is often different from budgeted expenditure (see Box 7).

Actual expenditure of any particular department may be *less* than budgeted expenditure for a number of reasons, including:
- slow and complex disbursement mechanisms;
- inability of spending departments to design programmes that comply with spending guidelines;
- instructions from the Ministry of Finance to make cuts in spending because of shortfalls in revenue or unexpectedly high spending in other departments.

Actual expenditure may *exceed* budgeted expenditure for a number of reasons, including:
- cost overruns on infrastructural projects;
- unexpected increases in statutory payments for welfare benefits and pensions;
- unexpected increases in debt repayments due to unexpected increases in interest rates.

In some countries it is common for there to be at least one supplementary budget during the financial year. So it is important that analysis of public expenditure looks at actual as well as budgeted expenditure wherever possible.

Box 7 Actual expenditure and budgeted expenditure

It is not necessarily the case that compliance with the Human Development expenditure ratios would ensure that there is adequate funding to cover the minimum core obligation to supply these services (see Box 3). That depends on the costs of supplying the minimum core amount of the services compared to the absolute amount of funding allocated. However, even when the minimum core is satisfied, human rights law requires analysts to continue to strive towards improvement; it is inherent in the meaning of 'progressive realization' that the obligation to move towards full enjoyment of human rights is a continuing one (see e.g. CESCR, General Comment 3, paras. 9, 11).

These ratios are useful benchmarks for the fulfilment of obligations of conduct, and can be used in monitoring whether a State is fulfilling these obligations. They are particularly useful to monitor expenditure cutbacks in the context of reduction of budget deficits (see Section 7). But the ratios are not useful in monitoring fulfilment of obligations of result. For a number of reasons, allocation of funding is not necessarily reflected in enjoyment of appropriate services:
- Budgeted funds do not always find their way to the point of service delivery, as the result of bureaucratic inertia (e.g. disbursement delays) or of corruption.
- Even if the funding does get through to the point of service delivery, there is no guarantee that services operate in ways that respect human rights, especially of poor people, and operate in ways that improve their lives.

It is necessary to 'follow the money' through to the outcomes and outputs of programmes to establish whether states are meeting their obligations to realize economic and social rights of poor people.

2.2 Achieving non-discrimination in the distribution of funding by social group: public expenditure on health in Mexico

In a groundbreaking study, Hofbauer, Lara and Martinez (2002) have evaluated the health budget in Mexico in relation to the right to health as set out in the International Covenant on Economic, Social and Cultural Rights, and in the Mexican Constitution, placing particular emphasis on the prohibition of discrimination in access. As they point out, the obligation not to discriminate is not subject to the clause on 'progressive realization' (Box 3). Rather it is an immediate obligation, in the sense that it does not depend on obtaining more resources, but redeploying existing ones. They investigate whether there is discrimination in the institutional and geographic distribution of resources, in terms of the access to health services.

The public health system in Mexico is divided into a social security system for those who have higher incomes and formal employment contracts (both public and private) (the 'protected population') and a decentralized fund for health services for those who are poor, do not have formal employment contracts and who rely on services funded through the Ministry of Health (the 'unprotected population'). The division in itself does not necessarily constitute discrimination. What matters is whether the availability of services is equitable for the two groups. Hofbauer et al. calculate yearly real per capita expenditure for the two groups and find that in 1998, the level for the unprotected population was less than half that for the protected population. The gap diminished a little over the period 1999 and 2000, but almost three quarters of public health expenditure still went to the protected population.

The distribution of funding by region within Mexico was also very unequal, with the poorest states having the lowest per capita health expenditures. These states are also the states where the indigenous people of Mexico are concentrated, and where health indicators are worst.

The procedures for decentralizing funding to states perpetuate the inequality. The first call on funding is to cover the costs of existing, unequal levels of staffing, equipment and buildings. This leaves only a small additional amount that is available for improving facilities in the worst-off states. Moreover, the total budget for new health infrastructure for the unprotected population fell between 1998 and 2002.

The researchers conclude that inequality is institutionalized in Mexican public expenditure on health services, so that resource allocation is discriminatory in its effects, judged by the benchmark that all segments of the population have a right to the same standard of health care, irrespective of where they live and which system delivers their health care.

It might be argued that there is some tension between the 'immediacy' of the obligation not to discriminate and the fact that redistribution of real resources like medical personnel and infrastructure cannot be achieved overnight. The researchers deal with this by arguing that the obligation not to discriminate requires urgent movement 'towards a set of clearly defined actions, aimed at achievable benchmarks. In this way, the reduction of existing gaps could be evaluated, and responsibility could be established in case of failure to achieve the goals agreed upon' (Hofbauer et al., 2002:23).

This case illustrates some key points about investigating whether the allocation of public expenditure is discriminatory in effect:
1. Identify different social groups. This is an important step because human rights law provides extra guarantees for vulnerable groups or those who suffer discrimination, whose rights must be protected even in times of severe resource constraints (see CESCR, General Comment 3, para. 12; CESCR, General Comment 6, para. 28; CESCR, General Comment 14, para. 18).
2. Identify how much expenditure per capita is being received by each group for a particular service.
3. Analyse whether any differences operate so as to reduce, perpetuate or increase inequalities between the groups.
4. Identify what can be done to remedy discriminatory outcomes.

2.3 Matching obligations with funding: the child support grant programme in South Africa

The South African constitution contains a comprehensive set of economic and social rights, including children's rights to basic nutrition, shelter, basic health care services and social services, including social assistance. The State has an obligation to 'respect, protect, promote and fulfil' these children's rights, irrespective of resource constraints, but the constitution does not specify the exact content of each of these rights.

A case study by two researchers at the Budget Information Service of the Institute for Democracy in South Africa (Streak and Wehner, 2002) investigates the adequacy of government funding for the child's right to social assistance via the child support grant programme. This programme offers a cash transfer to those caring for young children in poor households. The grant at the time of the study was for children up to the age of 6 living in the poorest 30% of households. It was initially R100 per month and was increased to R110 in the 2001 Budget and R130 in the 2002 Budget. To qualify, the caregiver must pass an income means test, and supply their identity document and the child's birth certificate. The implementation was to be phased in over a five-year period from 1 April 1998 to 31 March 2003, and targets were set for the number of children to be reached in each of the nine provinces by 1 April 2003.

The programme is implemented by the provincial governments. The funding to cover this, and most other provincial spending, is provided by the central government through a block grant, using a formula that takes account of both the judgement of the central government on how much public expenditure can in total be afforded and the relative needs of different provinces, related to the socio-economic profile of their populations.

However, the provincial government is not obliged to spend the money according to the notional budget heads implied in the formula.

Streak and Wehner investigate whether the provincial governments have allocated enough funding in their budgets for 2002/2003 to achieve the targets set for 31 March 2003 (see Box 8).

There are three steps in the calculations made by Streak and Wehner, 2002:

1. Estimate number of children each province must extend the grant to in 2002/3 for the target to be met, using data on the children already covered at end of March 2002 and on the targets.
2. Estimate how much it will cost provinces to pay the grant in 2002/3 to children already receiving it by March 31 2002 (including the administrative costs).
3. Estimate what is left in programme budget after deducting cost for existing beneficiaries, and whether it will be sufficient to cover the extension of the grant to the additional children identified in step 1, assuming a uniform rate of extension across the twelve-month period.

The principles are simple. Getting the data proved harder. Problems in the database of the Department of Social Development meant that data was not available for the number of child beneficiaries in March 2002. The numbers had to be estimated using data for February and May. There was no central database on provincial budgets and different provinces used different budget classification systems, making it hard to get comparable data from published sources. For most provinces, data had to be specially requested from the relevant provincial departments. There was also the issue of administrative costs. The researchers side-stepped such difficulties by assuming that they amount to 5% of the value of total grant payments; though there might be a case for expecting these to rise at the margin if those children not yet covered are from harder to reach families in more remote areas.

Box 8 Calculating the adequacy of funding for the child support grant programme

The result of the calculations showed that:

> 'in five of the nine provinces, the budgets are not enough to support the rate of expansion of access required to ensure that the number of children that government initially planned to reach by 31 March 2003 will be reached' (Streak and Wehner, 2002:26).

Inadequate funding had been allocated to realize children's right to social assistance, judged against the government's own targets.

Streak and Wehner go on to investigate how this could have happened, tracing it to design faults in the formula for transfers between the central government and provincial governments, which do not make explicit provision for funding the child support grant, and are based on a household income and expenditure survey conducted in 1995. They make recommendations about how this can be reformed.

This case illustrates some key steps in assessing the adequacy of funding a particular right in situations where that right has a domestic implementing mechanism and budget allocation:

1. Identify an already adopted government target, related to the realization of a particular right. It might be a target for number of beneficiaries of particular programme, as in the above case, but could be the implementation of a new law, or a particular outcome, such as an increase in adult literacy.
2. Identify the costs of meeting this target, allowing for direct costs and administrative costs. This will inevitably involve some element of 'guesstimate', as information will only be available about current costs at current scale of provision.
3. Identify what has been budgeted, and compare it with the costs. If there is under-funding, consider what could be done to generate sufficient funding.

2.4 Conclusions

In all three examples, the analysis went beyond the idea of making particular groups visible in the budget. Expenditures were evaluated in relation to specific benchmarks for priorities, equality and adequacy. The identification of these benchmarks was a key aspect of the human rights perspective.

Section 3

CEDAW and Government Budgets

CEDAW and Government Budgets

Section 3 sets out the key implications of CEDAW for government budgets and discusses the engagement of the CEDAW reporting mechanism with government budgets.

3.1 CEDAW: a standard of substantive equality and autonomy

The *preamble* to CEDAW specifically states that:
> 'States Parties to the International Covenants on Human Rights have the obligation to ensure the equal rights of men and women to enjoy all economic, social, cultural, civil and political rights'.

The *preamble* to CEDAW begins by reaffirming faith in 'the dignity and worth of the human person and in the equal rights of men and women'; and notes that states which ratify CEDAW have 'the obligation to ensure the equal rights of men and women to enjoy all economic, social, cultural, civil and political rights'. It also draws attention to 'the social significance of maternity' and states that 'the role of women in procreation should not be a basis for discrimination but that the upbringing of children requires a sharing of responsibility between men and women and society as a whole'. It ends with a recognition 'that a change in the traditional role of men as well as the role of women in society and in the family is needed to achieve full equality between women and men'.

Article 1 defines discrimination against women, as 'any distinction, exclusion or restriction made on the basis of sex which has the effect or purpose of impairing or nullifying the recognition, enjoyment or exercise by women … of human rights'.

In *Article 2,* States Parties agree to pursue 'by all appropriate means and without delay a policy of eliminating discrimination against women'. In particular they undertake to 'refrain from engaging in any act or practice of discrimination against women and to ensure that public authorities and institutions shall act in conformity with this obligation'; and to 'take all appropriate measures to eliminate discrimination against women by any person, organization or enterprise'.

In *Article 3,* States Parties agree to take 'all appropriate measures, including legislation, to ensure the full development and advancement of women, for the purpose of guaranteeing them the exercise and enjoyment of human rights and fundamental freedoms on a basis of equality with men'.

Article 4(1) recognizes the legitimacy of 'temporary special measures aimed at accelerating *de facto* equality between men and women'.

Article 5 enjoins States Parties to take all appropriate measures 'to modify the social and cultural patterns of conduct of men and women, with a view to achieving the elimination of prejudices and customary and all other practices which are based on the idea of the inferiority or the superiority of either of the sexes or on stereotyped roles for men and women'.

The rest of the Convention spells this out in greater detail with respect to particular issues like trafficking in women, participation in political and public life, education, employment, health, rural development, legal rights, marriage and the family, etc.

(See Appendix 1 for the full text of CEDAW.)

These articles show that CEDAW mandates both substantive and formal equality and recognizes that formal equality alone is insufficient for a State to meet its affirmative obligation to achieve substantive equality between men and women (CEDAW, General Recommendation 25, para. 8). Formal and substantive equality are 'different but interconnected concepts' (CESCR, General Comment 16, para. 7). Formal equality generally prohibits the use of distinctions between men and women in law and policy. It assumes that undifferentiated or identical treatment of men and women is best suited to achieve equality between them (CESCR, General Comment 16, para. 7). Substantive equality goes one important step further and looks at the impact of laws, policies and practices on women. Under the substantive equality model, laws and policies that formally treat men and women identically and are not intentionally discriminatory, are considered discriminatory if they have a disproportionately negative impact on women. In this way, substantive equality requires governments to achieve quantitative and/or qualitative 'equality of results' (CEDAW, General Recommendation 25, para. 9). To meet Convention obligations in this regard, States must give women an 'equal start' and provide an 'enabling environment' for women to enjoy equality (CEDAW, General Recommendation 25, para. 9). To do this, States are under an obligation to take note of biological and socially constructed differences that may necessitate non-identical treatment, while working to transform those socially constructed differences that are a result of discrimination (CEDAW, General Recommendation 25, para. 9). The model of substantive equality embodied in CEDAW also requires States to address the causes of historically embedded discrimination that prevent the achievement of substantive equality between men and women (CEDAW, General Recommendation 25, para. 9).

3.2 Implications of CEDAW for government budgets

The achievement of substantive equality for women requires government action to ensure that the state functions without discrimination against women, and that the state works to overcome inequality in households, communities, markets and businesses. Unlike the Convention on the Rights of the Child, there is no specific article in CEDAW that links 'appropriate measures' to resources, but it is inconceivable that the 'appropriate measures' to achieve substantive equality between women and men would have no implications for public finance.

Government budgets affect people in multiple ways: their primary impact is through distributing resources to people via expenditure and claiming resources from them via tax and other measures. They also have secondary impacts via their impacts on job creation, economic growth and inflation. It is not possible to sum up the total impact of the budget on males and on females in just *one* set of indicators and use this to judge whether the budget is non-discriminatory and advances the achievement of substantive gender equality. If large amounts of data are available, it is possible to use micro-simulation models to examine the primary impact of direct taxes and direct income transfers (such as government grants to parents or to poor people) on the incomes of the adult population, disaggregated by household income group, and to see how far this reduces the income inequalities that arise from the operation of the private sector (markets and businesses). But that is only feasible for high-income industrialized countries, and even in them, it leaves out large areas of expenditure and revenue and does not capture the secondary impacts. Moreover, such models typically do not disaggregate the primary impacts by sex, and so do not examine gender equality.

Therefore, this report recommends a step-by-step approach, examining particular dimensions of the budget separately, taking into account their interactions where appropriate and possible. Some key dimensions are identified below.

3.2.1 Public expenditure

Public expenditure is required to fund the 'appropriate measures' repeatedly mentioned in CEDAW. All too often gender equality measures (such as plans to implement the Beijing Platform for Action) are introduced without a clear appropriation of funding for their implementation. There is a lack of clear and binding guidelines to spending Ministries requiring them to allocate their funds so as to realize such plans, and inadequate funding for the body (such as the Ministry of Women's Affairs) that is meant to oversee the realization of the gender equality plans.

Some gender equality measures may be relatively low cost in budget terms, such as the removal of laws that explicitly discriminate against women. But even this requires some funding for the Department of Justice (or comparable Ministry). New laws to promote equal opportunities and the advancement of women require funding if they are to be effectively implemented. For example, equal opportunity laws require a body to monitor their implementation, to provide training and advice to employers and employees, and to support women in litigation for equal opportunities. Gender equality measures without budgets are only half-measures. It is important to close the gap between funding and policy. Debbie Budlender (2003) has produced a useful list of questions that can be used to monitor how much money the government has allocated to measures introduced to implement CEDAW.

CEDAW not only requires funding to be allocated to implement 'appropriate measures', it also requires that there should be no substantive discrimination in the distribution and impact of public expenditure in general. This is particularly important in relation to Article 10 (elimination of discrimination in education); Article 11 (elimination of discrimination in employment); Article 12 (elimination of discrimination in health); Article 13 (elimination of discrimination in other areas of economic and social life); and Article 14 (elimination of discrimination against women in rural areas). The funding of 'temporary special measures aimed at accelerating *de facto* equality between men and women' is anticipated by Article 4(1). States should consider adopting such temporary special measures where there is a need to both accelerate access to equal participation and accelerate resource redistribution (CEDAW, General Recommendation 25, para. 39). In the case of budgets, this may require, for example, the adoption of temporary special measures to ensure women's participation in government decision-making processes regarding budget formation, content and implementation. This can include measures such as financially assisting and training women candidates and setting quotas for women's appointment to public positions within government (CEDAW, General Recommendation 23, para. 15).

3.2.2 Public revenue

CEDAW positions women as autonomous citizens, possessing their own rights and obliges States Parties to treat them as such, not merely as dependents of men. Article 16 requires that in family relations, men and women should be treated as equals, with the same rights. This implies that women must be treated as autonomous claimants on, and contributors to, the budget rather than as dependents that benefit from and contribute to government budgets via their relations with male family members.

Thus revenue must be raised in ways that do not discriminate against women and do not perpetuate those traditional roles that are incompatible with substantive equality, such as assigning men the role of the family 'breadwinner' and women the role of their dependents. Tax systems must not be designed and implemented in ways that amplify pre-existing gender inequalities. For instance, systems of taxation should not be designed in ways that reinforce women's unequal access to the labour market.

If fees are charged for public services, they must not operate in ways that result in substantive inequality between women and men. If publicly owned assets are sold, the impact of privatization must not jeopardize gender equality and the full development and advancement of women, either via the labour market or via the markets for goods and services.

3.2.3 Macroeconomics of the budget

Aggregate expenditure and revenue must be managed in ways that create adequate fiscal resources for the elimination of discrimination and the full development and advancement of women. Cuts in expenditure should not be designed in ways that add to the amount of unpaid work that women have to do in families and communities. Sufficient tax revenue should be raised to provide adequate funding for the measures that are necessary to implement CEDAW. Debt repayments must not be allowed to crowd out funding for services essential for the realization of CEDAW. The rich countries must take up their obligations to assist the poorer countries by providing resource flows to sustain adequate fiscal resources for CEDAW realization.

3.2.4 Budget decision-making

Article 7 of CEDAW requires that women should participate equally with men in budget decision-making and the exercise of related legislative, judicial, executive and administrative powers (CEDAW, General Recommendation 22, para. 5). This means that women should participate equally with men in a number of different capacities, including as government officials and ministers; as members of legislatures; as members of public boards and trade unions; and members of the judiciary (CEDAW, General Recommendation 22, para. 5). This requirement applies to all stages of the budget cycle: budget formulation; legislation; implementation; and auditing and evaluation.

3.3 CEDAW reporting and government budgets

The latest Guidelines (issued in 2003) on what States Parties should include in their report to the Committee on the Elimination of Discrimination Against Women do not contain any specific reference to budgets, though they do require an explanation of the 'practical' as well as the 'legal' measures taken to give effect to the convention. Moreover, they require information on the actions taken to implement the Beijing Platform for Action (United Nations, 1995) and the further actions agreed at the Beijing+5 meeting in June 2000. The Beijing Platform for Action and the Beijing+5 Outcome Document of the 23rd Special Session of the General Assembly (United Nations, General Assembly 2000) both make reference to the relationship between implementation and public finance (see Box 9).

The *Beijing Platform for Action* (United Nations, 1995) refers to the need to conduct gender analysis of budgets, and to adjust public spending to ensure equality between women and men, in the following paragraphs:

Financial Arrangements

345. This will require the integration of a gender perspective in budgetary decisions on polices and programmes, as well as the adequate financing of specific programmes for securing equality between women and men.

National level

346. Governments should make efforts to systematically review how women benefit from public sector expenditures; adjust budgets to ensure equality of access to public expenditures ...

International level

358. To facilitate implementation of the Platform for Action, interested developed and developing country partners, agreeing on a mutual commitment to allocate, on average, 20% of official development assistance and 20% of the national budget to basic social programmes, should take into account a gender perspective.

The review of implementation of the Beijing Platform for Action, conducted in 2000, also showed a concern for the implications of government budgets for gender equality. The *Outcome Document* stated that:
'Limited funding at the State level makes it imperative that innovative approaches to the allocation of existing resources be employed, not only by Governments, but also by NGOs and the private sector. One such innovation is the gender analysis of public budgets, which is emerging as an important tool for determining the differential impact of expenditures on women and men to help ensure equitable use of existing resources. This analysis is crucial to promote gender equality'.

Box 9 Beijing Platform for Action and government budgets
(United Nations, General Assembly 2000, para. 36))

In the years since the Beijing Declaration, the CEDAW Committee has begun to make more specific reference to the role of government budgets in relation to women's human rights. One example is the *General Recommendation 24 on Women and Heath,* issued in 1999 (United Nations, Committee on the Elimination of Discrimination Against Women, 1999a) (see Box 10).

The Committee issued *General Recommendation No 24 on Women and Health* in 1999, which contained the following paragraphs:

17. The duty to fulfill rights places an obligation on States Parties to take appropriate legislative, judicial, administrative, budgetary, economic, and other measures to the maximum extent of their available resources to ensure that women realize their rights to health care. Studies such as those which emphasize the high maternal mortality and morbidity rates worldwide and the large numbers of couples who would like to limit their family size but lack access to or do not use any form of contraception provide an important indication for States Parties of possible breaches of their duties to ensure women's access to health care. ... The Committee is concerned at the growing evidence that States are relinquishing these obligations as they transfer State health functions to private agencies. States Parties cannot absolve themselves of responsibility in these areas by delegating or transferring these powers to private sector agencies. States Parties should therefore report on what they have done to organize governmental processes and all the structures through which public power is exercised to promote and protect women's health. ...

30. States Parties should allocate adequate budgetary, human, and administrative resources to ensure that women's health receives a share of the overall health budget comparable with that for men's health.

Box 10 Government expenditure and women's health

(United Nations, Committee on Elimination of Discrimination Against Women, General Recommendation 24, 1999a.)

Other examples can be found in some recent Concluding Comments issued by the Committee after the consideration of reports by States Parties. For instance, in reference to Luxembourg in 2000, the Committee 'welcome[d] the [Women's] Ministry's interest in, and support for, proposals to conduct a gender analysis of the entire State budget. This will contribute to a better understanding of the way in which women and men benefit from governmental expenditures in all areas' (United Nations, Committee on the Elimination of Discrimination Against Women, 2000a, UN Doc. A/55/38, para. 393).

In 2002, when reviewing Fiji's report, the Committee 'commend[ed] the efforts of the State Party to strengthen gender mainstreaming and monitoring through the gender budget initiative, and a gender audit project' (United Nations, Committee on the Elimination of Discrimination Against Women, 2002a, UN Doc. A/57/38, para. 43).

The first State Party report to make substantial references to gender equality and government budgets was South Africa in its initial report in 1997. Another State Party that has recently mentioned the government budget in its report to the CEDAW committee is France (see Box 11).

The Committee has, on at least one occasion, asked a State to conduct a gender analysis of its budget and to report on the results. In its concluding comments concerning Austria in 2000, the Committee 'request[ed] the Government to ensure, on a regular basis, the evaluation and assessment of the gender impact of the federal budget as well as governmental policies and programmes affecting women' (United Nations, Committee on Elimination of Discrimination Against Women, 2002b, UN Doc A/55/38, para. 226). However, this request does not seem to be made on a regular basis, and it has not been explicitly incorporated into the CEDAW reporting guidelines.

No guidelines have yet been suggested for standards that should be used in the evaluation and assessment of government budgets from a CEDAW perspective. The first step is to make women visible in budgets, in the way that the CRC has called for children to be made visible in budgets (see Box 5). But this is not sufficient. It is important to identify and apply evaluative criteria that judge budgets against the CEDAW standard of substantive equality between women and men.

Gender and the Budget in the Initial South African Report (1997)

Among the important points from the report (United Nations, Committee on the Elimination of Discrimination Against Women, 1997) are the following:

- The Financial and Fiscal Commission, which advises government on the allocation of government revenue, has an allocation formula which favours the more rural provinces where women predominate, and thus has an implicit bias in favour of women.
- In his budget speech of March 1996, the then-Minister of Finance, Chris Liebenberg, committed his department to the development of:
  - o a gender-disaggregated statistical database
  - o gender-disaggregated targets and indicators
  - o a gender-sensitive performance review mechanism.
- The Women's Budget Initiative: Since late 1995 the Gender and Economic Policy Group of the Joint Standing Committee on Finance and the Ad Hoc Joint Committee on the Improvement of Quality of Life and Status of Women has worked with NGOs to produce reports analysing the extent to which various departments use their budgets to prioritize and implement provisions which would lead to an improvement in the lives of women.

Gender and the Budget in the Fifth Report of France (2002)

The CEDAW report of France (United Nations, Committee on the Elimination of Discrimination Against Women, 2002b, UN Doc. CEDAW/C/JOR/2) specifically mentioned 'an increase in State resources devoted to achieving equality between men and women' and the introduction in 2000 of a yellow budget paper on women's rights and equality) that provides an account of public expenditure on behalf of women's rights and the promotion of equality between women and men. It incorporates gender-equality indicators for each Ministry. The yellow budget paper on women's rights and equality is a legal requirement, introduced at the request of parliament. It functions as an information and monitoring tool. The report states that:

'As both a "mainstreaming" tool and a tool for measuring the impact of public policy on men and women, the yellow budget paper on equality is an essential steering mechanism, through which public actions can be directed and adjusted to ensure that equality between men and women can progress and take genuine effect'.

Box 11 Gender and budgets in States Parties' reports

3.4 Evaluation and assessment of the gender impact of budgets

Conducting a CEDAW-compliant evaluation and assessment of the gender impact of budgets implies answering a number of questions, including:

- What criteria should be used to determine whether there is equality of access to public expenditures? (as required by Articles 2(1) and 3 of CEDAW and detailed in para. 346 of the Beijing Platform for Action.)
- What criteria should be used to determine whether there is adequate financing of specific programmes for securing equality between women and men? (as required by Article 3 of CEDAW and detailed in para. 345 of the Beijing Platform for Action).
- What methods can be used to assess whether women's particular economic, social and cultural rights receive a share of the overall health budget comparable with that for men's particular economic, social and cultural rights, taking into account their different needs? (e.g. as required by CEDAW General Recommendation 24, para. 30 in relation to women and health).
- What criteria should be used to assess the gender impact of the state budget? (as requested by the CEDAW Committee in its Concluding Comments on the report by Austria).
- If reliance is placed on gender budget initiatives to ensure that the State conducts its budget in compliance with CEDAW, then what constitutes an effective gender budget initiative?

Gender budget initiatives in some countries have been grappling with these questions. The next section discusses some of the characteristics of gender budget initiatives and their relation to women's human rights.

Section 4

Gender Budget Initiatives and
Women's Human Rights

Gender Budget Initiatives and Women's Human Rights

There is no one template for a gender budget initiative (GBI). As befits a process of innovation taking place in a wide variety of socio-economic and political contexts, there has been considerable diversity and experimentation. A multiplicity of actors has been involved: government minister and officials (especially women's ministries, sometimes Ministries of Finance), parliamentarians, policy research NGOs, women's advocacy groups and academics. GBIs have often been supported by grants from foundations and from development cooperation agencies (see Budlender, 2000; Budlender et al., 2002; Budlender and Hewitt, 2002; UNIFEM, 2002). This section provides a brief overview of the varying modalities of GBIs. The primary aim of GBIs to date has been to make gender visible in government budgets. Some GBIs have also aimed to assess the impact of government budgets on gender equality outcomes.

4.1 Government GBIs

A wide range of governments in both developed and developing countries have taken some steps to analyse their budgets from a gender perspective. The pioneer was the Government of **Australia,** which began a pilot initiative in 1984, and in 1987 launched an annual Women's Budget Statement, issued as part of the federal budget papers. This lengthy document (of about 300 pages) attempted to examine the whole budget, tax as well as expenditure, for its likely implications for women in Australia, documenting how women were expected to benefit (Sharp and Broomhill, 2002; Sawyer, 2002). The gender focus on Australian budgets was promoted by gender equality advocates who had become officials and Ministers. It had three goals:
- to raise awareness within government of the gender impact of the budget and the polices funded;
- to make governments accountable for their commitments to gender equality;
- to bring about changes to budgets and the policies they fund to improve the socio-economic status of women.

Sharp and Broomhill (2002) judge that there was some success in achieving each of these goals, but successes were limited by political factors and by the changing macroeconomic climate. All the States and Territories that make up Australia subsequently introduced some form of women's budget statement. The format developed by Rhonda Sharp for use in South Australia has been particularly influential and is shown in Box 12.

Rhonda Sharp developed a threefold classification of government expenditure for use in South Australia, and this has since been widely disseminated and adapted in various ways to make gender visible in government budgets. As presented in Budlender and Sharp (1998), the format distinguishes:
- specifically targeted expenditures to women or men in the community intended to meet their particular needs (example: women's health programme; domestic violence counselling for men);
- equal opportunity expenditure by government agencies on their employees (example: special training for disadvantaged groups; paid parental leave);
- general or mainstream budget expenditures by government agencies, which make goods or service available to the whole community (example: literacy classes; agricultural support services).

Expenditures in the first two categories can often be easily identified from budget documents, but evidence suggests that gender-specific or equal opportunities programmes are generally very small, no more than 1 or 2% of budget expenditure. The conclusion drawn by Sharp was that it was essential to analyse the gender impact of the mainstream, non-gender-specific expenditures.

Box 12 Three ways of classifying public expenditure from a gender perspective

The election, in the mid-1990s, of a new government which believed that market liberalization was more important than public finance, led to a suspension of the production of Women's Budget Statements at the federal level, though the practice was continued in some of the Australian States and Territories. In 2001, the Australian Labour Party committed itself to the re-introduction of the Women's Budget Statement if it returned to government, but failed to win the elections.

The Australian example was one of the inspirations for a **Commonwealth Secretariat** initiative to promote the use of gender budget analysis by governments as a response to the challenges of economic restructuring. A menu of tools which might be used for this was assembled (for more details see Appendix 2). Beginning in 1997, the Commonwealth Secretariat supported five Commonwealth countries in testing some of these tools to conduct gender analysis of the budgets and services of selected Ministries. (The countries were South Africa, Sri Lanka, Barbados, Fiji Islands, and St Kitts and Nevis). A notable feature of this initiative was the leadership role of the Ministry of Finance in each country. Some useful analysis was carried out, and the opportunities and constraints for using some of the tools were further clarified. However, it proved difficult to get sustained commitment from the Ministries of Finance in the five countries to institutionalize the analysis and to use it to improve their budgets, polices and programmes (Hewitt, 2002). Nevertheless, the use of gender budget analysis was endorsed by the Meeting of Commonwealth Ministers of Finance in 2002.

Another pioneering government was the Government of **The Philippines,** which pursued a very different strategy, focusing on ensuring funding for its Gender and Development (GAD) strategy (Reyes, 2002; Caharian and Lampauog, 2001) (see Box 13).

Beginning in 1995, a provision was included in the General Appropriations Act mandating all government agencies to set aside a proportion of their allocation to 'projects designed to address gender issues'. In 1996, the proportion was set at 5% as a minimum. This became known as the GAD Budget. It is monitored by National Commission on the Role of Filipino Women (NCRFW). The number of government agencies submitting reports about their GAD plan and GAD budget had reached 40% of government agencies by 1999 and the average allocation to the GAD budget was 0.6% of total government expenditure (NCRFW, 1999). The major problem in compliance seems to be a lack of understanding in government agencies about how to design projects 'to address gender issues', and how to classify their activities into the required three categories of 'women-specific, building institutional mechanisms, and gender mainstreaming'. The strength of the initiative is that it does require all government agencies to begin thinking about the gender dimensions of their activities and is thus an impetus for gender mainstreaming, but its weakness is that at best it only covers 5% of public expenditure and does not cover the revenue side of the budget at all. The NCRFW, together with the Department of Budget Management and the National Economic Development Authority, is investigating ways of moving beyond the 5% GAD budget to look at the rest of the budget.

Box 13 The GAD budget in the Philippines

Since 2000, in a growing range of countries, governments are seeing gender budget analysis as an important tool for mainstreaming gender in their policies and programmes. For instance, in Europe there are government initiatives at the national level in Belgium, the Nordic countries, Ireland and the UK; and at the regional level in Scotland, the Basque country and Emilia Romagna. In Asia, work has begun in India and Nepal. In Africa, Kenya, Malawi, Rwanda, Mozambique, the United Republic of Tanzania and Mauritius are among the governments that have done some gender analysis of their budgets. In Latin America, Chile has introduced gender analysis into the process by which departments bid for funds from the national budgets, while in Mexico analysis has been done of the budgets of the Ministries of Social Development and of Health.

4.2 Collaboration between parliamentarians and civil society organizations in GBIs

In several countries the political leadership for gender analysis of government budgets has come from elected representatives in legislatures, working more closely with civil society organizations. The Women's Budget Initiative (WBI) in **South Africa** originated in 1994 through a coalition of civil society activists and parliamentarians—particularly Pregs Govender—who was a member of the parliamentary Joint Standing Committee on

Finance, and Debbie Budlender, of the policy research NGO the Community Agency for Social Enquiry, who coordinates the gender budget analysis. It came out of a profound mobilization of South African women in the Women's National Coalition as apartheid came to an end. The Women's National Coalition, which drew women together across race, party and class, drew up a Charter for Effective Equality. The WBI reflected the determination of the many newly elected women parliamentarians to see the Charter become a reality (Govender, 2002) (see Box 14). The South African WBI has explicitly used a rights-based approach in its analysis of the budget for housing (Pillay, Manjoo and Paulus, 2002). This is discussed in more detail in Section 5.

Debbie Budlender, who leads the WBI analysis and edits its annual publication, notes that the term 'women's budget' may be something of a misnomer (Budlender, 2000). The WBI does not advocate for a separate budget for women, or confine its analysis to the figures in the budget document. It begins from an analysis of gender inequality and the policies that government is introducing to address this, and goes on to consider questions of policy, programmes and performance. It is a form of policy monitoring and audit and is used to inform parliamentarians so that they are able to understand better the gender implications of the government budgets, and to exercise their parliamentary scrutiny function more effectively.

The standard method employed is to take the government's policy framework sector by sector and go through the following steps:
- Review gender issues in the sector;
- Analyse the appropriateness of the policy framework.
- Examine the extent to which the allocation of resources reflects a serious commitment to the policy goals.
- Examine how the resources have actually been utilized (e.g. how many male and female members of the population have benefited and at what cost).
- Assess the longer-term impacts on male and female members of the population, identifying to what extent their lives have improved.

As well as producing publications with technical analysis, the South African WBI produces popular handbooks in a number of languages for use in workshops with the women for whom it is advocating. It is engaged in a long-term process of capacity building so that there is a well-informed demand for budgets that deliver the promises of the South African constitution.

The five-step method of analysis used by the South African WBI has been disseminated to groups in many other countries. It has also been incorporated into a manual (Budlender and Sharp, 1998) used in training government officials in a wide range of developing countries in which governments have expressed an interest in gender budget analysis. This approach has many useful lessons for monitoring whether budgets comply with CEDAW.

Box 14 The five-step method of the South African Women's Budget Initiative

Uganda is another country in which parliamentarians have provided the political leadership for a GBI, working in conjunction with civil society. The GBI, which began in 1997, has been spearheaded by the Forum for Women in Democracy (FOWODE), an NGO established by women MPs. In cooperation with researchers from Makerere University, and government planners, the GBI has researched three sectors—education, health and agriculture—producing reports and policy briefings that have been used by members of parliament in their scrutiny of the budget. In the words of Winnie Byanyima, formerly one of the leading parliamentarians in the GBI, their findings 'have given credibility and respect to the subject. Male parliamentarians who have joined the project say that this work helps them to speak up for their women constituents' (Byanyima, 2002:131).

4.3 GBIs initiated by civil society

In yet other countries, the lead has been taken by NGOs that have often gone on to develop collaborative relations with governments and parliaments. For example, in 1997, an NGO, the **Tanzania Gender Networking Programme** (TGNP), began to analyse the Tanzanian budget using the same approach as the South African WBI. The aim of the Tanzania Gender Networking Programme was:

'to examine the national budgeting process from a civil society perspective to see how public resources are allocated in national and local budgets and to assess how this allocation impacts women and other groups, such as youth and poor men. … The exercise seeks to lay the foundation of an effective consensus-building campaign to influence the public, policy-makers, legislators and government officials on the necessity of increasing resources towards programmes to benefit women and other disadvantaged members of society' (Rusimbi, 2002).

Later, the Swedish International Development Agency began funding a parallel exercise in the Ministry of Finance, and subsequently TGNP was brought in as consultants to the government to conduct training based on their research and to develop guidelines for gender mainstreaming. The 2000/2001 Budget Guidelines mandated all ministries to prepare their budgets with gender mainstreaming objectives in mind. TGNP has also been invited to contribute to related processes, such as the Public Financial Reform Management Programme, the Public Expenditure Review and the Poverty Reduction Strategy Paper.

In **Mexico** the process was somewhat similar (Hofbauer, 2002). Gender analysis of the allocations for women's reproductive health services budget was initiated in 1999 by Foro, a network of women's organizations, and one of the network members, Equidad de Genero (an NGO working to develop the capacities of women elected to public office) began conducting public finance workshops for women leaders. In 2000, Equidad joined forces with Fundar, a think-tank devoted to applied budget research, in a joint project that began by analysing anti-poverty programmes. One important aim was to monitor the extent of compliance with the Social Development Department directive that every anti-poverty programme should strive to allocate 50% of its total resources to women. The type of participation open to beneficiaries was evaluated and it was found that the participation open to poor women was to contribute their unpaid time to keep the costs of the programme low, rather than participation in 'the definition of the problem, in the identification of possible solutions or in the design of the programmes that are being implemented' (Hofbauer, 2002:15). The conclusion reached was that:

'the majority of the programmes fail to acknowledge the structural obstacles, difficulties and limits placed on women and, by doing so, reproduce and even aggravate existing imbalances. Traditional roles of women are not only upheld, but further relied on to successfully carry out the programs, such as in the case of unpaid work. Women's capacities to organize and play more active roles within their communities and development strategies in general go unrecognized, and receive very little financial support' (Hofbauer, 2000:16).

Since the change in government in 2000, the NGOs have worked more closely with some government departments, especially the Ministry of Health, and with women elected to the legislature, to bring about increases in allocations to programmes important for women's health.

In **India,** the Karnataka Women's Information and Resource Centre (KWIRC), based in Bangalore, has initiated a project with poor, and often illiterate, elected women representatives at the local level with the aim of enabling them to build budgets from below. The project takes as its point of departure that 'gender equality is recognized as part of the fundamental human rights as enshrined in the Indian constitution' (Karnataka Women's Information and Resource Centre, 2002:4). Many more women are now elected to village councils as a result of the constitutional amendment of 1993, which requires that one third of the seats on the councils be reserved for women. However, the KWIRC found that women elected representatives are frequently excluded from discussions of the budget, and the requests they made for funding for projects in their constituencies ('wards') were given less priority than those made by men elected representatives. The KWIRC concluded that 'this is because of gender discrimination and gender bias shown by the authorities while allocating works and distributing benefits. As a result, most of the women members could not undertake development works in their respective wards' (KWIRC, 2002:50).

4.4 GBIs explicitly focused on women's human rights

There is at least one example of a government-led GBI that is explicitly linked to compliance with CEDAW—that of the city of **San Francisco** in the USA. The USA has not ratified CEDAW, but in 1998 the San Francisco Board of Supervisors and the Mayor enacted an ordinance to implement the principles underlying CEDAW. The CEDAW ordinance requires the city government to ensure that it eliminates discrimination and ensures equal opportunity, through its budget, employment practices and provision of services. With the help of the consulting group Strategic Analysis for Gender Equity (SAGE), a city task force examined the services, employment and budgets of two city departments, the Juvenile Probation Department and the Department of Public Works, in the light of CEDAW. The outline of the guidelines used is provided in Box 15.

Services

Step 1 Gathering and Analyzing Gender Disaggregated Data and Reports
  A. Relevant Reports/Studies
  B. Services and Population Served
Step 2 Assessing the Differences in Services between Women/Girls and Men/Boys
  A. Designing and Implementing Services
  B. Contracting for Services
  C. Evaluating Services
  D. Community Involvement
Step 3 Formulating Recommendations for Action

Employment Practices

Step 1 Gathering and Analyzing Gender Disaggregated Data and Reports
  A. Relevant Reports/Studies
  B. Analyzing Workforce Composition
Step 2 Assessing the Differences in Employment between Women/Girls and Men/Boys
  A. Recruitment
  B. Professional Development
  C. Benefits
  D. Anti-discrimination Policies
Step 3 Formulating Recommendations for Action

Budget

Step 1 Gathering and Analyzing Gender Disaggregated Data and Reports
  A. Relevant Reports/Studies
  B. Overall Budgets
Step 2 Assessing the Differences in Budgets between Women/Girls and Men/Boys
  A. Services
  B. Employment
Step 3 Formulating Recommendations for Action

Box 15 San Francisco guidelines for gender budget analysis
(Strategic Analysis for Gender Equity and San Francisco Commission on the Status of Women, 1999.)

The guidelines placed particular attention on the intersection between gender and other forms of inequality, requiring other forms of disaggregation, such as by race, age, language, etc. They included the contracting of service provision to NGOs and small businesses, and the mechanisms for community involvement with service providers. Moreover, departments were required to consider recommendations for change.

It was found that while the services of the Juvenile Probation Department were originally designed to serve young men and boys, the Department had moved to introduce services designed to meet the needs of girls and young women, who in 1999 comprised 25% of the users of the Department's services. However, the Department of Public Works needed to introduce training on how to design, implement and evaluate services from a gender perspective. In both Departments there was a need for further action to eliminate discrimination based on sex and race. The Juvenile Probation Department had proved able to carry out a gender analysis of its budget, which revealed that 17% of its budget was spent on services utilized by girls. The Department of Public Works had not been able to provide comparable data. The follow-up focused primarily on better collection of sex-disaggregated data, and the creation of a more equal workplace.

The objective of compliance with CEDAW led to this initiative but it was exploratory and its scope was limited. No attempt was made to draw out the detailed implications of CEDAW for the city budget as a whole, or to develop benchmarks for evaluating the allocation of expenditure among programmes. There was no discussion of the revenue side of the budget. Nevertheless, it was an important pioneering initiative.

The GBIs in the Andean region **(Bolivia, Colombia, Ecuador** and **Peru)** aim to bring together a wide range of actors from government, legislatures and civil society within an explicit framework of the promotion of women's economic and social rights (Pearl, 2002). The rights-based approach of these initiatives does not take the form of analysis of the quantity of funding allocated to different uses in relation to particular human rights treaties or constitutional guarantees. Instead, it focuses on another element of a rights-based approach: the principles of accountability and transparency (see Section 8.2 for further discussion). These principles are integral to a rights-based approach because they ensure good governance, which is in turn required for the effective implementation of human rights (CESCR, General Comment 14, para. 55; General Comment 15, para. 49). The GBIs in the Andean region aim to ensure that States observe these principles by engaging in an analysis of budget processes, especially at the municipal level, to evaluate the extent of women's ability to hold governments to account, and the scope for enlarging this ability:

> 'One of the dimensions that has acquired the most importance in women's organizations and among the female municipal authorities themselves is facilitating the exercise of transparency and the call for accountability. This involves certain costs: in some provincial and district municipalities of Peru, for example, there have been cases of harassment of female administrators who have developed budget monitoring and surveillance initiatives. This highlights the need to generate mechanism to guarantee this right, especially in rural areas' (Vargas-Valente, 2002:111).

Some GBIs have advocated for quantitative quotas in the distribution of funding. For instance, a GBI in the municipality of Quito in Ecuador, organized by an NGO, the Women's Political Coordinating Organization, argued for a rule that at least 30% of the beneficiaries of municipal projects should be women. Also that 30% of municipal contracts should go to women (Pearl, 2002: 32). This may be effective as an *ad hoc* way of increasing the numbers of women beneficiaries, but it is not clear how the benchmark of 30% was determined.

As noted in Box 11, in 2000 the Government of **France** introduced, at the request of parliament, a budget report on women's rights and equality. It is intended to provide parliamentarians with a tool to effectively measure and monitor public expenditure on efforts to promote women's rights and gender equality. It does not aim to evaluate whether the budget as a whole is in compliance with CEDAW. The report documents budget allocations aimed specifically at women and girls (such as a special guarantee fund that supports the establishment of women-owned businesses and grants made for the operation of shelters for women who have experienced domestic violence). It also identifies spending on awareness-raising or capacity-building activities designed to enable policy-makers and budget officials to address gender inequalities. In 2000, these two types of expenditure amounted to about 40 million Euro in a total national expenditure of about 260 billion (Philippe-Raynaud, 2002:138).

4.5 Questions to ask about GBIs

Given the diversity of GBIs, it is important to seek more information from states that report that there is, or is planned to be, a GBI operative within their country:

- What kind of GBI is planned or is operative in the country?
- What are the roles of the government, parliament and civil society?
- What is the role of the Ministry of Finance and the Office of the Budget?
- Is it institutionalized in ongoing, regular, transparent procedures?
- Do women enjoy equal participation in budget decision-making?

- In what ways has it made women and girls visible in the budget?
- What impact is it expected to have, or has it had, on women's substantive enjoyment of equality?
- What benchmarks or standards are used to assess the impact?
- How do the results of the analysis influence the formulation and implementation of budgets?

Debbie Budlender (Budlender et al., 2002:123) summarizes good practice in the organization of GBIs by referring to *'the triangle of players'*:
- progressive elected politicians
- effective government institutions staffed with well-trained officials
- active and well-informed coalitions of NGOs.

Effective and sustainable GBIs are generally based on the interaction of all three.

Rhonda Sharp, adviser to the south Australian GBI, points to a different triangle (Sharp, 2002:88), a *'triangle of goals'*:
- Raise awareness and understanding of gender issues and the impacts of budgets and policies.
- Make governments accountable for their budgetary and policy commitments.
- Change and refine government budgets and policies to promote gender equality.

She also points to a hierarchy between these goals, with the achievement of the first being necessary for the achievement of the second; and the achievement of the first two being necessary for the achievement of the third. In her assessment, there are many examples of success in achieving the first two goals.

It is much harder to achieve the third goal. As Pregs Govender, former chair of the Parliamentary Committee on the Improvement of the Quality of Life and Status of Women in South Africa, points out, a government's budget reflects its priorities. An end to discrimination against women and the promotion of women's empowerment is not necessarily high on the list of priorities, despite the state having ratified CEDAW. Creating a budget that is consistent with gender equality and supportive of the advancement of women generally means a change in priorities, and there are often strong forces opposed to this. In many countries it is proving difficult to move from analysis conducted by civil society and parliaments to action taken by governments (Budlender, 2000; Hofbauer, 2003). If the analysis were to establish that some dimension of the budget is in violation of CEDAW, then this might contribute additional mobilizing power. The definitional structures and legitimacy provided by CEDAW constitutes a recognized framework that can be used to fortify claims that certain core issues (e.g. the prohibition on non-discrimination) are inalienable. This can be particularly important for marginalized groups, such as women, who may not otherwise have the social, economic or political power to ensure governments adequately address their needs in budgeting processes. The use of the framework of CEDAW also enables groups to tap into broader regional and international networks of women's organizations working on these issues.

Section 5

Analysing Public Expenditure
Programmes from a
CEDAW Perspective

Analysing Public Expenditure Programmes from a CEDAW Perspective

This section draws upon examples of gender budget analysis to consider how public expenditure might be monitored for compliance with CEDAW. The gender implications of programmes to reform the management of public expenditure are discussed in the final part of this section. The gender implications of the macroeconomic dimensions of public expenditure, including the level of total public expenditure, and its expansion and contraction are considered in Section 7.

5.1 Monitoring public expenditure for compliance with CEDAW: Starting points

Expenditure is usually broken down into:
- debt-servicing charges
- expenditure on government activities.

In poor, highly indebted countries, payment of interest on foreign debt often exceeds expenditure on public services.

The expenditure on government activities is generally presented in budget documents in a number of ways:
- by administrative agency, specifying how much money each Ministry or public sector agency would be allowed to spend in the coming financial year;
- by economic function, breaking down total expenditure into a current account (e.g. salaries and consumables, such as paper and telephone calls), and a capital account (e.g. equipment, such as computers, and construction of buildings and other infrastructure);
- by programme, specifying the type of activities to be funded (e.g. primary health care, hospitals, medical research); recently, this has been further elaborated in some countries, both rich and poor, to a system of 'performance-oriented budgeting' in which there are targets and performance indicators for each programme (Sharp, 2003).

To monitor compliance with CEDAW, it is important to examine expenditure by programme. In this section we consider ways of monitoring:
1. Priority given to gender equality and the advancement of women in distribution of public expenditure among programmes;
2. Presence of discrimination against women and girls in the distribution of public expenditure;
3. Adequacy of public expenditure for realization of obligations to gender equality;
4. Gender equality in the impact of public expenditure.

It is important to look at all four dimensions because a high priority for gender equality in distribution of funding does not guarantee that sufficient public expenditure has been allocated to meet obligations, nor that there is real gender equality in the enjoyment of public services, nor that the outcome of the budget is greater gender equality.

It is also important to recall that this monitoring of expenditure applies to both gender-specific programming (which may be targeted exclusively to males or exclusively to females) and programming that is not specifically targeted to one sex or the other. This latter type of programming may appear to be gender neutral, but cannot be taken at face value, as its impact may be far from neutral. States are obliged to monitor both types of programming to ensure that they enhance substantive equality. This scrutiny is necessary because programming targeted to males is not necessarily discriminatory against females; it may promote *de facto* equality (for example, an anger-management programme target at teenage boys). Nor does programming targeted to females necessarily promote gender equality; it may reinforce unequal stereotypes. Moreover, not all non-targeted programming will be equally beneficial to males and females. On the latter point: on the one hand, it is clear that *de facto* equality will not be realized simply through the implementation of programmes that, on the face of it, are gender neutral (CESCR, General Comment 16, para. 8 and para. 13). This is because such programmes may fail to consider existing inequalities between men and women and may instead reinforce women's subordinate role or traditional gender stereotypes.

In monitoring expenditure by programme, it is also necessary to bear in mind the three different types of measures for which CEDAW provides. This is necessary because each measure has different elements against which a particular government policy will need to be assessed to determine whether it complies with CEDAW. These three types of measures have been set out in the Introduction and will be briefly recapped here. These measures are: general measures to improve the position of women and to guarantee their full enjoyment of economic, social and cultural rights; temporary special measures to accelerate the achievement of *de facto* (or substantive) equality between women and men (Article 4(1)); and permanent gender-specific special measures necessitated by biological difference (Article 4(2)). The particularities of monitoring of expenditure pursuant to temporary special measures as opposed to permanent special measures can be taken as an example here. Article 4(1) makes it clear that the temporary special measures to accelerate *de facto* equality do not constitute discrimination. It is also clear from Article 4(1) that the adoption of temporary special measures 'shall in no way entail as a consequence the maintenance of unequal or separate standards' and that 'these measures shall be discontinued when the objectives of equality of opportunity and treatment have been achieved'. Thus, a key element of monitoring of expenditure through temporary special measures is to determine whether such measures should be continued or discontinued, that is whether the objectives set out in Article 4(1) have been achieved. The CEDAW Committee has clarified that temporary special measures 'must be discontinued when their desired results have been achieved and sustained for a period of time' (CEDAW, General Recommendation 25, para. 20). This is a different 'end point' than for gender-specific special measures necessitated by biological difference (Article 4(2)). These measures are permanent in nature and last until their review is required by the scientific and technological knowledge mentioned in Article 11(3) (CEDAW, General Recommendation 25, para.16).

It would be useful to be able to examine programme expenditure on public services jointly with direct taxation but the micro-simulation models required for this do not disaggregate by sex but by household income level (for an example of analysis that disaggregates by household income group, see Sutherland et al., 2004). Moreover, large amounts of data are required for such analysis, and this is usually not available in lower income countries. Thus, expenditure will be treated separately from revenue.

5.2 Priority given to promotion of gender equality in distribution of public expenditure between programmes

In Article 3 of CEDAW States Parties agree to take, 'all appropriate measures, including legislation, to ensure the full development and advancement of women, for the purpose of guaranteeing them the exercise and enjoyment of human rights and fundamental freedoms on a basis of equality with men'.

If programmes that promote gender equality and the full development and advancement of women could be identified, and the expenditure on these programmes could be identified, then it would be possible to calculate the share of public expenditure going to such programmes. This could be tracked over time and one country could be compared with another. It might be possible to reach some international consensus on a benchmark comparable to the human development expenditure benchmarks (see Box 6). This would be particularly useful for monitoring compliance with article 3 of CEDAW. The Government of France's budget paper on gender equality and women's rights, discussed in the previous section, is a possible example.

Country	Share of public expenditure targeted to women (%)			
	1998/99	1999/00	2000/01	2001/02
India	1.02	0.94	0.88	0.87
Nepal	n.a.	0.40	0.40	0.60

Box 16 Expenditures targeted exclusively to women in India and Nepal
(India: NIPFP, 2003:64; Nepal: Acharya, 2003:35.)

5.2.1 Expenditures targeted to women

However, there are many complexities in identifying which programmes promote gender equality and the advancement of women. Several gender budget initiatives have tried to classify programmes in terms of their gender implications, taking as their point of departure Sharp's three-step classification (Box 12), and modifying it to meet local conditions. The case of India and Nepal reveals some of the difficulties. Box 16 shows expenditures targeted exclusively to women in the two countries. In both countries the share is very small; in India it is higher, but falling over time, whereas in Nepal the share is smaller, rising over time. However, by themselves, the figures do not tell us much, since we have no benchmark against which to assess them. As mentioned above, not all expenditures targeted to women promote gender equality, and many programmes that are not specifically targeted to women have an equality-enhancing impact on women.

5.2.2 'Pro-women' expenditures

In both Nepal and India, analysts argue that there is a further range of programmes from which women derive substantial benefits, and they give these the label 'pro-women' programmes (Acharya, 2003:17; NIPFP, 2003:71).

In the case of India, the label 'public expenditure with pro-women allocations' was used to cover the 'women's components' of poverty alleviation programmes. This was a response to the Indian Government's practice of designating 'women's components' in programmes targeted at both men and women. For instance, the Ministry of Rural Development has 'special components for women in its programmes and funds are earmarked under "women's component" to ensure flow of adequate resources for their empowerment' (Ministry of Rural Development, 2000:11). Examples include:
- a micro-enterprise development programme for poor people in which 30% of the opportunities are reserved for women;
- a programme to provide assistance in house construction for poor people in which priority is given to widows and unmarried women; and
- a programme of employment creation for poor members of the Scheduled Castes and Tribes in which 30% of the employment opportunities are reserved for women (Senapaty, 2000a).

This practice of reserving places for women in programmes that serve both men and women goes back to the time of the Sixth Plan (1980-85) (UNIFEM, 1998:4). It is a continuation of a longstanding policy of reserving places for deprived or socially excluded groups, notably the Scheduled Castes and Tribes. It is not easy to determine how much is actually spent on the women's components. In the case of the Scheduled Tribes there is a specific budget heading where all the money spent on programmes reserved for them must be recorded, but this does not apply to the women's component (Senapaty, 2000a: 9). NIPFP (2003) contains estimates for the years 1995/1996 and 2002/2003, which are shown in Box 17.

Country	Share of pro-women expenditure in total expenditure				
	1995/6	1999/00	2000/1	2001/2	2002/3
India	3.89	n.a.	n.a.	n.a.	2.05
Nepal	n.a.	13.6	14.2	13.8	n.a.

Box 17 Pro-women expenditures in India and Nepal
(India: NIPFP, 2003:71; Nepal: Acharya, 2003:35.)

An analysis of expenditure in Nepal also used the category 'pro–women' to refer to some types of expenditure (see Box 17) but in the absence of an Indian-style 'women's component' system, proposed the following criteria (Acharya, 2003:17):
- Women's involvement: Participation is a necessary condition for empowerment.
- Women's employment opportunities: Does the program increase work opportunities for the poorer sections of the population, particularly women/men from the poorer households?

- Do such programs have positive impacts on overall gender relations?
- Impact on women's workload: Do the project activities reduce women's drudgery and workload?
- Impact on women's social and household decision-making roles: A pro-women programme is expected to enable women to participate more in decision-making processes both within and outside their households.
- Do women derive direct benefit from income-generating, health and education activities?

These are helpful criteria but it is hard to apply them *a priori*. They are more appropriate for conducting an impact analysis than for categorization of expenditure allocations.

On the face of it, the data in Box 17 might be taken to imply that Nepal is better than India at ensuring women benefit from public expenditure. However, these estimates cannot be directly compared because the definition of 'pro-women expenditure' used in the Nepal analysis is much broader than that used in the case of India. For instance, it includes all expenditure on primary education, whereas education expenditure is excluded from Indian estimates.

5.2.3 Empowering expenditures

Nirmala Banerjee proposes yet another way of classifying expenditure in her analysis of gender and public expenditure in the state of West Bengal in India. She argues that many programmes targeted specifically to women serve to reinforce traditional roles, and spending on them should not be counted as equality-promoting expenditure: 'But if our overall aim is to harness the state's help in achieving true equality between men and women, we need to push for policies that not merely assist women to fulfill their traditional roles, but also to promote them in roles that will change existing gender positions' (Banerjee, 2003:16).

She suggests a different classification (Banerjee, 2003:16-18):
- relief policies, targeted to specific groups of women in distress (e.g. widows);
- gender-reinforcing assistance, which provides for women's 'needs in accepted gender roles' (e.g. programmes that address women's reproductive functions);
- equality-promoting schemes, 'which are meant specifically to remove some gender-based handicap of women', including schemes such as crèches to allow women to work and extra toilets for girls in schools.

The first two categories of programme help meet women's immediate needs, but for longer-run changes, the third type of programme is essential. Banerjee argues that 'even if the allocation to schemes of the third kind is relatively small, it is essential that the balance, over time, shifts in their favour' (Banerjee, 2003:18).

A tension between gender-reinforcing and equality-promoting aspects of the Mexican poverty alleviation programme, *Progresa*, has been identified by Colinas (2003). The programme, which ran from August 1997 to 2002, provided cash assistance to mothers in poor families, on condition that they sent their children to school and to the clinic for check-ups and vaccinations, and took care of family health and nutrition. On the one hand, the programme reinforced the responsibility of women for the care of the family. On the other, it made payments directly to women, even those in male-headed households. Moreover, the grants for sending girls to secondary school were higher than for sending boys to secondary school, to counteract the tendency for poor girls to drop out of school earlier than poor boys. '*Progresa* shows implicit contradictions, because on the one hand, the programme aims to challenge women's subordination but on the other hand, relies on women's traditional role in its operation mechanisms' (Colinas, 2003:34).

These complexities suggest that it is not possible to identify *a priori* which programmes promote gender equality and the advancement of women. It is necessary to investigate the content and impact of programmes in a particular social context. This means it is difficult to construct *a priori* benchmarks comparable to the *Human Development* expenditure benchmarks. It would be even more difficult to construct them in ways that are comparable across countries. A simple, quantitative, internationally applicable benchmark for a gender equality priority ratio does not seem feasible.

5.3. Presence of discrimination against women and girls in the distribution of public expenditure

It is likely to be much more feasible to monitor distribution of expenditures to specific programmes to see if there is *de jure* or *de facto* discrimination. Below we consider some examples and the lessons that may be drawn from them.

5.3.1 Separate programmes

A first step investigating this would be to consider whether there are programmes that formally exclude females (or males). Very often there are such programmes in the fields of health or education or sport, for instance. The division itself does not necessarily constitute discrimination as defined in Article 1 of CEDAW. The rationale for the exclusion needs to be considered. For example, a country that maintains separate schools for boys and girls and justifies differences in per capita expenditure on these schools on the basis of a preference for male education would clearly be discriminatory and violate Article 2(1) of CEDAW. It would also infringe particular articles of CEDAW, such as Article 10(b) which requires that males and females should have access to the same curricula, the same examinations, teaching staff with qualifications of the same standard and school premises and equipment of the same quality'. There may, however, be a case for exclusion of one sex or the other if it is demonstrated that males and females have different needs that can be best met by separate programmes, and that the existence of these programmes will enhance the equality of men and women. This last element is often dispositive, since it requires States to demonstrate that their aim in creating separate programmes is to enhance women's substantive equality, something that is often impossible with separate programmes for females and males.

5.3.2 General programmes with individual beneficiaries

Most expenditure is on general programmes that do not formally exclude either sex. Here the first question is whether the laws governing access discriminate against women, either directly or indirectly. Such discrimination is often found in the laws governing access to income transfers, such as family allowances, health insurance, social security and retirement benefits. These laws often treat women as merely dependents of male bread-winners and give women less favourable access than men. In many cases independent entitlements can only be established though engagement in paid work in 'formal' jobs in the public sector or large firms, excluding the contribution to society that is made through 'informal' employment and through the unpaid work of caring for families and communities. Such rules tend to result in women having less income security and being more at risk of impoverishment than are men. They make it more difficult for women to leave abusive relationships.

CEDAW specifically calls for equality of rights to social security, 'particularly in cases of retirement, unemployment, sickness, invalidity and old age and other incapacity to work' (Article 11(e)). It also calls for equality of rights to family benefits (Article 13(a)).

States Parties' reports often do include discussion of discrimination in the laws governing these areas of provision and of the measures they are taking to remove it. For instance, the second periodic report of Jordan, in 1999, acknowledged that there are elements of discrimination against women in provisions relating to family allowances, health insurance, social security and retirement benefits, and discussed progress towards the removal of such discrimination (United Nations, Committee on the Elimination of Discrimination Against Women, 1999, UN Doc CEDAW/C/JOR/2, para. 137).

Even if the laws governing access are not discriminatory, the distribution of public expenditure may still be unequal as between males and females. In the next few sections we consider how to monitor this. We consider programmes with individual beneficiaries, such as education, training programmes, employment creation programmes and poverty alleviation programmes. To check for equality in the distribution of public expenditure, the first step is to obtain data on expenditure and outputs of the programme; the second is to obtain sex-disaggregated data about the beneficiaries of programmes, either from household surveys or from administrative data held by government agencies. In many cases sex-disaggregated data is not readily available, and a major task of GBIs is to search for such data. Budlender (2003) has a helpful checklist of the kinds of questions that need to be asked about the beneficiaries of programmes.

5.3.2.1 Gender distribution of education expenditure

Article 10 of CEDAW provides that: 'States Parties shall take all appropriate measures to eliminate discrimination against women in order to ensure them equal rights with men in the field of education' and sets out in sub-sections (a) to (h) a series of measures that the State must in particular ensure: 'the same conditions for career and vocational guidance, for access to studies and for the achievement of diplomas in educational establishments of all categories in rural as well as in urban areas' (10(a)); access to the same resources (e.g. curricula, teaching staff, premises) (10(b)); elimination of stereotypes on roles of men and women (10(c)); same opportunities for scholarship benefits (10(d)); same opportunities to access continuing education (10(e)); 'reduction of female student drop-out rates and the organization of programmes for girls and women who have left school prematurely' (10(f)); 'same opportunities to participate actively in sports and physical education' (10(g)); and access to information to ensure health and well-being of families (10(h)).

Both the general, and many of the specific, obligations on States listed in Article 10, require, at minimum, gender equality in enrolment rates in primary, secondary and tertiary education. Insofar as boys and girls are present in equal numbers in the school age population, equal enrolment rates also implies that boys and girls should have equal shares of total school enrolment. Ending gender disparity in educational enrolment is also one of the Millennium Development Targets. If the enrolment rates of boys and girls are different, then the expenditure will not be equally divided. The distribution of expenditure by sex can be calculated using sex-disaggregated expenditure incidence analysis (one of the tools identified in Appendix 2). The basic method for this is given in Box 18; some examples are given in Box 19.

1. Estimate for any given year the unit cost of providing the service, e.g. the cost of a school place for a year—this can be done by dividing total expenditure on schools by the number of school places provided or the number of children who actually attend school. If fees are charged to attend school, these should be deducted.

2. Estimate how many girls and how boys attended school in that year. Enrolment figures are often used. But if substantial numbers of children drop out of school, then it would be better to adjust enrolment figures for dropout rates.

3. Multiply the unit costs by the number of girls in school to get the amount of public spending going to girls.

4. Multiply the unit costs by the number of boys in school to get the amount of public spending going to boys.

5. Compare the two, either on a per capita basis, or in terms of the share going to each sex.

Box 18 Sex-disaggregated expenditure incidence analysis

Where boys and girls are present in equal numbers in the school age population, equal enrolment rates implies equal shares of educational expenditure. It is important to bear in mind that equality in the distribution of expenditure does not guarantee equality in the ultimate benefits that stem from this expenditure. For instance, girls and boys may be equally enrolled in school, but girls may fail to complete their schooling. Disparity in completion rates may result from families valuing longer-term education needs of boys over that of girls; by conditions that jeopardize the safety of girls on their way to and from school (CESCR, General Comment 16, para. 30) and thereby discourage continued attendance; and by traditional or stereotyped views which confine girls to earlier marriage or maternal roles that disrupt their completion of formal education. Even if completion rates are equalized, the financial return to education may be lower for women than for men. Differences in financial returns to employment can result from lack of equal remuneration for work of equal value; gender stereotypes in hiring practices; and unfavourable work conditions in occupations in which the majority of employees are women.

The figures in Box 19 indicate that girls are not getting equal shares of expenditure on education. This is not because governments are deliberately channelling resources to boys or have discriminatory laws governing access. The schools are equally open to boys and girls. The inequality in the distribution of expenditure is

India: Central government spending on elementary education in 2002/2003
Per capita expenditure going to girls: Rs.323.48
Per capita expenditure going to boys: Rs. 388.91(estimated by NIPFP, 2003)

West Bengal: State spending on elementary education in 1999/2000
Share of expenditure going to girls: 43.5%
Share of expenditure going to boys: 56.5% (estimated by Banerjee, 2003)

Cote d'Ivoire: Spending on primary education, 1995
Per capita expenditure going to girls: CFAF 6135
Per capita expenditure going to boys: CFAF 8252
Share of expenditure going to girls: 41.6%
Share of expenditure going to boys: 58.4% (estimated by Demery, 2002)

Box 19 Examples of sex-disaggregated education expenditure incidence analysis

because families are not sending girls to school at the same rate as boys. Nevertheless, the State has a responsibility here because there are measures it is required to take under CEDAW to persuade and enable families to send girls to school at the same rate as boys. Such measures include those provided for in Article 10 of CEDAW and temporary special measures that can be adopted under Article 4(1) to accelerate the achievement of substantive equality. These measures can include:
- providing scholarships for girls
- providing separate school toilet facilities for girls and boys
- providing more women teachers.

To meet obligations under CEDAW, the governments mentioned in Box 19 need to assess why substantive equality has not been achieved in education, and to analyse to what extent, and in which ways, adjustments in public expenditure will realize this goal. However, changes in how public expenditure on education is distributed between boys and girls will often be an insufficient (though necessary) step towards discharging obligations under CEDAW. This is because the requirement of substantive equality under CEDAW means that it is not enough to just redistribute public expenditure in ways that seek to close the gender gaps in school enrolment. Instead, the measure of a State's compliance with CEDAW is the *effects* of this redistribution on the provision of an education in which girls enjoy substantive equality. Redistribution of public expenditure on education will not be sufficient to secure girls' substantive equality in education unless it includes finance for other measures that a State is obliged to take under CEDAW, such as measures to ensure that girls complete their education and do not drop out of school, and transformation of curricula to eliminate stereotypes which inhibit women's enjoyment of substantive equality. Ensuring that there is gender equality in the enjoyment of financial benefits from education is even more challenging, since it requires measures to end discrimination in the labour market.

5.3.2.2 Gender distribution of expenditure on training programmes for farmers

CEDAW Article 14 focuses on the rights of rural women, and specifically requires States Parties to 'take all appropriate measures to eliminate discrimination against women in rural areas'. This includes ensuring that rural women have equal rights to obtain all types of training, including 'the benefit of all community and extension services, in order to improve their technical proficiency'. This means that rural women must themselves be treated as producers, not merely as farmers' wives.

The requirement for formal equality in CEDAW means that there is a presumption that women's share of enrolments in, and completions of, such training programmes should be in proportion to their presence in the relevant target population. In some cases, in which women comprise the majority of farmers in a particular community or of those farmers undertaking a particular activity, formal equality implies that women should have the proportionate majority of places in training programmes targeted to that group. In cases where women are a minority of the relevant group of farmers, then formal equality implies that women should have a proportionate minority of places in training programmes targeted to that group.

However, because CEDAW also mandates substantive equality and recognizes that formal equality is insufficient for a State to meet its obligations, it also allows for evidence rebutting this presumption, for example by showing that proportionate enrolment shares is not sufficient to achieve *de facto* equality and that additional activities, such as temporary special measures, are necessary to meet the different training needs of members of rural populations. An example would be where women, or men, are in a minority in a particular target group because of stereotypes that limit women's, or men's, participation in some particular activity. In such a case, it would be appropriate to introduce special programmes designed to increase the participation of women, or men, in the activity.

This requirement of substantive equality makes judgments about the presence or absence of gender equality in the distribution of funding more nuanced. Box 20 discusses an example for government-funded agricultural training programmes in Sri Lanka. It is clear that in this case, definite conclusions cannot be drawn from sex-disaggregated figures on numbers of farmers receiving training. More information is required about how the programmes operate.

Among 113,078 farmers receiving field training from the Department of Agriculture in 1996, for every male there were only 0.07 females (Department of National Planning, Ministry of Finance and Planning, Government of Sri Lanka, 2000:35). Clearly, women did not receive an equal share of training places.

However, according to official statistics, women account for 34% of workers in agriculture (meaning that for every male agricultural worker, there are about 0.45 women). It could be argued that the standard for judgment should be the ratio of 0.45 women to each man in each course.

Judged against this standard, there were wide variations between programmes, in some of which women were under-represented and in others of which they were over-represented. The under-representation of women was particularly marked in the major programme, field training in crop production. The over-representation of women was particularly marked in training for agricultural processing.

However, it might be argued that the appropriate benchmark to use is not the ratio of women to men in agricultural work in general, but in relation to the particular agricultural tasks that women and men do. Since women and men specialize in different agricultural tasks, they are likely to choose different kinds of training. It would be useful to compare expenditure per beneficiary on the programmes on which women were over-represented with expenditure per beneficiary on the programmes on which men were over-represented. Do the former get less funding per capita than the latter? If so, is this an example of discrimination? Or is it justified by the different requirements of different kinds of training (e.g. for special equipment)?

To investigate how far the patterns of participation do reflect choices and how far gender-specific barriers, further investigation would be needed, including interviews with actual and potential beneficiaries. It might be argued that government-funded training programmes have a duty to try to modify stereotyped roles for women and men in agriculture, in so far as they disadvantage women. In this case, evidence might be sought of measures to attract women and men to attend the training courses in which they are under-represented.

Box 20 Participation of men and women farmers in training programmes in Sri Lanka: What counts as non-discrimination?

5.3.2.3 Gender equality in the distribution of expenditure on public employment creation programmes

Article 11(1) of CEDAW requires that 'States Parties shall take all appropriate measures to eliminate discrimination against women in the field of employment in order to ensure, on a basis of equality of men and women, the same rights …' as men in the field of employment. Article 11 proceeds to set out in sub-sections (a) to (f) the rights that a State shall, in particular, ensure. Article 11 is aimed at the obligations of the State to end discrimination against women and to ensure equality in all employment contexts. It has relevance to public employment creation programmes designed to provide employment for poor people. These employment programmes (like any other employment activities) must meet CEDAW's requirement of substantive equality, which in turn means that they must produce equality of results (CEDAW, General Recommendation 25, para. 9). This means that women should have the same income levels and working conditions as men in such programmes and should be fairly represented in such programmes.

An appropriate benchmark to use as a starting point in assessing women's representation in such programmes is the proportion of jobs going to women in such programmes compared to the proportion of women in the target unemployed population. If women's share of the employment created is less than their share of the unemployed population, this gives cause for concern that the programme may be operating in a way that discriminates against women. On the other hand, if women's share of employment is higher than their share of the unemployed population, this gives cause for concern that the programme's benefits may be too low, since programmes with low benefits tend not to attract unemployed men. Because of inequality in the economy and society, men tend to have a higher 'reservation wage' than women. That is, unemployed men tend to require higher wages and benefits than do women to attract them to take up employment.

Box 21 shows an example of gender analysis of an employment creation programme in South Africa. The analysis suggested the programme was operating in a way that discriminated against women; and the government planned to adjust the programme to rectify this.

The 1998 Budget Review of the government of South Africa reported on employment in the Community Based Public Works Programme, to which R250 million had been allocated between 1994 and 1998.

'A 1997 evaluation of the program found that the quality of the assets produced was exceptionally high compared to similar programs elsewhere in the world. It found the 599 projects to be well-distributed geographically with respect to the relative poverty profiles of the nine provinces ...

Of those employed on the projects, 41 per cent were women ... While the figure for women is lower than the female proportion of the population in the rural areas in which the projects operate, it is almost certainly higher than would have been the case without explicit targeting. Unfortunately, the evaluation suggests that women were often assigned the more menial jobs, that their average wages were lower, that they were generally employed for shorter periods than men and that they were less likely than men to receive training. Thirty-seven per cent of men who were employed received training, compared to 32 per cent of women. The evaluation results have formed the basis of the Department's current plans to fine-tune the program and further improve targeting'.

Box 21 Gender equality in the National Public Works Programme in South Africa
(Republic of South Africa, 1998)

5.3.2.4 Gender equality in the distribution of expenditure on poverty alleviation programmes

The requirement of substantive equality under Article 3 of CEDAW means that States must undertake activities that concretely improve the position of women in relation to resources and power (CEDAW, General Recommendation 25, para. 8). Such activities include poverty alleviation programmes. In addition to Article 3, other articles that would provide for the adoption of poverty alleviation programmes for women include Article 13, which states that 'States Parties shall take all appropriate measures to eliminate discrimination against women in other areas of economic and social life in order to ensure, on a basis of equality of men and women, the same rights ...' and lists the rights which must in particular be guaranteed). Since many rural women live in poverty, the specific obligations that States have towards this subset of women are also relevant to poverty reduction programming.

Some governments have tried to promote greater equality in the gender distribution of expenditure on poverty alleviation and rural development programmes through the use of quotas. For instance:
- Indian 9th plan (1995-2000) has a women's component requiring 30% of expenditure of a variety of poverty alleviation programmes to go to women.

- In Mexico in the late 1990s, the Ministry of Social Development had a policy that 50% of beneficiaries of poverty alleviation programmes should be women.
- In South Africa, the code of conduct for special public works programmes states that 60% of the beneficiaries should be women. In the skills development programmes 54% of the beneficiaries are meant to be women and 85% black South Africans.

The rationale for the choice of the stipulated percentages is not always clear. The Secretary for the Ministry of Women and Child Development, Government of India, was quite frank about this at a Workshop on Gender Budgets organized by UNIFEM in Delhi, July 2000. As the workshop report puts it:

'Mr Chaturvedi questioned the sanctity of the number 30 percent and stated it is really an ad hoc number. ... The crucial issue is the need of the sector, if it is education or health, perhaps we need to spend much more than 30 percent (even 75 percent) on women' (Senapaty, 2000b:3).

The quotas in South Africa do reflect the needs of different groups and relate to the percentage of women (and black people) in the target group (poor people and people who need skills development). Thus a good benchmark would be that the female proportion of beneficiaries of poverty alleviation programmes should be equal to the female proportion of the population in poverty. However, in certain circumstances CEDAW may require States to do more than just meet this benchmark. The exact State obligations will ultimately depend on what is required to ensure substantive equality for women, including specific groups of women. For example, it may be necessary to adopt temporary special measure that allow for the targeting of a specific group of women in poverty in order to accelerate the substantive equality of women subject to multiple grounds of discrimination (e.g. black poor rural women). The CEDAW Committee has explicitly encouraged temporary special measures to be directed, where necessary, to women experiencing multiple discrimination, including rural women (CEDAW, General Recommendation 25, para. 39).

5.3.3 Programmes that provide 'public goods'

There are many important public services whose use cannot be broken down into individual units, consumed exclusively by this or that person. Instead they go to whole groups (households, communities, society as whole). In many cases, one person's use of them does not stop other people also benefiting from the facility at the same time. For example, street lighting, paved roads, sanitation systems, defence and policing. These services are described by economists as 'public goods'. It is not possible to analyse the distribution by sex of expenditure on these programmes in quite the same way as for programmes that deliver services on an individual basis.

However, we can do some gender analysis once we recognize that men and women frequently utilize 'public goods' in different ways and have different priorities for the provision of such goods. So the benefits are not equally divided between them. Surveys can be done to collect information on direct utilization by men and women of many public goods. The fact that men's use of them does not exclude women's use of them does not mean that men and women will utilize them in equal measure. If women live in the seclusion of the household, they will not make much use of public parks. If men leave the neighbourhood each morning for paid work and do not return until the evening, they will not make much use of local facilities such as paved roads and sanitation systems. If men are not victims of domestic violence to the same extent as women, they will not make as much use of policing services that aim to reduce domestic violence. Not surprisingly, different patterns of use may tend to lead to men and women having different priorities for public expenditure on public goods (see Box 22).

The distribution of expenditure on public goods can be analysed in terms of gendered priorities—comparing the funding allocated to those prioritized by men with those prioritized by women. A focus on priorities would be particularly useful for those public goods that are more in the nature of national 'overheads' not directly utilized by households—defence, dams, trunk roads, ports, for instance—where it does not make sense to speak of the distribution of expenditure to men and women, but it does make sense to speak of meeting men's priorities or women's priorities. A focus on priorities is necessitated by the principle of participation which requires that all women be able to contribute on equal terms with all men in decision-making about how the budget should be spent (see further Section 1.3.8). The principle of participation means that the State must ensure that different groups of women have an equal opportunity to articulate their priorities and that the space for participation is not monopolized by privileged women's groups (e.g. wealthy urban women) at the expense of others (e.g. poor

Here are three examples of different in men's and women's priorities, drawn from a guide to creating infrastructure that will fairly serve the needs of all (Reed et al., forthcoming):

- **Three Crowns Community, Totonicapan, Guatemala**

The men refused to take any initiative in solving a problem with drinking water, as water for domestic use is not their priority. The women formed a committee, looked for better water sources and obtained external funding to construct a better facility. Once the women were able to get the funds, the men began to support them and do the necessary construction work.

- **Guyana, Amerindian community**

The needs and priorities of the community were discussed with an aid agency at a community meeting attended by both men and women. The priority of women was for water, since they had to walk some miles to a spring. The men wanted a road to be constructed to increase opportunities for income generation. During the meetings no consensus could be reached.

- **Nkayi, Zimbabwe**

Only men were on the dam committees, which managed water for cattle.

Hand-dug wells, used mainly for domestic purposes, were almost the exclusive domain of women. Boreholes, which supplied water for cattle and for domestic use, were used by both men and women, and conflict arose over the priorities of different users. Cattle watering generally took precedence over domestic use.

Box 22 Gendered priorities for public goods

rural women). The obligation on States to ensure substantive equality also acts as a check to ensure that meeting priorities does not reinforce inequalities among differently situated groups. Both this obligation and the principle of participation requires attention to the process of decision-making about budgets, which will be considered in more detail in Section 8.

The issue of gender difference in priorities has been addressed by a quota in the Indian state of Kerala, where the state government has stipulated that 10% of expenditure allocated for implementation of local development plans should go to priorities identified by women. As with the quotas mentioned earlier, it is not quite clear why this particular percentage has been chosen.

Another way of conducting a gender analysis of expenditure on public goods is via a geographical distribution of infrastructural facilities. Insofar as men and women are distributed in different ways by location, this throws some light on the gender distribution of such facilities. For instance, if females constitute a higher proportion of the rural population than males (as they do in many poor countries), and the share of infrastructure expenditure going to rural areas is lower than that going to urban areas, such a distribution of funding would be a case of *de facto* discrimination against women. Moreover, it would be in contravention of Article 14 of CEDAW, which requires that 'States Parties shall take all appropriate measures to eliminate discrimination against women in rural areas'.

5.4 Developing benchmarks for adequacy of public expenditure for CEDAW obligations

CEDAW implies a need to go beyond the question of whether expenditure is distributed equally, because it would be possible to have a non-discriminatory distribution of funding, but insufficient funds to carry out all the measures which are vital for the 'full development and advancement of women'. Here it is important to read CEDAW in the light of the International Covenant of Economic, Social and Cultural Rights, with its requirement for 'progressive realization', and its implication that core minimum standards should be met (see Box 3).

To develop benchmarks for adequacy requires going beyond financial inputs to look at required activities, outputs and outcomes. It requires:

- agreement on the outcomes to be achieved
- investigation of the activities and outputs required to achieve the agreed outcomes
- investigation of the costs of providing these activities and outputs
- comparison of the costs with what has been allocated in the budget.

Developing such benchmarks also requires that account be taken of how women's unpaid work often represents a hidden subsidy to public programmes. There is reason to believe that this subsidy has been growing in many countries, as the delivery of social programmes is contracted out to NGOs and community organizations (often in the name of 'self-management' or 'partnerships'). Gender analysis of the budget of the municipality of Villa El Salvador in Peru examined this hidden subsidy. It investigated a food assistance programme that takes up one third of the municipal budget and is supported by 3 million US dollars annually. The programme relied on the unpaid work of women in the municipality to distribute the food. The study, by Arlette Beltran, examined the amount of time this took, and estimated what it would have cost if the municipality had had to pay for this time at the minimum wage rate. The cost would have been equal to 20% of the budget for this programme (Pearl, 2002:39).

Gender budget analysis in Mexico found a similar phenomenon. An investigation of a major anti-poverty programme, *Progresa,* found that it relied heavily on the unpaid work of women who were already overburdened. The implementation of the programme at the grass roots relied on 46,521 voluntary workers, mainly women, who worked on average 29 hours per month without pay. Some beneficiaries expressed the view that the meagre cash grants they obtained were not worth the overall effort required to comply with the programme's demands (Hofbauer, 2003).

Women's unpaid contributions that are genuinely voluntary are not against the spirit of CEDAW. Nor are contributions from beneficiaries who do have spare time. For instance in South Africa, poor women can obtain housing subsidies to build a house provided they are willing to contribute their own labour. In this case women are able to do so because in the townships there are no employment opportunities and they have time on their hands. Where there is cause for concern is when those poor women, who already have many demands on their time, find they can access public services only by making unpaid contributions to the running of public programmes. Care must be taken that unpaid voluntary work does not become another kind of user fee, paid in time rather than money, and that inadequate funding is not perpetuated by hidden subsidies of women's unpaid work.

Once a benchmark has been established and funding is found to be inadequate, it is also important to consider how more resources can be found, in ways that are in compliance with CEDAW. This might imply:
- redistribution of funding between programmes
- measures to increase tax revenue
- increased foreign aid flows
- extension of debt relief.

5.4.1 Adequacy of funding for implementation of domestic violence policies

A pioneering analysis looked at the adequacy of the budget for the implementation of the Domestic Violence Act in South Africa (see Box 23). The issue of funding for domestic violence policies was also addressed in a gender analysis of the national budget of Barbados, 1998/99 (see Box 24).

A comprehensive method for identifying how much government funding is needed for adequate implementation of domestic violence policies in Latin America and the Caribbean has been developed, in consultation with women in the region, by the International Centre for Research on Women (ICRW, 2003). This follows an investigation of domestic violence policies and laws in seven countries in the region (Chile, Costa Rica, Dominican Republic, Ecuador, El Salvador, Mexico and Peru). It was found that:
- In no case was there an appropriation in the national budget for domestic violence programmes and interventions when the law was enacted or the plan of action formulated.
- Subsequent funding of programmes to address domestic violence came out of general budgets of a number of Ministries and/or from international donors. It was often insecure and generally inadequate to meet the needs of women.

The Domestic Violence Act 116 was introduced in 1998, and is an expression of the commitment of the state to eliminate domestic violence in line with its CEDAW obligations, and with the South African constitution, which states that 'Everyone has the right to freedom and security of the person, which includes the right to be free from all forms of violence from either public or private sources'. NGOs welcomed the Act but were concerned that insufficient resources were being allocated for its implementation. The Gender Advocacy Programme, a Cape Town-based NGO, commissioned the study that identified in detail shortfalls in the budgets of the Departments of Safety and Security, Justice and Welfare/Social Services, in areas such as training for police and officials, and victim support services in the Western Cape Province

Source: Goldman and Budlender, 1999.

Three examples of significant findings are:

- Although there would be the need for additional police time to implement the Act, there was a general shortfall of funding for police officers. Although the approved complement of police officers was 161,755 posts, there was no funding for 35,755 of them.

- Although there was a budget allocated for training police officers in the implementation of the Act, the third of the funding that was supposed to come from an international donor had been delayed, and no specific funding had been made available to the Western Cape training manager, who therefore was constrained to do the training 'cheaply' allowing for just 3 to 4 hours at each police station, though local NGOs with extensive knowledge of policing of domestic violence thought that 5 to 6 hours would be necessary.

- Although there was R500,000 funding for shelters for victims of violence in 1999/2000, there were no proposals to increase this. Moreover, the funding did not cover the full costs of the shelters, which were run by NGOs.

The study was innovatory in also identifying ways of making available the additional resources required to implement the Act by changing priorities and improving efficiency:

- Further resources for the implementation of the Domestic Violence Act by the South African Police Service could come by levying a charge on the budgets of all police programmes and transferring it to the implementation of a 'women's safety plan'. In effect this would be reallocating police time towards women's safety.

- 'Money being wasted by the Department of Justice could be used instead to implement the Act. Business Day (20.8.1999) notes that the justice budget has "serious shortcomings, poor checking and control and non-compliance with directives". One security official apparently claimed for 2,323 hours of overtime, which would have meant an average of 6.3 hours per day overtime for 365 days a year'.

Source: Goldman and Budlender, 1999:53.

Box 23 Funding the implementation of the Domestic Violence Act in South Africa

- Implementation is often carried out by NGOs which themselves make additional contributions in terms of both cash and unpaid work.
- User fees are charged for services, such as provision of legal documents and conduct of laboratory tests in a number of countries.

The first step in analysing the need for funding is to identify the activities necessary to implement the law. This has to be followed by an estimate of the costs of funding an adequate level of these activities. These estimates will be rough orders of magnitude, as there are a lot of unknowns, and data is frequently not available in the required format. In the case of services dedicated to victims of domestic violence, this requires an estimate of the costs of providing the service to one woman and her children, and an estimate of the number of women likely to need the service in each year. The former requires information on how many women actually use the service in a year, and the annual costs of providing the service (staff, supplies, overheads). The latter requires

The budget of the Ministry of Social Welfare provided some funding for a shelter for battered women, consisting of 380,000 Barbadian dollars for one year, to cover the start-up costs of a shelter run by an NGO which was opened in November 1999. The NGO estimated that it takes 900 Barbadian dollars to house one adult shelter resident per month; more for residents with children. The shelter is designed to provide accommodation of up to 3 months, together with counselling and support in dealing with legal, welfare and police departments. There was no indication that the Ministry would provide ongoing funding to cover these costs. The shelter had been able to attract some donations from the private sector but these were insufficient. Moreover, the shelter did not have space for all the women who wanted to come. The members of the NGO had to use personal contacts to temporarily house and transport abused victims, putting the volunteers at considerable personal risk. The funding for the shelter was inadequate and insecure. Moreover, there was no provision in government housing policy for low-cost long-term housing for women domestic violence survivors and their children. As a result, several of the women had been unable to find suitable accommodation after leaving the shelter, and their children had been taken into institutional care.

Box 24 Funding for shelters for battered women in Barbados
      (St Hill, 2000.)

an estimate of the prevalence of domestic violence, and the needs that victims have for different services. Generally there is more danger of under-estimating the costs than of over-estimating the costs. However, spending money to prevent violence against women will in time reduce costs to other parts of the budget, such as health and policing. The method will be piloted in a number of Latin American countries.

The UN Millennium Project has developed methods for estimating the costs of the services required to achieve the Millennium Development Goals. Of particular interest is the method developed by the Project Secretariat and the Taskforce on Goal 3, Gender Equality and Women's Empowerment, to ensure the inclusion of necessary services not covered by the other goals. Particularly relevant is the inclusion of services that protect women's rights and enable women to claim their rights (e.g. Gender Equality Commissions, counseling services, legal services, media campaigns) (Taskforce on Gender Equality, UN Millennium Project, 2005:130-137).

5.4.2 Adequacy for funding for women's housing rights

An analysis of the adequacy of funding to meet the housing rights of poor women in South Africa has been undertaken by the WBI in South Africa (Pillay, Manjoo and Paulus, 2002). Adequacy was assessed in relation to housing policy and the provisions of the South African Constitution, which protects the right of access to adequate housing and the right to equality. Poor South African women face particular problems in enjoying adequate access to housing. Historically, housing has been allocated via male heads of household and disproportionate numbers of poor women live in informal settlements. Female household heads have often been discriminated against in access to housing. Poor women are very dependent on public housing to meet their needs. There has recently been an important case on housing rights heard by the Constitutional Court in South Africa (see Box 25).

The WBI analysis of the national housing budget in South Africa showed that although there was projected to be a modest increase in allocation to housing between 1998/89 and 2004/05, this was not sufficient to meet the backlog of unmet needs. Pillay et al. found that 'the housing budget constitutes only 1.5 per cent of total government expenditure, compared to the national housing goals of allocating 5% of government expenditure to housing'. In the Western Cape, a relatively wealthy province, the provincial government contended that insufficient housing funds had been transferred to it by the national government. However, Pillay et al. pointed out that the provincial government had substantial other funding from the national government, which was not tied to specific programmes, and suggested that some of this could be re-allocated (Pillay et al. 2002:25). Moreover, the provincial government could change the way it spent money on housing to meet needs more effectively and reduce the backlog more quickly:

Mrs Irene Grootboom was the lead plaintiff in a case heard by the Constitutional Court in 2000. Mrs Grootboom and about 900 other poor people in Wallacedene, Western Cape Province, had nowhere to live, and claimed that the municipality was failing to provide adequate access to housing. They first took their case to the Cape High Court, basing the case on two provisions of the constitution:

- Section 26 which states that 'everyone has right of access to adequate housing' and that the state 'must take reasonable legislative and other measures, within its available resources, to achieve progressive realization of this right';
- Section 28(1)(c) which says that children have a right to shelter.

The case was eventually heard by the South African Constitutional Court, which found that the state's housing programme could not be considered reasonable if it did not address the needs of those in extreme conditions of poverty and homelessness. It was not enough that the programme showed progressive realization in terms of the statistical average if it failed to respond the needs of the most desperate. The Court noted that 'effective implementation requires at least adequate budgetary support by national government' within the state's available resources. However, it failed to address how the availability of resources is to be determined. It did not require the government to increase its overall budget for housing. The Court did clarify that all three levels of government—national, provincial and local—have obligations to realize the rights to housing and act upon its judgment.

The response of the national government was to develop policy guidelines for the provision of emergency housing, and to require the provincial governments to reserve between 0.5 and 0.75% of their housing budgets as a contingency fund to meet emergency housing needs.

Box 25 Women's right to housing in South Africa

'One example for the short term is the use of existing rental stock to provide emergency relief for people, and especially women and children, who are homeless and destitute. A more sustainable alternative is increased support and liaison with successful cooperatives that have demonstrated the ability to save and build quality homes, such as the SA Homeless People's Federation. This is preferable to supplying commercially built houses to a select few who quality for financing, but who are left with an extremely small top-structure of dubious building standards and quality' (Pillay et al, 2002:26).

The case of funding for housing in South Africa is also significant to illustrate the scope for judicial review of executive decisions. A key lesson that emerges from the Grootboom case is that the role of the courts in reviewing executive economic policy very much depends on the separation of powers as defined in a State's constitutional and other domestic arrangements. In the case of South Africa, the Court was able to make a declaratory order requiring the State to act to meet the obligation imposed on it by section 26(2) of the Constitution (concerning the obligation to devise, fund, implement and supervise measures to provide relief for those in desperate need) and to require the Human Rights Commission to monitor and assess the State's compliance with the judgment. In other countries there can be more of a reluctance from courts to review budget allocations on the basis that these are a matter for executive decisions on economic policy (Hirschl, 2000). However, it is very important in this regard to emphasize that when courts assess the parameters of a State's obligation and find that a State is not fulfilling a particular right, remedying this deficiency will necessarily require a State to adjust its budget allocations even though the precise terms on which it does so may not necessarily be dictated by the court.

5.5 Gender equality in the outcomes of public expenditure

The allocation of funding is only the first step in the budget process. The **Inputs** of funds must be translated into:
   Activities (e.g. operation of health and education services, delivery of income transfers, construction of infrastructure, etc.);
   Outputs (e.g. number of patients treated, children enrolled in school, grants given, miles of roads built, etc.);

Outcomes (or **Impacts** or **Results**) (e.g. health status, educational qualifications obtained, people raised above the poverty line, economic growth achieved).

How far a State Party has met its obligations of conduct can be measured by looking at the allocation of expenditure. To investigate how far obligations of result have been met requires an investigation of outcomes.

The outcomes will fail to promote gender equality and the advancement of women if:
- funding fails to get through to the activities due to factors such as lags in disbursement, corruption, etc.;
- activities funded do not effectively produce outputs that are non-discriminatory and gender-equitable;
- outputs fail to produce improved gender equality outcomes.

For a full picture we need to follow the money from the budget appropriations to the activities and outputs it funds and investigate the substantive outcomes in terms of gender equality and the advancement of women. Useful tools are expenditure-tracking studies, beneficiary assessments, and quantitative investigations of budget outcomes. Gender-sensitive performance-oriented budgeting may be helpful in ensuring that public expenditure produces outcomes that are in compliance with CEDAW.

5.5.1 Tracking expenditure from a gender equality perspective

Expenditure tracking traces what happens to funds once they have been appropriated in the budget. For example, a study of the education system in Uganda in the period 1991/95 found that only 30% of the funds appropriated for grants to be paid to schools actually reached the schools (Abbo and Reinikka, 1998). The bottleneck was the district education office which was not disbursing the funding to the schools. Measures were taken to address this problem, including informing parents of the grants their local schools should be receiving, and by 2000 about 90% of the funds were reaching the schools. Bottlenecks in disbursement are very common and have been identified in many gender budget studies.

An example of a gender equality-focused expenditure-tracking study is provided in an analysis of the new District Primary Education Programme, Haryana, India (Senapaty, 1997). This programme had three objectives:
- retention of children in school and improvement of their achievement levels
- improving access to schooling
- capacity building.

Programme guidelines recognized the need for a special effort to reduce gender disparity in education. Most of the expenditure directed to the second and third objectives was for new managerial structures and in-service training of trainers. Very little was made available directly to schools. An average sum of Rs2,000 was to be provided per school per annum to be spent by the head teacher and the Village Education Committee and Rs500 to each teacher for preparation of teaching materials, but this was a tiny fraction of the total budget. Expenditures focussed directly on girls' education amounted to about 12.6% of the total budget, and almost all of this was on materials and training for the District Institute of Education and Training and the State Council of Educational Research and Training. A high proportion of the finance was used to create new managerial structures and provide new training for upstream staff, without much discernible impact on service delivery to users. No specific measures were included in the DPEP to reduce the costs to poor families of sending girls to school.

Some measures to reduce the costs of sending girls to school were supposed to be already in operation. Grants were supposed to be available to promote schooling of girls, including free textbooks, free uniforms or uniform allowances and attendance allowances. Teachers complained that none of these were received on a regular or timely basis. Moreover, although schooling was meant to be free, parents were required to make regular payments to school funds.

5.5.2 Investigating the views of the beneficiaries

As mentioned above in Section 1.3.8, a rights-based approach to construction of programmes and activities requires consultation and participation of those affected. Even if the funds get through to the agencies delivering the services, the activities may not be very satisfactory from the point of view of the beneficiaries. Hofbauer (2003:10-11) gives the example of reproductive health services for indigenous people in rural Mexico. She quotes a study that found that the services focussed on women as the ones responsible for reducing fertility and promoted methods such as pills, intra-uterine devices, injections and sterilization. They did not promote fertility control as a shared responsibility of men and women. Medical staff had insensitive, even racist, attitudes and disregarded the ideas of indigenous women about the body and sexuality. The women who were supposed to benefit from the services found interactions with health professionals difficult and intimidating. All of this implies that the health services were not being delivered in ways that respect women's human rights.

Several gender budget studies in India have investigated the views and experiences of beneficiaries of poverty alleviation programmes. In West Bengal, Nirmala Banerjee and Joyanti Sen investigated a major anti-poverty programme that focussed on the delivery of subsidized credit via self-help groups and local branches of state-owned banks. The programme was not specifically targeted to women but women were the majority of those who had entered the first stage of the programme, the formation of self-help groups: 'In the two-year period from March 2000 to April 2002, approximately 35,635 self-help groups had been formed in the state. Of these, 90% were women's groups' (Banerjee and Sen, 2003:29). Field work revealed that men were not very interested in joining the self-help groups because the additional earnings that this would generate were very low. Women, however, were always interested in supplementing their cash income, even if the amounts were very small. Women had joined the programme in large numbers but the programme was not operating in a way that respected their human rights, and ensured their full development and advancement (see Box 26).

Interviews were conducted at the end of 2002 with about 200 members of 15 self-help groups (SHGs) in three districts. Most groups were at the initial stage, where they could get a subsidy from the state to form a revolving fund. Only three groups had reached the stage where they were able to establish links with the banks and get credit, and these were groups that had been in operation since 1996. Very few participants understood the complex financial arrangements in the scheme. They did not know to what they were entitled and accepted whatever they were given. The economic activities undertaken by the groups were mainly a continuation of their traditional activities. No new skills were being introduced and the scale of the enterprises remained very small. The members of the groups did not know that they had a right to supporting services, such as training and market information. Women's traditional roles were being reinforced and their workload increased by a programme organised in a top-down way:

'In our interviews with beneficiaries, it was repeatedly pointed out by the women how joining SHGs had increased their workload. This was mainly because joining the SHGs had provided them with some supplementary work, but the new activities could not generate enough income for them to give up any of their earlier tasks ...

Perhaps the worst aspect of the programme is that at no point have the beneficiaries been consulted'.

Box 26 Beneficiaries views of an anti-poverty programme in West Bengal
(Banerjee and Sen, 2003:49, 50.)

5.5.3 Quantitative investigations of budget outcomes

A gender-sensitive investigation of budget outcomes requires the identification of appropriate gender-sensitive outcome indicators. Two sorts of indicators are required:
- female-specific indicators, such as the maternal mortality rate and the female literacy rate
- gender gap indicators, such as the ratio of the female literacy rate to the male literacy rate.

Some relevant outcome indicators can be found in the Millennium Development Goals Database (see Elson and Keklik, 2002 for further discussion). There are also many relevant outcome indicators in Budlender (2003).

However, the issue in monitoring government budgets from a CEDAW perspective is the link between gender equality indicators and government budgets. Some forms of gender inequality are not easily reduced by budgetary policy, such as the gender wage gap in the labour market. Others can be reduced by budgetary policy, such as the gender gap in incomes after the payment of taxes and receipt of income transfers. It is important to identify gender equality outcomes that can plausibly be linked to budgetary policies. Some governments are beginning to specify indicators for the gender equality outcomes they are aiming to reach through their budgets (see the examples of South Africa and France in Box 11). However, others are reluctant to do so because they argue that the degree of gender equality depends on many other factors apart from government budgets.

It seems plausible that health and education outcomes do bear some relation to public expenditure on health and education services, provided that funds are effectively spent on these services, and that other aspects of budgetary policy do not weaken the impact of these services. However, some quantitative studies of public expenditure find a weak link between specific outcomes and specific expenditures. This may be because:
- funding is not spent effectively
- other factors intervene.

These other factors may be:
- external to a particular programme but internal to the budget itself (e.g. expenditure on water and sanitation services affects health outcomes);
- external to the budget as a whole (e.g. drought, war).

There may be disagreement about which factors are external and which internal. For instance, poverty affects health and education outcomes. The degree of poverty may be considered to be primarily the result of factors external to the budget (e.g. the natural resources of a country; the terms of trade it faces in international markets). But the degree of poverty may also be linked to the revenue and macroeconomic dimensions of the budget, for which government does bear some responsibility. (For further discussion of these issues see Mehrotra and Delamonica, forthcoming.)

The GBI in Mexico is beginning to investigate budget outcomes. The NGOs, Fundar, Foro and Equidad are evaluating the impact of public expenditure on health services on maternal mortality in two states, Chiapas and Oaxaca. These two states have the highest maternal mortality rates in Mexico. Maternal mortality is closely related to lack of access to health care and emergency services. The investigation will involve fieldwork research on access to and quality and availability of maternal health services (Hofbauer 2002:94).

It would be best to combine quantitative studies of budget outcomes with expenditure-tracking studies and beneficiary assessments to get a full picture of the reasons for budget outcomes. A failure to improve gender equality outcomes may be the result of any combinations of the following:
- insufficient funding allocated in the budget
- insufficient funding reaching the point of service delivery
- inappropriate design and delivery of services
- factors external to the particular programme
- factors external to the budget as a whole.

5.6 Gender equality and the reform of public expenditure

In many countries measures are being introduced to reform the management of public expenditure, with the aim of making it more efficient. Some of these changes may make it easier to introduce gender equality criteria into public finance, but there is also potential for the introduction of measures that will not promote gender equality. Among the reforms are:
- performance-oriented budgeting
- decentralization of expenditure and services
- narrower targeting of public expenditure
- privatization of public services.

Many governments are introducing various forms of performance-oriented budgeting that aim to make a closer link between inputs of finance and outcomes for the people of a country. This presents both dangers and opportunities (Sharp, 2003). The usual performance criteria may lead to gender-unequal outcomes because they ignore women's unpaid contributions to public services and do not include the *quality* of outputs. The criteria are:
- economy (purchasing inputs at least financial cost)
- efficiency (minimizing financial cost per unit of output)
- effectiveness (maximizing outcomes for given outputs).

Nevertheless, there are opportunities, including introduction of gender-aware output and outcome indicators, and introduction of gender equality as a fourth performance criterion. UNIFEM is currently supporting the Government of Morocco to introduce gender into its newly emerging performance budgeting system.

Decentralization of expenditure and services to lower tiers of governments is widespread. This is supposed to improve services by building closer links between providers and users, and promote greater participation of citizens in decision-making. However, there is a danger that the power of existing local elites will be increased rather than reduced and that inequality between regions will grow, neither of which will improve the position of poor women (Grynspan, 2003). In order to mitigate some of these effects, decentralization must be accompanied by additional capacity building for those involved in decisions on budgets at local level.

Narrower targeting of public services is supposed to benefit deprived groups by concentrating scarce resources on them. However, narrow targeting has hidden costs. Vandemoortele (2002:59) identifies the following:
- cost of mis-targeting: it is difficult to identify the poor, especially poor women;
- cost of administration: narrower targeting requires more checks on beneficiaries;
- cost to beneficiaries of documenting eligibility and claiming benefits;
- cost of non-sustainability: if people who are not poor are not beneficiaries of services, political commitment to maintain their scope and quality falls.

Privatization of public services typically means that charges for services rise. This may lead to expanded coverage of services and provision of services for groups that lacked access to publicly owned services. But there is a danger that groups who already had access will lose it as they can no longer afford to pay.

Rebecca Grynspan, former Vice President of Costa Rica, argues that women need to take a critical look at these reforms, as they may have 'perverse effects on women, in terms of their access to quality services and of the increasing and unpaid workload implicit in many reforms' (Grynspan, 2003:99).

5.7 Conclusions

It is not possible to identify *a priori* from budget headings which programmes promote gender equality and the advancement of women. It is necessary to investigate the content and impact of programmes in specific social and economic contexts. This means it is difficult to construct *a priori* benchmarks comparable to the Human Development expenditure benchmarks. It would be even more difficult to construct them in ways that are comparable across countries. A single, simple, quantitative, internationally applicable benchmark for a gender equality expenditure priority ratio does not seem feasible. Rather the criterion needs to be whether governments have adopted adequate measures to eliminate discrimination in public expenditure and to promote substantive gender equality.

For programmes that are open to both women and men as individuals, calculations can be made of the share of expenditures going to each. It some cases, such as education, where boys and girls are usually present in roughly equal numbers in the school-age population, the appropriate starting point is equal shares for boys and girls. But there needs to be allowance for evidence that this is not sufficient to achieve substantive equality; sometimes additional expenditures may be needed for girls to attract them to courses of study (such as science and technology) in which the representation of girls is low, and sometimes additional expenditures may be needed for boys to attract them to courses of study (such as in care services) in which the representation of boys is low.

In other cases, where males and females are not equally present in the target population, the appropriate starting point or benchmark for equality may be that women's share of expenditure should be equal to their share of the relevant population (e.g. of farm workers, unemployed people, poor people). However, this runs the risk of preserving the traditional roles of women and men, to the disadvantage of women. So consideration would need to be given to financing measures, including temporary special measures, to address gender gaps in programme participation to achieve the overall goal of substantive equality.

The distribution of expenditure on public goods cannot so easily be partitioned between women and men. But frequently women and men use public goods in different ways and have different priorities for expenditure on public goods. Analysis can be conducted of how much is spent on public goods that are priorities for men and how much on those which are priorities for women, to establish whether the priorities of each are being equally served.

The adequacy of funding for the implementation of particular measures can be evaluated by costing the activities required for implementation, and comparing this with the amount allocated. This can be a complex undertaking when several Ministries are required to undertake complementary activities, as in the case of implementing laws to combat violence against women. Costing of measures to promote gender equality is being undertaken by the UN Millennium Project and there may be some lessons to share from this.

Programmes with inadequate funding are often subsidized by women's unpaid contributions to the programme. While unpaid contributions that are genuinely voluntary are not against the spirit of CEDAW, there is cause for concern if poor women, who are already over-burdened find that they can access a service only by making unpaid contributions of their time.

The impact of programmes on gender equality can best be judged using a combination of expenditure-tracking studies, beneficiary assessments and quantitative investigations of outcomes using gender-sensitive indicators.

Reforms of management of public expenditure may have benefits for women, but there are also dangers. Gender-aware performance-oriented budgeting presents new opportunities to introduce gender equality as a performance indicator, but it also presents dangers, especially if indicators of economy, efficiency and effectiveness do not take into account women's unpaid work.

Gender budget analysis can contribute in many ways to the analysis of public expenditure from a CEDAW perspective. The main difficulties are obtaining sex-disaggregated data about the use of services, and determining what standards of equality to use in making the assessments.

Section 6

Analysing Public Revenue from
a CEDAW Perspective

Analysing Public Revenue from a CEDAW Perspective

This section considers how the revenue side of the budget might be monitored for compliance with CEDAW. It draws on a recent report on gender impacts of taxation (Barnett and Grown, 2004) and on the work of a number of GBIs. The revenue side of the budget sets out the amount of revenue that the government expects to raise and the sources from which it intends to raise it. From a CEDAW perspective, the *total* amount of revenue must be sufficient to ensure 'the equal rights of men and women to enjoy all economic, social, cultural, civil and political rights', and the revenue must be raised in ways that are consistent with the same goal of substantive equality.

6.1 The revenue side of the budget

Revenue analysis involves many technicalities but fundamentally, revenue systems are social and political systems. As the UN Economic Commission for Latin America has pointed out:

'The strength or weakness of public finance reflects the strength or weakness of the "fiscal covenant" that legitimizes the role of the state and the scope of government responsibilities in the economic and social spheres. The absence of a generally accepted model of what the State's goals should be undercuts any possibility of consensus on the amount of resources it should manage, the source of its revenues and the rules for allocating and utilizing them. An explicit or implicit political agreement between the various sectors of society as to what the State should do, on the other hand, helps legitimize the amount, composition and orientation of public expenditure and the tax burden necessary to finance it' (ECLAC, 1998:I-7).

Human rights treaties may provide an important foundation for strengthening the 'fiscal covenant'.

The question of the adequacy of the total amount of revenue will be considered in Section 7 on Analysing the Macroeconomics of the Budget from a CEDAW Perspective. In this section we consider the gender equality implications of particular ways of raising revenue, especially tax revenue, and the gender implications of tax reform.

Governments raise revenue from a number of sources, including:
- direct taxes on personal incomes and on the profits of corporations
- payroll taxes, paid by employees and employers
- property taxes
- indirect taxes on good and services
- user fees for public services
- fees for licenses
- income from public enterprises and property
- interest on financial assets
- sale of public sector assets
- foreign aid grants.

In designing revenue policy, governments have to balance the effectiveness of the policy in raising revenue with the impact of the policy on economic and social behaviour. Sometimes a measure that is effective in raising revenue has undesirable economic and social impacts, as shown by a case of licences to sell alcohol in India (see Box 27).

In the 1980s, the government of the State of Andhra Pradesh in India wanted to raise revenue to subsidise the price of rice. It did so by actively promoting the production and distribution of a cheap alcoholic drink (called arrak) because revenue could be raised from the public auction of state licenses to sell arrak. In five years, revenue from liquor licenses increased by over 400%. However, the increased availability of arrak resulted in increased rates of alcohol abuse among poor men and negative impacts on household income available to meet the needs of poor children and poor women. It also led to an increase in domestic violence against women and children. In 1992, poor women in Andhra Pradesh began an anti-arrack campaign, and the state government was induced to prohibit the sale of arrack and withdraw licenses. The women suggested other ways of raising revenue, but these met with opposition from wealthier groups, and eventually the state government re-introduced alcohol licenses, despite their negative effects. This case is documented in the film *When Women Unite: The Story of an Uprising* by Nata Duvvury and Shabnam Virmani.

Box 27 Effective in raising revenue but negative impacts on poor women
(Barnett and Grown, 2004:21.)

This section does not examine all forms of revenue, but concentrates on taxes (especially personal income tax, Value Added Tax (VAT) and excise tax) and user fees for public services like water and sanitation and health and education.

The structure of tax revenue varies with the level of national income (Barnett and Grown, 2004:12-13):
- In low-income countries, about two thirds of tax revenue is raised through indirect taxes, including trade taxes (such as tariffs on imports), excise taxes (such as taxes on alcohol and cigarettes) and broad-based taxes on goods and services, such as General Sales Tax and VAT.
- In high-income countries, indirect taxes account for only about one third of tax revenue. The other two thirds comes from direct taxes. The share of trade taxes in tax revenue is much higher in low-income countries than in high income countries; over one third, compared to less than one hundredth.
- In low-income countries, income tax accounts for just over a quarter of tax revenue, while in high income countries, it accounts for over a third of tax revenue.

As tax payers, all women are affected by broadbased indirect taxes like VAT, but poor women, especially in developing countries, are likely to be outside the direct scope of personal income tax, since there is generally a minimum income below which there is no liability to pay income tax.

There is an argument for always considering the implications of tax jointly with the implications of expenditure, on the grounds that inequality in the payment of tax may be off-set by compensating redistribution through expenditure. This issue will be considered from time to time in discussion of direct and indirect taxes, but in practical terms it is very hard to establish the gender dimensions of the joint effects of taxation and expenditure because of lack of data; uncertainties about actual payment of taxes and actual access to the benefits of expenditure; and lack of sex-disaggregated models for computing the effects.

6.2 Evaluating tax systems: the public finance approach

Public finance experts typically judge tax systems in terms of three criteria:
- equity
- efficiency
- ease of administration.

Tax reforms are designed with these criteria in mind.

6.2.1 Equity

Equity in taxation refers to the idea that taxes should be fair. To judge this we need measures of how much tax people pay and criteria of 'fairness'.

Two measures of tax paid are commonly used:
- Tax burden, defined as the statutory tax payment obligation as a percentage of the tax payers' disposable income. In the case of taxes on businesses, the burden can to some extent be shifted by raising prices to pass on the cost to customers, or reducing wages to pass on the cost to employees.
- Tax incidence measures who is actually paying the tax, when the tax burden is shifted in part or in whole, to consumers and employees.

Two interpretations of fairness have been used in discussion of taxes:
- Benefits received: This criterion implies that fairness means that people should pay tax in proportion to the benefits they receive from public services.
- Ability to pay: This criterion implies that those with higher incomes should pay a larger share of the tax than those with lower incomes, that is, the tax system should be *progressive.*

There is a widespread support for 'ability to pay' as a principle, since those who most need public services are usually those least able to pay for them. This can easily be built into income tax through introduction of the following measures:
- a threshold income below which no tax is paid
- tax credits or deductions for support of children
- a range of tax rates, with higher tax rates for higher income groups.

But it is not so easy to build in to indirect taxes, such as trade taxes and VAT. These taxes are generally *regressive* in the sense that poor people contribute a higher share of their income to payment of such taxes than do rich people. Indirect taxes can be made less regressive through the following measures:
- exemptions for items purchased primarily by poor people
- lower rates on items purchased primarily by poor people
- higher rates on items purchased mainly by rich people.

Even if the principles of 'ability to pay' and 'progressive taxation' are accepted, there are further problems to confront in the design of income tax:
- aggregation of different types of income
- selection of the tax unit
- clarification of the principles of horizontal and vertical equity.

Aggregation of different types of income

Some income tax systems aggregate all sources of personal income (wage income from employment; non-wage income from running a business and from receiving interest and dividends and rent), and levy a single tax on the total. (This is known as a global system and is characteristic of high income countries, though many low-income countries are introducing such systems.) Some countries have separate systems of tax for each source of income. (This is known as a schedular system and is typically found only in low-income countries.)

Selection of tax unit

The tax unit might be an individual or a group of individuals. Where the tax unit is a group, it is generally determined on the basis of marriage. Unmarried people living together are generally not able to be taxed as a group. Married people are required to file a joint tax return on their combined income in some countries, and in others they file individual tax returns. Most high-income countries previously had joint filing, but many have now moved to individual filing. Most low-income countries require individual filing for at least some sources of income (typically on wage income) but often have joint filing for non-wage income. One reason for joint filing is the view that it results in a more progressive system.

Horizontal and vertical equity

The principle of horizontal equity is that all persons in the same circumstances should be treated in the same manner; while the principle of vertical equity is that persons in differing situations should be treated in an appropriately different manner (Young, 2000). The problem is defining what counts as 'the same circumstances', and what counts as 'appropriately different' (see Box 28).

> **The problem of operationalizing these concepts in tax systems is illustrated by the following example (adapted from Barnett and Grown, 2004: 22):**
>
> *Horizontal equity:* Consider two households both earning 60,000 rupees a month. Applying the principle of horizontal equity to their incomes, they would be considered the same for tax purposes in a system of joint filing. But if one household earns this income through the labour of one wage earner and the other from two wage earners, are the two households in the same circumstances?
>
> *Vertical equity:* Consider two individuals both with a wage income of 50,000 pesos. One saves part of the income for retirement and therefore gets additional income from interest on the savings, while the other spends all of her income. Applying the principle of vertical equity to their incomes, the saver pays more taxes. But the non-saver may consume more public services in retirement due to her lack of income. Is the tax system treating them in an 'appropriately different' manner, or is the saver being unfairly treated?
>
> ---
>
> **Box 28 Horizontal and vertical equity in tax systems**

6.2.2 Efficiency and neutrality

Economists argue for efficiency in taxation, which sounds like a good idea—who would be in favour of inefficiency? But it is important to examine how 'efficiency' is defined before coming to a conclusion.

Efficiency has a very particular meaning in the neo-liberal theory of public finance. It means the achievement of a situation that is 'optimal' in the sense of the maximization of the output produced from existing resources, with the existing pattern of property rights, so that it is impossible to make someone better off, in terms of the output available to them, without making someone else worse off. Using this definition, a situation can be optimal when most of the output in a country accrues to a few wealthy individuals who live in the lap of luxury, while the majority of the people are malnourished.

This theory of efficiency also assumes that an 'optimal' output is achieved through the private decisions of people buying and selling in competitive markets. Almost all the taxes that governments levy are regarded, in this perspective, as 'inefficient', because they change the outcome from what it would be in competitive markets. This is because taxes typically have an impact not only on people's disposable income, but also on people's decisions about paid employment, consumption, savings, investment, and so on. These impacts are considered to be 'distortions' because they result in losses in output, compared with what is hypothesized would prevail with competitive markets and no taxes.

The only taxes that are considered not to have this kind of impact are the kind of taxes where people have to pay the same amount irrespective of whether they participate a little more or a little less in markets. These taxes are called lump-sum taxes, and include poll taxes and hut taxes. However, these supposedly efficient taxes are precisely the taxes that modern governments do not make much use of because they are totally unrelated to ability to pay and are regarded as so unfair that many people do not regard them as legitimate.

If 'distortions' (as measured against behaviour in a hypothetical perfectly competitive economy) are impossible to eliminate completely, then, from the public finance perspective, an efficient tax system is one that minimizes the 'distortions'. This is the conceptual framework that informs much of the design of tax reforms in developing countries.

An alternative approach would be one that defines efficiency, not in terms of non-distortion, but in terms of achieving collectively agreed social and economic objectives, considering a much wider range of objectives than maximum output from existing resources and lack of impact on 'private' decisions. This would take into account that taxes do indeed typically have an impact on people's behaviour as well as on their income, and that it is important to avoid ways of raising revenue that seriously jeopardize important economic and social objectives, even if they raise a lot of revenue in the short run.

Tax lawyers often argue for *tax neutrality,* by which they mean that the tax system should not provide more incentives for one type of behaviour as compared to any other. This position has been endorsed by some advocate for women's equality. For instance, tax lawyer Claire Young argues for neutrality of the tax system in relation to social choices:

> 'Social choices, such as the choice to marry or to live in a common-law relationship or to remain single, should not be made as a consequence of any preferential tax treatment that would ensue from choosing one lifestyle over another' (Young, 2000:3).

We may agree with Young in this instance, but her argument for neutrality depends on the judgment that each type of behaviour is equally valuable. We may legitimately wish to use the tax system to encourage some types of behaviour more than others, in circumstances where private behaviour has external, public effects on other people; for instance, to encourage health-promoting behaviour by taxing cigarettes and alcohol more than fresh fruit and vegetables or to discourage polluting behaviour by taxing the use of cars more than the use of bicycles.

Of course, social judgments about the value of different lifestyles may change. In the context of Canada, Christa Freiler et al. argue that:

> 'The tax system does not exist in a vacuum. It arises from and embodies societal values. … For example, when non-marital co-habitation was less socially acceptable and less prevalent than it is today, legally married couples were entitled to tax credits and deductions were not available to co-habiting couples. It was not until 1992 that the definition of spouse was extended to include common-law couples, and they could claim the benefits of these provisions. The battle of same-sex spouses to achieve neutrality in the tax system with respect to their orientation was only very recently resolved …' (Freiler et al, 2001:5).

6.2.3 Ease of administration

Ease of administration is the third consideration that public finance experts emphasize. Tax law prescribes the types and rates of tax, but tax revenue depends on effective implementation of this law and a willingness to comply with it. Factors such as low literacy, poor communications infra-structure, a large number of very small businesses and a poorly trained and poorly paid tax department all make implementation of tax law more difficult. Moreover, rich people, with access to tax lawyers and accountants and powerful politicians, find it easier than poor people to evade or avoid paying taxes. (Tax evasion is not declaring taxable income or transactions; tax avoidance is maneuvering within the tax rules to reduce tax liability). Tax inspectors may turn a blind eye to evasions by rich people, while they harass poor people, and extract so-called 'unofficial charges' as well as those required by law. Trade taxes are easier to administer than most other taxes, but even so are vulnerable to smuggling, and in any case trade liberalization policies reduce the scope for trade taxes. Direct taxes are widely regarded as harder to administer. The inherent difficulties of administering direct taxes are compounded in many countries by complex systems of special allowances, deductions and deferrals. VAT is regarded as easiest to administer and its use has expanded rapidly, but it is a regressive tax.

Simple tax systems are easier to administer and may secure greater compliance from tax payers and officials. The rules are more transparent and that may make it easier to hold governments accountable for the tax regime. But the impact of the rules is not always transparent, and is often far from progressive. A single rate of VAT on all goods and services is one of the simplest taxes, but results in a higher tax incidence on poor people than on rich people.

Clearly it is a difficult task to balance the achievement of different objectives in taxation. But many of these difficulties are social and political rather than technical. Jamaica, which has a per capita income only about a third of that in Chile, has a tax revenue to GDP ratio of 29 per cent, compared to 17 per cent in Chile (Huber, 2003:13).

A weak fiscal covenant makes it much harder to achieve a well-functioning tax system. Since human rights treaties do set out an important set of States Parties' obligations, they may provide an important anchor for a stable fiscal covenant, even though they do not contain any explicit reference to taxation. For example, the universally recognized and agreed framework of human rights can lend legitimacy to the proposed role of the State and extent of government responsibilities. Further, human rights law seeks to minimize disparities (such as those in relation to wealth or education) and include–through the principles of non-discrimination and participation–various sectors of the community in decisions about the role of the State, which in turn provides a stronger foundation for the fiscal covenant.

6.2.4 Tax reforms

Over the past 20 years, tax systems in many countries have been reformed in ways that are supposed to promote faster economic growth through removal of 'distortions' and creation of incentives for private investment. The key measures have been reduction of direct taxes on profits of corporations and on high earners; reduction of trade taxes; and extension of broad-based sales taxes such as VAT.

Advocates of such reforms, including the World Bank and IMF which stipulate such reforms as conditions for adjustment loans, argue that such reforms reduce the incentives for tax evasion and tax avoidance. However, tax evasion and tax avoidance have remained fundamental problems in many countries. There has been a growth of tax havens that offer big businesses and rich individuals the possibility of keeping their accounts 'offshore', and beyond the reach of national tax inspectors.

These reforms have made tax systems more regressive, with a higher proportion of tax being paid by poorer households. This is obscured by the tendency to present data on the distribution of tax payments which cover only personal income tax. A greater share of this is generally paid by people in the middle- and higher-income brackets. But VAT and General Sales Tax are paid by everyone. Once such taxes are included, it becomes evident that tax reforms in many countries have tended to increase the tax contribution of poor households. However, there are few quantitative studies available on the impact of tax reforms on the overall distribution of household income in poor countries, and those that are available are not disaggregated by sex (Huber, 2003).

6.3 Evaluating tax systems: CEDAW principles

The Convention on the Elimination of All Forms of Discrimination Against Women does not contain any explicit reference to taxation. Nor do the documents produced by the CEDAW Committee. However, as outlined above in Section 1, the Convention's general principles of non-discrimination and substantive equality can be brought to bear upon taxation.

In view of the fact that the distributional effects of taxation are generally discussed in terms of the impact on households, rather than on individuals, it is particularly relevant that Article 1 specifies that marital status is not an acceptable basis for any 'distinctions, exclusions or restrictions' which impair women's equality with men in the enjoyment of human rights. The Convention gives women rights as individuals.

Other provisions that are particularly important for taxation are the following:

Article 2 requires that States Parties must 'take all appropriate measures, including legislation, to modify or abolish existing laws, regulations, customs and practices which constitute discrimination against women'.

Article 5 requires that States Parties shall take all appropriate measures.
(a) To modify the social and cultural patterns of conduct of men and women, with a view to achieving the elimination of prejudices and customary and all other practices which are based on the idea of the inferiority or the superiority of either of the sexes, or of stereotyped roles for men and women.
(b) To ensure that family education includes a proper understanding of the role of maternity as a social function and the recognition of the common responsibility of men and women in the upbringing and development of their children, it being understood that the interest of the children is the primordial consideration in all cases.

Article 13 requires States Parties to ensure that men and women enjoy the same rights to family benefits.

Article 15 says that 'States Parties shall accord to women equality with men before the law'.

Article 16 requires that 'States Parties shall take all appropriate measures to eliminate discrimination against women in all matters relating to marriage and family relations'.

Also particularly relevant is General Recommendation 21 (made in 1994) on Equality in Marriage and Family Relations. This clarifies that the form and concept of the family can vary from State to State, but whatever form it takes 'the treatment of women in the family both at law and in private must accord with the principles of equality and justice for all people' (para. 13). Also, 'A stable family is one which is based on principles of equity, justice and individual fulfilment for each member. Each partner must therefore have the right to choose a profession or employment that is best suited to his or her abilities, qualifications and aspirations' (para. 24). Moreover, para. 26 refers to 'a woman's right to enjoy financial independence'.

Taken together, these articles and General Recommendation 21 imply that there must be no discrimination against women in tax systems. Women must be treated as equal to men in tax laws as individual, autonomous citizens, rather than as dependents of men. Moreover, the impact of tax laws (in terms of tax burden/incidence and incentives for particular kinds of behaviour) should promote substantive, and not merely formal, equality between women and men, including egalitarian family relations.

The idea of discrimination against women informs the framework for evaluating the gender dimensions of tax systems that has been suggested by economist Janet Stotsky (1996:1). She distinguishes:
Explicit gender bias against women in the formulation of tax laws:
- 'Explicit forms are specific provisions of the law or regulation that identify and treat men and women differently'.
- Explicit discrimination is intentional.

Implicit gender bias against women in the impact of tax laws:
- 'Implicit forms are provisions of the law and regulations that, because of typical social arrangements and economic behavior, tend to have different implications for men than for women'.
- Implicit discrimination may be intentional or inadvertent.

There is much that is useful in Stotsky's framework and it has been used by Barnett and Grown (2004). But it has some important limitations, since it is based on the idea that bias (which is a normative term, implying injustice) stems from treating men and women differently, and that a non-biased system would treat them the same. As tax lawyer Claire Young argues, we need to recognize that in order to achieve substantive equality, different groups in society may require different treatment. Different treatment is not necessarily biased treatment. This recognition is undergirded by CEDAW, which allows for different treatment when that treatment is aimed at overcoming discrimination.

6.4 Applying CEDAW principles to personal income tax

It is easier to see how CEDAW principles might be applied to monitoring personal income tax than to other taxes and more work has been done on gender and income tax than on other kinds of taxes. Here we examine four dimensions of personal income tax in the light of CEDAW:
- Content of tax rules
- Tax burden/incidence
- Behavioural incentives
- Impact of tax on gender inequality in income.

6.4.1 Income tax rules

These refer to the rules about whether there is joint filing or individual filing of tax returns of married people; the system of income tax exemptions and allowances (sometimes called 'tax expenditures' because they are fiscally equivalent to collecting a tax and spending some of it on a rebate); and the structure of tax rates.

Joint filing refers to a system in which the personal income of a married couple, from whatever source, is aggregated and included in a joint tax return. Joint filing was common in the industrialized countries but many have moved to individual filing. Joint filing is less common in developing countries because they more often have schedular income tax in which different types of income (e.g. wage income and property income) are subject to different tax rules.

Explicit bias against women in joint filing

Stotsky identifies two kinds of explicit bias against women in joint filing:
- Husbands having sole responsibility for filing. There is explicit bias against wives if it is husbands who have responsibility for filing the tax return, and the wife has no separate existence as a tax payer. For example, France until 1983; the UK until 1990 (Stotsky 1996:6).
- Allocation of tax exemptions and allowances to husbands, not wives. There is explicit bias against wives if certain tax allowances and exemptions are available only to the husband. For example, allowances for married men for the expenses of supporting a household, but not for married women; allowances for children that married men but not married women may deduct from their incomes. For example, many countries in Middle East and North Africa (Barnett and Grown, 2004:33).

Stotsky argues that *explicit* discrimination is less frequently found in joint filing than in individual filing systems, since the tax paying unit is the couple. (This means that, for instance, it is not possible to have *explicit* differences in the tax rates for men and women or to allocate a wife's property income to her husband for tax purposes.)

Individual filing refers to a system in which each person who is liable to income tax files an individual return. This system recognizes women as individual tax payers, but may still be subject to several forms of explicit bias against women.

Explicit bias against women in individual filing

Stotsky identifies three forms of this:
- Allocation of tax exemptions and allowances to husbands, not to wives. For example Jordan (though the exemptions may be accorded to the wife at the request of her husband, or if she is the sole breadwinner) (Stotsky, 1996:5).
- Attribution of the non-labour income of the wife to the husband. Many countries have rules in which profits, rents, dividends and interest are regarded as the income of the husband and are included on his tax return, even if in fact they accrue to the wife. In many countries the profits of family businesses are regarded as the income of the husband, irrespective of the wife's roles in the business. For example, this happens in Tanzania. (Stotsky, 1996:4)
- Higher tax rates for married women than for other tax payers (unmarried women, married and unmarried men). For example, South Africa, in the early 1990s (Smith, 2000:10).

Explicit bias against women is easiest to identify and criticize. It is mentioned in some countries' reports to the CEDAW committee under Article 13 (a), the right to family benefits. For instance, the report submitted by Jordan in 1999 acknowledges that there is discrimination between the spouses with respect to tax relief and reports that 'nongovernmental organizations are calling for this provision to be amended so that the granting of such tax relief to the wife would no longer require the husband's consent'.

This kind of discrimination against women in tax relief rules is prevalent in many other developing countries. For instance in Senegal, a woman cannot claim tax allowances for dependents, even if she is the sole breadwinner, unless her husband formally relinquishes his status as head of household, under the Family Code. This kind of provision in the tax law is in breach of CEDAW.

A few countries have allowances that are only available to women. For instance, in Singapore, a married women with a child can claim a basic child tax allowance and is also entitled to additional allowances 'if she has elected to be charged to tax in her own name and has passed at least three subjects at one sitting at the examinations for the General Certificate of Education or has obtained an equivalent or higher educational qualification'. These allowances are also available to widows, divorcees and married women living separately from their husbands. The allowances depend on the number of children and are a percentage of their mother's earned income (Stotsky,1996, quoting International Bureau of Fiscal Documentation,1995). The allowances are designed to promote higher fertility of educated women, which is why they are given to women rather than men. Although such allowances need to be further scrutinized in the context of the whole taxation system, at first glance they introduce impermissible distinctions between different groups of women (educated versus uneducated; married women versus family units in which a marital relationship has not at any stage featured); violate Article 5(a) of CEDAW which calls on States to take measures to transform stereotypical roles of men and women; infringe CEDAW provisions which require the

State to ensure that both men and women have the same rights and responsibilities during marriage, as parents and in other arrangements with regard to children (Articles 5(b); Article 16(1) (c), (d), (f) irrespective of their marital status (CEDAW, General Recommendation 21, paras. 17-20); and have potentially adverse effects on married women's labour supply, in contravention of Article 11 of CEDAW. Indeed, the CEDAW Committee has called upon States to address hidden discrimination in social security and taxation systems among different groups of women (Belgium, CEDAW, A/51/38 (1996) 22 at para. 191).

Many countries have been reforming their tax rules to eliminate explicit bias against women. The example of South Africa has been analysed by the Women's Budget Initiative and is discussed in Box 29.

From 1914 to 1987 the household was the tax unit and the income of married women was taxed jointly with their husbands. Moreover, a married woman's income was subject to a higher rate of tax than the income of an unmarried person (both male and female) and that of a married person (which was taken to be male, unless a woman could show she was the main breadwinner).

From 1988, the salary of married women was taxed separately.

From 1990, the trading income of married women was taxed separately.

From 1991, the investment income of a married woman was taxed separately.

In 1995, a single income tax rate structure was introduced, applicable to all individuals irrespective of sex or marital status, replacing the system of unmarried persons, married persons, and married women. There was also the same allowance for the amount of income exempt from tax; and the same allowance for contributions to retirement annuity funds.

Box 29 Elimination of explicit discrimination against women in the Personal Income Tax rules in South Africa
(Smith, 2000.)

As Smith (2000) points out:
'The removal of this form of discrimination was necessary in terms of the South African constitution. There was clearly what is termed "formal" discrimination, in that women and men were explicitly treated differently. The situation is, however, not so clear in terms of outcomes, or what is termed "substantive discrimination" '.

This point refers to the impact of tax rules on the tax burden/incidence of different types of households, rather than the formulation of the rules themselves, and is one of the most contested issues in the evaluation of personal income tax. It is discussed in section 6.3.2.

We now turn to the issue of *implicit bias* against women in tax rules. This is not so immediately apparent but tends to persist even when explicit bias has been eliminated.

Implicit bias against women in joint filing systems

Wives tend to face a higher *de facto* tax rate on their income than their husbands. This happens because women usually earn less than their husbands, but their income is taxed at a rate determined by the aggregate of their own and their husband's income. This tends to put them in higher tax bracket than they would be if only their own income was considered. Economists describe this bias in terms of the women having a higher marginal tax rate:
'Joint tax filing by married couples in the progressive tax system results in the lower-earning spouse, who is usually the woman, facing a higher marginal tax rate on her first dollar earned than she would have as an individual and than her husband' (Anderson, 1999:699).

What this means is that, in fact, a lower-earning wife pays a higher tax rate than her husband, even if there is no formal rule that says she must. This is often referred to as the 'marriage tax' on women. It is generally considered to operate as a disincentive for women to participate in the labour market, because of the low after-tax earnings she will obtain. This is discussed further in Section 6.4.3. Of course, if the husband is the lower-earning spouse, it is he who pays the marriage tax, but such cases are the exception. Contemporary systems of gender relations mean that it is typically the wife who is the lower earning spouse.

Implicit bias against women in individual filing systems

In individual filing systems, married women do not face higher marginal tax rates on the income they earn, but will do so on their non-labour income if this is attributed to their husbands. Even if there is complete individual filing of all income, there can still be an implicit bias against women deriving from the treatment of tax allowances or tax credits (see Box 30 for the case of Canada).

In Canada, tax payers with a financially dependent spouse may claim the spousal credit, which is reduced by income earned by the dependent spouse. Moreover, a non- or low-earning individual who lacks sufficient income to claim other personal credits, such as the disability tax credit, the caregiver credit and the over-65 years credit, can transfer these to a higher earning spouse. In some cases higher-income tax payers can use tax avoidance arrangements to shift their tax burden to a lower earning spouse. For instance, one spouse can assume tax for the interest and dividends earned by the other in a particular year, shifting the tax burden from the high–income earner to the low-income spouse, whose income is then taxed at a lower rate. The Income Tax Act does not stipulate that the higher-income spouse be male, and so appears to be gender neutral. However:

'Women are more likely to be the "dependent spouses" than men, partly because they are more likely to assume child and elder care responsibilities. Further, because men generally have higher income than women, the beneficiaries of many tax concessions that transfer income or tax credits between spouses are men.

... While women, in principle, are able to use the same tax shelters as men, provided their incomes are high enough, their lower earnings prevent them from doing so. This kind of indirect and often unintended inequitable impact of a tax ... measure has to be considered a form of systemic discrimination. Whether intentional or not, the Canadian tax system results in gender discrimination because of rules that seem, on the surface, fair and gender neutral, but are not. It is designed without taking into account that in Canada today economic, social and political power is still predominantly in the hands of men'.

Box 30 Implicit bias against women in individual filing personal income tax systems
(Freiler et al. 2001:8-9.)

6.4.2 Income tax burden/incidence

In the case of personal income tax it is not necessary to distinguish between tax burden and tax incidence because the payer cannot shift the burden to others in the way that a business can. The burden/incidence of personal income tax is the ratio of tax payment to disposable income. It can be calculated for various categories of tax payer from data on tax returns. However, in many countries the income tax return does not include the sex of the person filing the return, and governments do not give sex-disaggregated data on income tax payers. An exception is South Africa, where, in 1998, there were 2,263,079 people registered for payment of personal income tax of which 1,516,263 (67%) were men and 746,816 (33%) were women (Department of Finance, Government of South Africa, 1999, quoted in Smith, 2000:9). As Smith points out, men's share in total income tax payments would be even greater than their share as tax-payers because men predominate in the higher income brackets where tax rates are highest.

The Gender Responsive Budget Initiative conducted by the State of Oaxaca, Mexico, has taken steps to ensure that in future the tax payers' register includes data on the sex of the tax payer, and plans to publish data on the share of taxes paid by women and by men. A first analysis shows women contribute 34% of the total revenue from local direct taxes, much higher than the popular perception of women's contribution. Women's aggregate earnings are about 37% of men's, and women are concentrated in the lower earnings levels (Cos-Montiel, 2004).

It is important to emphasize that gender equality in taxation incidence does NOT mean that men and women should pay equal shares of the total income (or payroll) tax payments, either in relation to a particular employer or the country as a whole. The principle of 'ability to pay' in taxation implies that men's share should be higher because their share of total taxable income is higher than that of women The Uganda report does not provide data on women's share of total taxable income earned by employees, but uses the benchmark of men's and women's share of employment and argues that since women comprise 32% of the employees and pay 32% of the tax bill, the income tax system is 'gender neutral' (in terms of tax burden). However, if, as is likely, women are more concentrated in the lower grades of employment than men, they may earn less than 32% of total earnings in the Uganda Revenue Authority.

A more appropriate measure is the tax burden, disaggregated by sex (i.e. ratio of tax paid by women to disposable income earned by women, compared to the ratio of tax paid by men to disposable income earned by men). The principle of progressive taxation implies that the income tax burden should be higher for those with higher incomes, so there is a case for arguing that the average tax burden on men should be *higher* than the average tax burden on women. It is currently difficult to operationalize this measure because the data required is rarely available. What is very often available is data on the income tax burden of different types of household.

It is important to consider the income tax burden of different types of household because tax rules can produce tax burdens that are not neutral as between different types of household. There has been considerable discussion of two intertwined issues:
* the treatment of households with only one adult earner compared to the treatment of households with two adult earners;
* the treatment of the income in kind produced by unpaid domestic work.

In the USA, the tax burden of a married couple in which one spouse participates in the labour market and one spouse stays at home and does unpaid domestic work is lower than that of a married couple in which both partners participate in the labour market. This is criticized by feminists in the USA as a system that favours traditional, patriarchal marriage in which there is a male breadwinner and a dependent wife (Anderson, 1999).

In some countries, the tax burden of one-earner households is higher than that of two-earner households. For instance, the income tax rules in South Africa mean that a household with only one earner has a higher tax burden, that is pays more of its income in tax) than a household with the same level of money income and two earners (see Box 31). Does this mean that the one-earner household is discriminated against? Smith (2000), in a contribution to the Fifth Women's Budget Report, suggests that it does.

Consider two households, each consisting of two adults and two children, and each having the same level of total money income. Each earner is taxed individually.

In Household A, the income is generated by two earners: a husband, earning R2,000 per month, and a wife, earning R1,000 a month. The other members of the household are their two children.

In Household B, the income is generated by a single mother who earns R3,000 per month. The other members of the household are her non-earning mother and her two children.

Applying the tax rules in operation in 1999/2000 (after the removal of formal discrimination against women) the total tax payable per year by household A is R850, while the total tax payable by household B is R3,460.The tax burden on the household with one earner is over four times the burden on the household with two earners.

Box 31 Tax of one-earner and two-earner households in South Africa
    (Smith, 2000.)

Comparable arguments are raised in Canada, where a one-earner couple pays more tax than a two-earner couple with the same income. In Canada, the claim of groups like REAL Women of Canada is that the tax system discriminates against traditional-type families with a male breadwinner and a female full-time home-maker. Philipps (2002) argues that this claim ignores the substantial tax-free economic benefits created by the homemaker's unpaid work, which reduces the amount of expenditure that a household needs to make on things like child care, meals, cleaning services, etc.

American economist Julie Nelson suggests that horizontal equity requires that tax systems should take into account the value of the output of unpaid work done in the home, as well as the value of income earned out-side the home (Nelson,1996). If this is not done, she argues that there will be unfair treatment of households in which both husband and wife do paid work, as compared to those with a male breadwinner and a dependent female homemaker (see Box 32).

Consider two pairs of spouses in a joint taxation system like that of the USA.

Couple A comprises two spouses each earning $20,000 in the market and each producing goods and serv-ices in the home worth $10,000. Their total joint income is $60,000. They are taxed on the $40,000 they earn in the market.

Couple B comprises one spouse earning $30,000 in the market and one spouse producing $30,000 worth of goods and services in the home. They are taxed on the on the $30,000 one of them earns in the market.

The tax bill of couple A is higher than that of couple B, though both couples both have the same amount of total income.

Box 32 Taking the value of unpaid work into account in evaluating tax burdens
    (Anderson, 1999; Nelson, 1996.)

The same argument is made by tax lawyer Claire Young (1999:4):
> 'The issue is that the value of women's labour in the home is "earned income in kind", a form of imputed income, and one that gives a personal benefit either to the person who performs it or to other members of the family. Ignoring its value for tax purposes is problematic. Unless the tax system recognizes the value of household production, either by taxing it or by giving tax relief to women who work outside the home in the paid labour force, those women are at a disadvantage when compared to women who work exclusively in the home. In effect, women who work outside the home have to purchase household services or forgo leisure time in order to provide for themselves and their families'.

The CEDAW Committee has recognized the economic significance of unpaid domestic work in General Recommendation 17, which recommends that States 'quantify and include the unremunerated domestic activi-ties of women in the gross national product' (United Nations, Committee on the Elimination of Discrimination Against Women, 1991).

However, many advocates for gender equality are uncomfortable with the idea that unpaid domestic work should be quantified and included in the assessment of household income for tax purposes. There is concern that this would increase the tax bills of households in the lower money income groups more than it would increase the tax bills of households in the higher money income groups. Moreover, taxes have to be paid in money, and cannot be paid through unpaid domestic work (one cannot bake a cake and take it to the tax office as part of the payment of the tax bill). However, the value of unpaid work can be taken into account in ways other than increasing the tax bills of households where a lot of unpaid domestic work is carried out. For instance, its value can be recognized by giving tax allowances to women who participate in paid employment in order to offset some of the costs of buying substitutes for the unpaid domestic work they would otherwise do (Young, 1999:4).

These arguments suggest that in comparing the two households in South Africa (Box 31), we need to know if the grandmother in household B provides substitute child care, cooking, cleaning, etc., which the couple in household A have to purchase from their earnings or supply themselves by reducing their time for leisure and sleep. If this is the case, then household A has less total real income than household B and its lower tax burden could be justified on that ground. On the other hand, if the grandmother in household B is too infirm to carry out these tasks, then there is a case for a tax allowance for household B to support the grandmother as a dependent. However, it may be difficult to implement this, as it would require additional questions on the income tax form and some form of accompanying certification of infirmity.

These examples illustrate some of the complexity of judging whether or not particular distributions of tax burden discriminate against particular types of household. This complexity does not alleviate the requirement that States look closely at these questions. CEDAW requires that families be based on 'principles of equity, justice and individual fulfilment for each member' (General Recommendation 21, para. 4). Many gender equality advocates would argue that this implies the tax system should not result in a lower tax burden for patriarchal families with breadwinner husbands and financially dependent housewives who do not engage in paid employment, but should result in a lower tax burden families in which both husbands and wives undertake unpaid domestic work and are in paid employment. However, some women argue that this would fail to give equal treatment to women who have chosen to be exclusively homemakers compared to those women who have chosen to do both paid work and unpaid work (Philipps 2002). This is an example of the complexity of determining how equal treatment should take account of different ways of living.

One way of resolving this would be to argue that the fundamental principle that is relevant here is that women should be equally free to choose how to live their lives and governments should not provide incentives for any particular choice. This would imply that the income tax system should be neutral in the burden of taxation on different types of household (see 6.2.2 for previous discussion of the idea of tax-neutrality).

However, it may be argued that women do not make choices on how to live their lives in conditions of substantive equality, but in conditions in which stereotyped roles shape their choices. CEDAW Article 5 enjoins States Parties to take all appropriate measures 'to modify the social and cultural patterns of conduct of men and women' in order to achieve substantive equality. This suggests that the design of income tax systems should proactively promote an equal sharing of both paid and unpaid work between women and men, and not give incentives for the perpetuation of families with breadwinner husbands and dependent wives. The CEDAW Committee has, for instance, expressed concerns about taxation systems that perpetuate stereotypical expectations for married women (Germany, CEDAW, A/55/38 part I (2000) 29 at para. 314).

6.4.3 Impact of income tax on behaviour of men and women

Taxes not only raise revenue, they also provide incentives and disincentives to certain forms of behaviour. Sometimes a tax is specifically designed to promote or discourage certain kinds of behaviour. For instance, taxes may be levied on activities that cause pollution in order to discourage people from polluting. Sometimes the behavioural effect is an unintended by-product and may result in what Stotsky (1996) called implicit bias against women. There are two important ways in which personal income tax may promote behaviour that does not accord with CEDAW's standard of substantive equality. The first way is to discourage the participation of married women in the labour market. The second way is to discourage men's participation in unpaid domestic work.

Labour market participation of married women

As noted in 6.3.1 above, systems of joint filing in graduated income tax systems (with higher tax rates on higher incomes) imply a higher *de facto* rate of tax on secondary earners and are examples of implicit bias against women. This means that:
> 'wives generally receive less after-tax income on each dollar they earn than their husbands, and this is a significant disincentive for married women to enter the paid labour force' (Barnett and Grown, 2004:33).

There are many studies by economists that establish that this kind of implicit bias does indeed diminish the labour market participation of married women.

This behavioural incentive is in violation of CEDAW principles. For instance, it promotes the perpetuation of stereotyped roles for men and women (Article 5). It hinders women's right to choose a profession or employment that is best suited to her abilities, qualifications and aspirations (Article 11(a) and (c); GR21, para. 24). It is an obstacle to women's right to financial independence (GR21, para. 26).

This disincentive is not present in tax systems that have individual filing. This is a strong argument in favour of individualization of the tax system (de Villota and Ferrari, 2001). However, individualization of personal income tax results in a less progressive system (in terms of distribution of after-tax income between households) as compared to systems of joint taxation. There is thus some tension between a system of personal income tax that promotes gender equality and one that promotes class equality.

> 'Independent taxation is less progressive between households than joint taxation, because the incomes of partners are highly correlated. Inter-household inequality is an aspect of gender inequality; women are disproportionately members of poorer households that would gain from a more progressive system. However, separate taxation means that men and women are taxed on, and therefore face, incentives based on their own incomes alone. This can be seen as a step towards gender equality in employment, since it favors a household with two earners over a single-earner household with the same income. Separate taxation also improves women's bargaining power within households; as women usually earn less than their husbands, wives will generally gain from being taxed at an individual, rather than a joint, rate' (Himmelweit, 2002:61).

Moreover, systems with individual filing may still create incentives to perpetuate gender stereotyped roles through the operation of the system of tax allowances and tax credits. In Canada the tax unit has always been the individual, not the family, but nevertheless, Young argues that:

> 'Each provision applies to both women and men, and yet, as I discuss, women suffer significant substantive inequalities when compared to men in terms of the impact of the system on them' (Young 2000:14).

Similarly, in their study of responsibility for children and the Canadian tax system, Freiler et al. (2001) argue that there is gender bias in the Canadian tax system, even though it is not immediately apparent, because many of its provisions in practice reinforce the traditional male breadwinner/dependent female housewife model of the family.

One way in which this happens is through the reliance on tax allowances as the principal means of subsidizing child care. Women with low wages obtain little benefit from this because their tax liability is low. Removing labour market disincentives for low-income married women requires that child care be subsidized through transfer payments and low cost public child care services, as is done in many European countries.

Men's participation in unpaid domestic work

Tax provisions that are intended to compensate women for their unpaid care work or for the costs of substitute care may, if not carefully designed, create disincentives to men taking on more of the unpaid work of caring for others that has traditionally been seen as women's role.

In the UK, the Working Families Tax Credit, introduced in 1999, embodied such a disincentive (Himmelweit, 2002:62-63). The WFTC was introduced to provide an income supplement to families of poorly paid earners with children. It was designed to make sure that being in employment pays better than being on welfare benefits. It included a supplement if one parent works more than 30 hours per week, but this supplement could not be claimed if the parents decided to split this work between them, so that each do some paid work and some unpaid childcare work. It creates an incentive to maintaining the traditional division of labour, and a disincentive to sharing paid and unpaid work more equally between families.

In the case of Canada, Philipps (2002) points to the dangers that income tax credits for those who provide unpaid care may reinforce existing gender divisions of labour in which women are expected to carry out most of this work. Referring to Canada, she argues:

> 'At a time when public transfers and services are being withdrawn it will be tempting to accept tax measures that provide any degree of relief to strained household budgets or a modicum of much-needed political recognition for women's care work. However, the new federal caregiver credit and the various other tax reform proposals being advanced under the banner of valuing unpaid work do less

to advance women's economic equality or autonomy than to legitimate the privatization of social reproductive costs to women' (Philipps, 2002:70).

The discouragement of men's participation in unpaid domestic work is not in compliance with Article 5 of CEDAW which calls for States to take appropriate measures to promote the transformation of men's roles, as well as those of women; and to ensure the common responsibility of men and women in the upbringing and development of their children. Article 16 of CEDAW also requires a State to ensure that women and men have the same rights and responsibilities during marriage (Article 16(1) (c)); as parents (Article 16(1) (d)); and with regard to other arrangements (e.g. guardianship) with respect to children (Article 16(1) (f)).General Recommendation 21 also makes it clear that both parents have shared responsibility for the care, protection and maintenance of children, irrespective of their marital status (CEDAW, GR 21, paras. 17-20).

Philipps (2002) suggests that one way of creating incentives for both women and men to engage in both paid work and unpaid care work would be to provide a refundable caregiver tax credit to be divisible between the partners if they are sharing the unpaid care work equally.

Complex tax and benefit systems such as exist in the welfare states give rise to very complex systems of incentives and disincentives with complex implications for substantive equality between women and men. Sue Himmelweit, a UK economist who is part of the UK Women's Budget group, has put forward some useful principles for examining the gender impact of such systems (Himmelweit, 2002:64-65).

6.3.4 Impact of income tax on gender inequality in income

On average men typically have higher incomes than women, because they typically have more income generating assets and get a higher return on those assets. A progressive personal income tax system can to some extent offset this inequality, and narrow the gap between women's and men's net income. For the same reason, reductions in the standard rate of income tax tend to benefit men more than women.

The Government of Canada has devised some Economic Gender Equality Indicators that show the gender equality impact of the personal income tax (Clark, 2000):
  • total earnings index
  • total income index
  • after-tax income index.

The *total earnings index* compares the average earnings of women and men aged 18-64 and includes those who have no earnings for various reasons (for example, unemployment, disability or full-time child care at home). In 1997 (the latest year for which the index is available), the average earnings of adult women were Canadian $16,300 compared to Canadian $29,900 for men. This results in a gender equality index of 0.54, showing that women's average total earnings were 54% of men's. Inequality in earnings is somewhat offset by greater equality in other sources of income, as shown by comparing the total earnings index with the total income index.

The *total income index* compares the average total income on women and men, aged 15 or over, including all income, not just wages and salaries and self-employment income, but also investment and rental income, pensions, employment insurance, child and spousal support payments and government transfers. In 1997, the average income of Canadian women was Canadian $18,000 compared to Canadian $30,900 for men. This results in a gender equality index of 0.58, showing that women's average total income was 58% of men's. The inequality in total income is reduced by the operation of the personal income tax system.

The *total after-tax income index* compares the average total income of men and women after paying personal income tax (but does not take into account the payment of other taxes). In 1997, the gender equality index was 0.63, showing that women's average after-tax total income was 63% of men's.

Analysis of the gender distributional effects of changes in the personal income tax system can be done using micro-simulation models (which can also take account of the welfare benefit system). UK economist Holly Sutherland, a member of the UK Women's Budget Group, is a pioneer in this field and has conducted a gender analysis of the immediate distributional effects of the tax-benefit changes introduced in the UK in April 2000. To conduct this analysis it is necessary to make assumptions about how income is shared within households, and the results of the analysis differ according to the assumptions made.

Assuming that individuals keep all of their earnings and pay their own taxes, the analysis shows that a percentage point cut in the standard rate of income tax benefits men more than women. A much smaller percentage of women (37%) than men (64%) benefit from such a cut, and men gain nearly threes times as much as women on the average (Sutherland, 2000).

In the UK, the Treasury (equivalent to the Ministry of Finance) conducts regular analysis of the joint impact of the personal income tax and welfare benefit system on the net income of women and men. The analysis is not presented in the budget papers but its results are sometimes revealed in response to questions from Members of Parliament. For instance, the budget presented in 2000 was estimated to increase, on average, the net annual income at the disposal of women by £440, compared to £225 for men (Toynbee, 2001). Again, such estimates are sensitive to assumptions about how income is shared within households and the Treasury does not make public the assumptions that it has made.

A micro-simulation model capable of examining the distributional implications of tax and social programmes in South Africa has been developed by the National Institute for Economic Policy. It can examine class, race, gender and region (Adelzadeh, 2001). Such models can be very useful for examining the gender impact of policy changes, but they require a lot of expertise and a large amount of good quality data.

In general, personal income tax tends to reduce income inequality between women and men, even if the rules involve explicit and implicit gender biases. This is because the tax is progressive, and in general men earn more than women.

6.5 Applying CEDAW principles to indirect taxes

Indirect taxes are much more important for poor women in poor countries than is personal income tax. But the gender dimensions of indirect taxes are harder to analyse, since indirect taxes are not levied on persons but on goods and services.

The main indirect taxes are:
- Value Added Tax (VAT) (typically levied across the board at the same rate on a wide range of goods and services, though there may be different rates for different categories of goods, and some categories may be zero-rated (i.e. included in the system, but currently with a zero rate of tax) or exempt (i.e. excluded from the system);
- excise tax (a tax on the sale of selected goods, typically including alcohol and cigarettes);
- import and export taxes (often called 'trade taxes' or 'customs duties').

Here we examine four dimensions of indirect taxes in the light of CEDAW:
- content of tax rules
- tax burden/incidence
- behavioural response of men and women
- impact of tax on distribution of income between women and men.

6.5.1 Indirect tax rules

The rules for indirect taxes explicitly differentiate between different types of goods, and sometimes between different kinds of suppliers (domestic and foreign, large and small), but not between women and men. Therefore, there cannot be explicit gender bias in the rules for indirect taxes. (For examples of differential rates, see Box 33.)

However, there may be *implicit gender bias* in the rules for indirect taxes. Stotsky (1996) focuses on the implications of differential indirect tax rates and suggests that these can contain implicit gender bias in the presence of:
- gender differential consumption of different goods and services;
- gender differential supply of different goods and services (through gender differences in composition of the workforce in different industries).

Implicit gender bias and gender differential consumption of goods and services

Stotsky takes the view that an unbiased system requires that goods and services which are disproportionately consumed by females should not be taxed at a different rate than goods which are disproportionately consumed by males. Thus she argues that:
- High (as compared to the standard VAT) rates of excise tax on alcohol and tobacco are implicitly biased against men, because these goods are disproportionately consumed by men.
- Lower rates of VAT (than the standard rate) on medical care are implicitly biased against men, because these goods are disproportionately consumed by women.

This argument stems from Stotsky's view that bias comes from treating women and men differently. It depends on the assumption that consuming alcohol and tobacco and consuming medical care are equally socially valuable forms of behaviour and equally a matter of personal choice. However, many people would take the view that consumption of alcohol and tobacco is more a personal choice than is consumption of medical care. Moreover, women's reproductive health needs may mean that women require more medical care than do men. In addition, many people would take the view that consumption of alcohol and tobacco often has adverse effects on other people. For instance alcohol consumption is often associated with violent behaviour and smoking tobacco has adverse effects on the health of non-smokers as well as smokers.

Distinctions are widely made within public finance between:
- 'merit goods', which are socially valuable goods, with positive effects on the consumer and on others in society, and whose consumption should be encouraged (e.g. medical care, education);
- 'demerit goods', which are goods that may have adverse effects both on those who consume them and on others;
- basic necessities, which are essential for a decent standard of living; and
- luxuries, which are optional extras.

It is widely regarded as justifiable to tax merit goods and basic necessities at a lower rate than demerit goods and luxuries. If this is accepted, it is not violating the principles of gender equality to have higher tax rates for goods disproportionately consumed by men (and lower tax rates on goods disproportionately consumed by women), if the goods consumed disproportionately by men are 'demerit' and/or luxury goods, and the goods disproportionately consumed by women are 'merit' and/or basic necessities. This is an example of where the achievement of *substantive* equality in economic and social life (as required by CEDAW Articles 3 and 13) between men and women may require different treatment rather than the same treatment.

On the question of 'demerit'/luxury goods versus 'merit'/basic necessities, it can also be argued that higher taxes for 'demerit' goods (such as cigarettes and alcohol) is consistent with States' obligations with regard to the implementation of human rights, such as the implementation of the right to health under Article 12 of the ICESCR (see further Crow, 2004; Appleberry, 2001; Dhooge, 1998; Wike, 1996). In this regard, the CESCR has stated that a government is in violation of the obligation to protect the right to health when it 'fails to discourage production, marketing and consumption of tobacco, narcotics and other harmful substances' (CESCR, General Comment 14, para. 51).

The principle that it is legitimate to tax necessities in a different way from luxuries underpins the case made by women in many countries for zero VAT rating for the sanitary products that enable women to continue their usual activities during menstruation (see Box 34 for an example).

A woman in Kenya wrote to the Ministry for Gender, Sports and Culture, copying the letter to all women Members of Parliament and to the Ministers of Finance and Education, requesting that VAT should be waived on sanitary pads. She argued that lots of girls absent themselves from school when they are menstruating because they cannot afford sanitary pads. In 2004 her request was heeded, and at the National Aids Conference for Women, the President announced that the tax would be waived.

Box 34 VAT waived on women's sanitary products in Kenya

But it is important not to overstate the case for low or no VAT on goods disproportionately consumed by women. An analysis of taxation in Uganda argued for lower tax rates on a wide range of goods mainly used by women (see Box 35) on the grounds that this would recognize women's unpaid contribution to the economy and improve its productivity. But many of the goods identified are not basic necessities, not merit goods, and can only be afforded by well-off urban women.

'There is therefore a need to provide direct fiscal benefits to women members of society in recognition of this contribution [of unpaid domestic work] in order to enhance their productivity. There are three main categories of goods which are mainly used by women through which these benefits could be provided: (a) items of reproductive health and hygiene; (b) items that support the care economy such as child care; and (c) items that have an impact on time use and leisure.

The items with an impact on reproductive health and hygiene include toilet soap and soap for washing clothes, sanitary towels and pads, hair shampoo and mosquito nets, maternity equipment and maternity clothes.

Items with an impact on time use are goods which help women save time for more productive work. These include energy/power for cooking, paraffin, household dishwashers, Hoovers … clothes washers and cookers. Tax relief on these items can go a long way in improving productivity of women.

Items with an impact on the care economy include goods relating to childcare, care of the sick and elderly and domestic work. These include items for child day care facilities, children's foods such as Baby foods, infant milk, etc., mosquito nets, toys, children's clothing and child toiletries, and equipment for care of the elderly'.

Box 35 A call for lower taxes on items mainly used by women in Uganda
        (Wanyaka et al., 2003.)

This raises the question of *inequality between women.* Such tax reductions would benefit mainly well-off urban women. CEDAW does not say anything explicit about inequality between women, but does make special mention of the need to take account of the particular problems faced by rural women in Article 14, which obliges States to 'take all appropriate measures to eliminate discrimination against women in rural areas' and to ensure that rural women enjoy the right to 'adequate health care facilities', 'all types of training and education' and 'adequate living conditions, particularly in relation to housing, sanitation, electricity and water supply, transport and communications'.

CEDAW Article 14 reflects a concern with deprivation as well as with inequality. Not only should there be no discrimination against rural women in access to services, but services should also be 'adequate' to meet the needs of rural women. Underlying this Article is a concern that rural women are likely to be more deprived than urban women, and that in ensuring 'the full development and advancement of women', as required by Article 3, particular attention should be paid to improving the situation of deprived women. The CEDAW Committee and other treaty-monitoring bodies have recognized on several occasions the need to address women's 'deprivation' and poverty outside of the context of a comparison with similarly situated men. First, they have acknowledged that many women experience different forms and degrees of discrimination that come about through the intersection of multiple identity factors (e.g. race, colour, language, property or birth) (CEDAW, GR 25, para. 12; CESCR, General Comment 16, para. 5; see generally CERD, General Comment 25, Gender Related Dimensions of Racial Discrimination (2000)). The CEDAW Committee has further emphasized the need for States to take account of these differences that exist among women. For example, it has encouraged States, where necessary, to direct temporary special measures to women experiencing multiple grounds of discrimination, including rural women (CEDAW, GR 25, para. 38). Additionally, in the specific context of poverty and deprivation, the CEDAW Committee in its Concluding Comments on Brazil's combined initial, second, third, fourth and fifth periodic report (Brazil, CEDAW, A/58/38 part II (2003) 93) highlighted its concern about the differential impact of poverty on women in Brazil (specifically Brazilian women of African descent, indigenous women, female heads of household and other socially excluded or marginalized groups of women) and urged the State to 'ensure that its poverty eradication measures give priority attention' to these women 'through adequately funded programmes and policies addressing their specific needs' (paras. 110 and 111). Similarly, in its Concluding Comments on Argentina's fourth and fifth periodic reports, the Committee expressed its particular concern at the impact of poverty on women heads of households who are unemployed with dependent children; rural women; indigenous women; and the most vulnerable parts of the population (Argentina, CEDAW, A/57/38 part III (2002) 196 at paras. 356 and 357).

In the light of this, it could be argued that the revenue that would be lost through tax reductions on most of the items listed in Box 35 would be put to better use by providing better public services for rural women or other women suffering multiple grounds of discrimination. Or if there is no confidence that the revenue would in fact be used for this rather than, say, expanding the military, it would be better to concentrate tax reductions on items consumed by poor women. This is taken up in the discussion of tax incidence in 6.4.2.

Gender differential supply of goods and services

Stotsky also suggests that there is implicit bias if the pattern of import duties favours industries that primarily *employ* women (such as clothing) or those that primarily *employ* men (such as vehicles). The implication is that a gender-neutral system would offer the same level of protection to all industries. However, though such a system of equal protection might be gender-neutral in terms of equal incentives for female-labour intensive and for male-labour intensive industries, it would not address issues of gender discrimination in wages and promotions, and would not challenge stereotypical patterns of occupational segregation. Moreover, the 'full development and advancement of women' (called for in CEDAW Article 3) is hard to realize without the 'full development and advancement' of the countries in which women live. There are strong arguments to suggest that national development requires differential protection of different industries in different phases of development (Chang, 2002). This is a complex issue on which there is no simple benchmark of gender equality that can be used.

CEDAW Article 11, which deals with the elimination of discrimination in employment, does have implications for the implementation of reductions in import duties (which is a key component of trade liberalization). It obliges States to ensure that women and men are treated equally in the retrenchment of employment that often occurs in sectors where import duties have been reduced, and are treated equally in policies to provide social security for periods of unemployment, and in policies to create new jobs for those who have been retrenched.

It should be noted that retrenchment and re-employment are normal features of the operation of a dynamic capitalist economy. This occurs for other reasons beside trade liberalization, especially technological change and changing patterns of needs. CEDAW does not oblige a State to try to prevent women ever being retrenched, but to ensure that women are not discriminated against in the process of retrenchment (including through indirect discrimination whereby retrenchment has a disproportionate impact on women), and to ensure that women, equally with men, find new employment and maintain adequate standards of living.

A different aspect of gender differential supply of goods and services is that women tend to be disproportionately concentrated in the *ownership and management* of small enterprises and in self-employment, whereas large and medium enterprises tend to be more likely to be managed and owned by men. There is usually a minimum size of enterprise below which there is no liability to pay indirect taxes. This may give rise to implicit bias against women, though it may also in some cases create economic opportunities for women. This is best explored in the context of tax burden/incidence, and is considered in the next section.

6.5.2 Burden/incidence of indirect taxes

In considering indirect taxes, it is important to distinguish between the tax burden and the incidence of the tax. The tax burden falls upon the entity with legal responsibility for paying the tax to the government. Where this entity (be it a person or an enterprise) is engaged in selling the goods and services that are subject to the indirect tax, some or all of the burden of the tax can be shifted to those who consume the goods. When this happens, the incidence of the tax is different from the tax burden. The incidence of the tax is its ultimate impact on incomes of consumers.

Gender inequality and the tax burden of VAT

Enterprises paying VAT are liable to pay the tax on the value of the output sold and get a rebate of the VAT charged to them on the inputs they buy. (This means that the tax then falls on the value they have added, rather than on the value of their output.) Only enterprises that are registered for VAT can claim the rebate on the VAT paid on the inputs they have purchased. If there is a minimum size of enterprise that can register, or if women tend to register less than do men, this can result in a lack of substantive equality in tax burden between male and female owners of enterprises. This problem has been identified in recent gender budget studies in Uganda, South Africa and Vietnam (see Box 36).

Uganda

The threshold for VAT registration is Shs 50 million annual turnover. Only enterprises that are registered can claim rebate of the VAT they have paid on their inputs. This rule excludes informal enterprises (which women are more likely to be running) from claiming rebates for the VAT they have paid on items required to run their businesses, such as weighing scales, juice makers, popcorn makers, groundnut paste makers, salt, sugar, paraffin.

Source: Wanyaka et al., 2003.

South Africa

Enterprises with an annual turnover of R150,000 or more are required to be registered for VAT, and registration enables them to claim a rebate of VAT paid on inputs. The turnover of most women-owned businesses in the informal sector is well below this, yet they are unlikely to be able to avoid paying VAT if they buy inputs from formal sector businesses. On the other hand, for those women who own businesses above the cut-off line, registration involves costs in terms of the time required for administering the tax.

Source: Hartzenberg, 1996:234.

Vietnam

Businesses are exempt from paying VAT on inputs if they are below a 'minimum level of business turnover minus a reasonable cost of business operation', provided they are registered. The registration rate is lower for businesses owned by women than those owned by men. This means that women will be less likely to be able to claim rebate of payments of VAT on inputs than will men

Source: Van Staveren and Akram-Lodhi, 2003.

Box 36 Gender inequality in the burden of VAT in Uganda, South Africa and Vietnam

---

Gender inequality and the burden of trade taxes: the suitcase trade

In many countries small amounts of consumer goods can be imported without being subject to duties. This has given rise to informal cross-border trade, carried out mainly by women, who travel across the borders with goods in suitcases. Though this has proved to be an important economic opportunity for many women, it is precarious. Women traders are particularly liable to harassment, including demands for bribes and for sexual favours, by border guards and Customs officials (clearly a breach of CEDAW Article 11). Moreover, the tax concessions that make this trade viable may easily be withdrawn when the trade grows and becomes very visible. Women informal traders are not in as strong a position to lobby for the maintenance of tax concessions as formal trading companies (which are more likely to be male-managed). (For an example, see Box 37.)

In the 1990s, women from Azerbaijan, Bulgaria, Georgia, Lithuania, Romania, Russia and Ukraine entered Turkey as tourists. They bought consumer goods that were unavailable in their own countries, or only available at high prices, because import duty was charged on them. Taking advantage of duty-free concessions for small quantities of goods, they took the goods back to their own countries and sold them in informal markets. They did have to pay VAT on the goods in Turkey, and in 1996 the Turkish Ministry of Finance reported that VAT revenues from the suitcase trade were US$8.84 billion.

After 1996, the governments of Bulgaria, Romania and Russia withdrew the concession and began charging 20 per cent duty on the goods imported by the suitcase traders. The result was a sharp drop in the suitcase trade. In 1997, the Turkish Ministry of Finance reported that VAT revenue from the suitcase trade had fallen sharply to US$5.85 billion. By 1998, the trade had come to an almost complete halt. During the same period, larger scale import/export firms received other forms of tax concessions and subsidies.

Box 37 The suitcase trade in Eastern Europe
(Esim, 2000.)

However, although there is a gain to women informal traders in maintaining the duty-free status of small quantities of goods, there is a loss of revenue to the government. This revenue might have been used to fund services important to women. In general, concessions in indirect taxes that reduce the tax burden on producers and traders tend to benefit large-scale formal enterprises more than informal enterprises. Given that women entrepreneurs tend to be disproportionately concentrated in the informal sector, this represents an implicit bias against women. In their gender analysis of taxation in Uganda, Wanyaka et al. (2003) conclude that tax concessions in indirect taxes should be avoided.

Gender inequality and the incidence of VAT

Ultimately, the burden of VAT is transferred to the consumer, with enterprises acting as tax collectors. The incidence of VAT on consumers can be calculated as the percentage of the consumer's income that goes on paying the tax. The income and expenditure data required for this is generally only available at the household level.

VAT is a highly regressive tax. Lower-income households pay a higher proportion of their income in VAT than do better-off households, because lower-income households have to consume a higher proportion of their incomes to achieve an adequate standard of living than do better-off households. The South African Women's Budget Initiative has drawn attention to this problem in South Africa (see Box 38).

Because women tend to be more concentrated in lower-income households than are men, and female-headed households on average tend to have lower income than male-headed households, VAT not only has a higher incidence on poor households, it also has a higher incidence on women than on men. It results in substantive inequality between women and men.

The regressive incidence of VAT can be mitigated by zero-rating basic items on which poor households spend a lot of their income, especially food. Smith (2000:23) reports that in South Africa a selection of basic foodstuffs are zero-rated, including brown bread, maize meal, dried beans, milk powder, rice, vegetables and fruit. But some basic necessities are subject to VAT, including paraffin, which is used by poor people for cooking, lighting and heating. In the second report from the Women's Budget Initiative, the annual revenue loss to the government of zero-rating paraffin was estimated at R150 million in 1996 (James and Simmonds, 1997:240). To put this in context, the total raised from VAT in 1995/95 was R29,288.4 millions (Smith, 2000:8). James and

Annual Household Income	Total VAT paid in Rands	VAT paid as % of total tax paid	VAT paid as % of annual income
R18,000	1,799	86	10
R30,000	2,910	54	10
R75,000	6,141	25	8
R140,000	10,241	18	7

Box 38 Incidence of VAT on households in South Africa
Smith, 2000:22, quoting Department of Finance statistics published in 1998.

Simmonds (1997) argue that zero-rating of paraffin would be a very well-targeted form of assistance to poor households as there would be little benefit to rich households because they do not make much use of paraffin. This is a good example of the kind of case that needs to be made in arguing for zero-rating of a product, with a careful consideration of the scale of the revenue loss to the government and the distribution of the benefits between rich and poor households. A few years after publication of this analysis, VAT was lifted on paraffin.

Some countries have made VAT less regressive by not only having exemptions for some items, but also having more than one rate of VAT, with a lower rate on goods and services which account for a high proportion of expenditure of lower-income households or which are considered to be 'merit' goods. This makes administration more complex and is often argued to increase costs of tax administration and make tax avoidance easier.

An argument is often made that it is better to deal with the regressive effects of VAT by channeling the revenue raised to poor households in the form of public services. This point deserves serious consideration. However, the problem is that the incidence of the tax on poor people is certain while the benefits they may get from the revenue are uncertain. There is no direct link between poor people paying VAT and getting better public services. So it is important to ensure that governments do not place too much reliance on VAT as a source of revenue.

Comparing VAT and income tax

If a government wants to raise more revenue, raising the rate of income tax generally does more to achieve substantive equality between women and men than raising the rate of VAT or reducing the number of VAT exemptions.

If a government wants to reduce tax payments, exempting more basic items from VAT generally does more to achieve substantive equality between women and men than reducing the rate of VAT, and both are better than reducing the rate of income tax.

Gender inequality and the incidence of excise taxes

If an excise tax is levied on a good, for example alcohol, enterprises can raise the price of alcohol and pass on the tax so that its incidence falls on the buyer. The extent to which the tax can be passed on depends on how far buyers reduce their purchases when the price rises. If they do not reduce their purchases very much, their demand is said to be 'inelastic'. If they continue to buy the same amount even if the price rises, then demand is 'perfectly inelastic'. This means that all of the tax can be passed on in higher prices and all the incidence of the tax falls on the buyer. Typically, demand for alcohol is inelastic, but not perfectly inelastic, so while much of the incidence of the tax falls on the on the buyer, some falls on the seller.

Excise taxes can be progressive taxes if they are levied on goods that are only consumed by rich households (such as expensive cars), but if they are levied on goods consumed by both rich and poor households they are regressive.

Contributing to the South African Women's Budget Initiative, Goldman (2000) reports that excise tax in South Africa is strongly regressive in terms of comparisons between households:
- Poorest 10% of households spent 0.8% of their annual income in 1997 on excise tax.
- Richest 10% of households spent only 0.2% of their annual income in 1997 on excise tax.

However, unlike VAT, this regressive impact does not necessarily result in a greater incidence of the tax on women than on men, since women tend to consume less than men of many goods that are subject to excise tax (see Box 39 for an example from South Africa).

Alcohol consumption as a percentage of household income is lower in households in which a higher proportion of adults are women.

In households with no adult women, or where fewer than 10% of household adults are women, 0.26% of household income is spent on alcohol.

In households in which more than 60% of the adults are women, less than 0.10% of household income is spent on alcohol.

In households in which all the adults are women, only 0.04% of household income is spent on alcohol.

Box 39 Gender and expenditure on alcohol in South Africa, 1995
(Goldman, 2000:24.)

As argued in 6.4.1, the greater incidence of alcohol taxes on men than on women can be defended in terms of alcohol being considered a 'demerit' good that can have adverse impacts on the consumer and others. Purchasing alcohol is not equally socially valuable as purchasing paraffin, so even though the excise tax on alcohol is regressive, there is not the strong case for exempting alcohol that there is for exempting paraffin.

It may seem tempting to argue that the 'full development and advancement of women' (CEDAW Article 3) would be served by higher taxes on alcohol. For instance, this would permit more basic goods to be exempted from VAT, while maintaining the same level of revenue. But this needs further consideration in the light of the likely impact of the two taxes on the behaviour of women and men.

6.4.3 Impact of indirect taxes on behaviour of women and men

As noted above, consumers of alcohol do not reduce their purchase of alcohol very much if the price rises. This raises the question of how they continue to fund their purchases. If their income does not rise, they will have to cut back on something else.

There is a danger that men will respond to a rise in the price of alcohol by cutting back on spending on goods that benefit other household members. For instance, if they are responsible for paying the rent on the family home, they may get into arrears, putting the family in danger of eviction. Or if they are responsible for buying furniture or larger items of kitchen equipment, they may cut back on buying replacements as these wear out. Or if they are responsible for proving cash to their wives to purchase daily necessities, they may cut back on this. This kind of behaviour transfers the burden of a rise in alcohol prices to women and children within the household. An alternative behavioural response is for men to cut back on some other item of personal consumption, such as clothes or visits to the cinema. This would not shift the tax burden to other members of the household. There do not appear to be any studies about which behavioural response predominates.

Similar issues of response arise in relation to VAT. If there is a rise in VAT on daily necessities that women have the responsibility of buying, where do the cuts in household expenditure fall? There is evidence to suggest that when the price of basic household goods rises, women tend to cut back on their own consumption and to spend more of their time on producing home-made substitutes (collecting firewood from the forest, cultivating kitchen gardens, making home-baked food, sewing clothes at home, etc.).

They may also try to negotiate an increase in housekeeping money from their husbands. If they succeed, then some of the increased tax burden is transferred to their husbands.

Again, it is not clear which behavioural response predominates.

Nevertheless, there is a lot of evidence that women's bargaining power within households tends to be weaker than men's. This suggests that a plausible hypothesis is that men have more capacity to transfer the burden of indirect consumption taxes (like excise duties and VAT) to other household members than do women. Stereotyped gender roles are likely to result in an unequal situation where men tend to pass on the burden of increased indirect taxes on goods like alcohol to other household members, while women, as far as possible, tend to bear the burden themselves. Insofar as this is the case, indirect consumption taxes will have a substantially unequal impact on women and men, with a greater incidence on women than on men.

6.4.4 Impact of indirect taxes on gender inequality in income

The only study that appears to be available that considers how indirect taxes impact on income inequality between women and men examines the implications of trade taxes in Bangladesh and Ghana (Fontana, 2003). A computable model is built of each economy, incorporating both paid and unpaid work, and male and female labour. This is used to examine the hypothetical impact of a number of policies, including the abolition of import duties, and an equalization of import duties, on a number of gender variables, including the hourly wages of women in relation to those of men. The model assumes that with import liberalization, imports would rise but that those people retrenched in the import-competing sectors would find jobs in other sectors, especially the export sector, which is assumed to expand. The findings are shown in Box 40.

Abolition of import duties:

- In Bangladesh, women's hourly wages would rise, both in absolute terms and relative to men.

- In Zambia, women's hourly wages would rise, but men's would rise even more, thus widening the gap between male and female wages.

The difference stems from the different structures of the two economies. Abolition of import duties would provide an incentive for the garment industry in Bangladesh which employs a large number of women. In Zambia it would provide an incentive for the expansion of mining and commercial crops, which are disproportionately employers of men.

Equalization of all duties at 20 per cent, in place of differential duties:

- In Bangladesh, women's hourly wage would fall, both in absolute terms and relative to men's.

- In Kenya, hourly wages of women would fall, except for women with no education, but women's wages would rise relative to those of men, except for women with primary education.

Again the difference stems from the different structures of the two economies, especially in the female share of employment in the expending sector. In Bangladesh, this policy would lead to the fall in employment in the garment industry and an expansion of commercial crops (where only 3 per cent of the labour force was estimated to be female). In Zambia, the policy would lead to a decline in employment in the mining industry and an expansion in commercial crops (where about 40 per cent of the labour force was estimated to be female).

Box 40 Estimates of impact of changes in import duties on gender wage gap in Bangladesh and Zambia
(Fontana, 2003.)

This study illustrates an important general point: the impact of changes in indirect taxes on gender inequality in incomes is likely to depend on the structure of production and consumption. Indirect taxes might be equalizing or disequalizing, unlike personal income tax, which is always equalizing.

6.6 Applying CEDAW principles to tax reforms

The main issue to consider in applying CEDAW principles to the assessment of entire programmes of tax reform is the change in the balance between corporate and personal tax, and within personal tax, between direct and indirect taxation. The analysis in Section 6.5 suggest that if tax paid by corporations falls and by persons rises, and if, within personal tax, income tax rates are reduced and sales taxes are extended, the incidence of tax on women, especially poor women, will tend to increase.

This has been discussed by the GBI in South Africa, especially in the contribution by Smith (2000). He documents the dramatic shift in the composition of revenue from direct taxes in the period since 1988/89 away from corporate taxes to personal taxes (mainly income tax). In 1988/89, personal taxes accounted for 30% of total tax revenue, while corporate taxes accounted for 22%. By 1998/99, personal taxes accounted for 42%, while corporate taxes accounted for only 13%. In the 1999 Budget Review, the Department of Finance announced a far-reaching reduction of the rate of tax on companies 'in response to the challenge of globalization'. The lowering of corporate taxes has been a key element in the South African Government's Growth, Employment and Redistribution (GEAR) strategy, which is discussed further in Section 7. Smith notes that men are predominantly the owners and shareholders of companies in South Africa; and concludes that:

> 'The … lower revenues from company taxes then leaves a greater burden on indirect taxes to make up the required tax revenue. This again places a disproportionate and unfair tax burden on lower income earners, i.e. women and the poor'.

A study of the gender dimensions of tax reform in Argentina, Chile, Costa Rica and Jamaica found that with the exception of Jamaica, a greater reliance was placed on indirect taxes and concluded that:

> 'Women as lower income earners and as mothers responsible for the needs of the family, particularly if on fixed budget, are more negatively affected than men by changes that increase regressive indirect taxes' (Huber 2003:20).

However, Huber noted that in Jamaica the tax system was still overall progressive in its incidence because a wide range of basic goods and services are exempt from VAT, and the personal income tax system is progressive.

6.7 User fees

In the 1990s many countries introduced user fees for publicly provided services such as water and sanitation and health and education. The introduction of these charges was encouraged by the World Bank and the IMF as a way of raising revenue to improve the services, and to discourage inefficiency in the use of the services.

Human rights treaties do not imply that user fees are for public services are in themselves a violation of human rights, but they do oblige governments to limit charges in various ways. For instance:

- Explicit prohibition on fees for primary education in Article 13 of the International Covenant on Economic, Social and Cultural Rights, which states that 'primary education shall be compulsory and free to all'; and a requirement for the 'progressive introduction of free education' at the secondary and higher level. See further CESCR, General Comments 11 and 13 for discussion of the content of these requirements.
- Obligation to ensure 'economic accessibility' (affordability) of rights. This means that charges must not threaten or compromise basic rights (CESCR, General Comment 4, para. 8(c); CESCR, General Comment 12, para. 13; CESCR, General Comment 15, para. 12(c) (ii)) and that charges for services (public or private) should be equitable, affordable for all (including the socially disadvantaged) and not place a disproportionate burden of expenses on poor households as compared to wealthier ones (CESCR, General Comment 14, para. 12(b); CESCR, General Comment 15, para. 27).
- Obligation to 'fulfill' rights, which requires the State to ensure affordable services for everyone, including through pricing policies in which key services are low-cost or free, or where the government provides income supplements for fees (CESCR, General Comment 15, paras. 26, 27).

- Obligation to 'respect' rights, which is violated when there are discriminatory or unaffordable increases in the price of basic services (CESCR, General Comment 15, para. 44(a)).
- Core obligation (from which no derogation is permitted) to ensure accessibility of crucial services for all without discrimination, particularly for the most vulnerable or marginalized (CESCR, General Comment 14, para. 43(a); CESCR, General Comment 15, para. 37(b)).
- Responsibility to ensure that activities of private actors do not interfere with equal and affordable access to services (CESCR, General Comment 5, para. 11; CESCR, General Comment 12, paras. 20, 27; CESCR, General Comment 15, para. 24).
- Obligation to provide to women 'appropriate services in connection with pregnancy, confinement and the post-natal period, granting free services where necessary' in CEDAW Article 12. This is further clarified by CEDAW General Recommendation 24 on Article 12 which requires States Parties to remove 'all barriers' to women's access to health services, education and information (CEDAW, General Recommendation 24, para. 31(b)); report on how 'they supply *free services where necessary* to ensure safe pregnancies, childbirth and post-partum periods for women' (emphasis included in original text) (CEDAW, General Recommendation 24, para. 27); and report on 'measures taken to eliminate barriers that women face in gaining access to health care services and what measures they have taken to ensure women timely and affordable access to such services. Barriers include requirements or conditions that prejudice women's access, such as high fees for health care services' (para. 21).
- Obligation to ensure that disabled women have specific measures to ensure their equal access to education, employment, health services and social security (CEDAW, GR 18).
- Requirement to provide guaranteed access to sex education and family planning services, as provided for in Article 10(h) of CEDAW (CEDAW, GR 21, para. 22).
- Recognition that 'where there are freely available appropriate measures for the voluntary regulation of fertility, the health, development and well-being of all members of the family improves' (CEDAW, GR 21, para. 23).
- Obligation in CEDAW Article 14 to ensure rural women 'enjoy adequate living conditions, particularly in relation to housing, sanitation, electricity and water supply, transport and communications'.

However, the design and implementation of user fees have frequently failed to comply with these obligations. Fees have been introduced for publicly provided higher and secondary and even primary education. Fees for health, water, sanitation and electricity have been set at levels which are not affordable to poor people, and which result in a lack of substantive equality in access to public services.

Like indirect taxes, user fees are regressive. When they pay the fees, poor households spend a higher proportion of their income on these charges than do better-off households.

Just as in the case of indirect taxes, there is evidence of implicit bias against women and girls in the operation of these charges. The bias arises because of gender inequality in control of household income and gender inequality in prioritization of use of services.

6.7.1 Education

Poor parents often give priority to sons rather than daughters if they have to pay school fees. In Africa there is evidence that the introduction of school fees led to reduction in enrollment and greater drop-outs in children in poor families, with a greater fall in enrollment and a greater increase in drop-outs for girls (see Box 41). This is clearly in breach of obligations under CEDAW Article 10 to ensure women equal rights with men in the field of education.

Some schemes for levying school fees try to build in some mitigation for poor communities through co-payment schemes with higher levels of matching grants for poor communities. Some also provide scholarships for girls that cover fees (and for other expenses such as uniforms), an example of the kind of 'temporary special measures' aimed at accelerating *de facto* equality between men and women that are permitted by CEDAW Article 4 (see Box 42 for an example). Many countries have now abolished fees for primary education.

Zambia: After introduction of fees in early 1990s, school drop-out rates increased, but more for girls than boys.

Kenya: Nearly half the households in seven poor districts investigated for the 1994 poverty assessment had one or more children who had dropped out because of inability to pay fees. Girls were twice as likely to be withdrawn from school than boys.

Malawi: A rise in school fees in the mid-1980s was followed by a decline in enrollment, mainly among girls. When fees were eliminated in 1994, primary enrolment increased by 50 per cent, with the new entrants mainly girls.

Box 41 Impact of school fees on education of girls in Africa
       (Vandemoortele, 2002:58.)

The Community Education Fund provides matching grants to schools related to the amount the school has raised through charging fees, selling the output of school farms and voluntary contributions from parents. The size of the grant varies with the average income of the community:

- above average income—grant of 100% of funds raised
- average income—grant of 150% of funds raised
- below average community—200% of funds raised

This sliding scale makes it easier for schools in poor communities to charge parents less, and should reduce the bias against the schooling of poor girls.

The **Girls' Secondary Education Support Programme** provides direct financial assistance with fees and other school-related expenses to girls form poor families who are recommended by their primary school teachers as academically eligible on the basis of their exam results. In 1997, 359 girls were benefiting from this programme.

Box 42 Measures to reduce gender bias in user fees for education in Tanzania
       (TGNP 2004.)

6.7.2 Health services

Poor parents in many Asian countries often give priority to sons rather than daughters in seeking health care if they have to pay fees. Moreover, fees may discourage poor women more than poor men in seeking health care, because women have less income and less voice in household decision-making, and are encouraged by social and cultural norms to put their own needs last. In Africa there is evidence that user fees for health services have had this effect (see Box 43). This is in breach of CEDAW Article 12 which obliges states to ensure equality between men and women in access to health care services and to provide free services for maternal health where necessary. The CEDAW Committee in its General Recommendation 24 has clarified that the State must address both the biological and social determinants of different women's health (para. 6). In this vein, it has identified the need for States to address, in addition to biological factors, the socio-economic factors and psychosocial factors that affect women's health (para. 12(b) and (c)).

It is often argued that a system of user fees for health care has benefits because it is more transparent than the systems of 'informal' payments to medical staff, which are widespread in some public health systems in poor countries. It is argued that official user fees will lead to an improvement of services and that poor people can be exempted from paying them. However, inconsistencies in exemptions, abuse of exemptions and misappropriation of the fees have been documented (Nanda 2000) (for an example see Box 44). Studies in several countries show that exemptions tend to benefit better-off groups, such as hospital staff and their relatives, and civil servants. Poor people are unaware they can claim exemptions (Mackintosh and Tibandebage, 2004). A few governments in Africa, including Uganda, have now abolished fees for public health services.

Kenya: Introduction of user fees (amounting to half a day's pay for a poor person) in government outpatient health facilities led to a big reduction in use of health services for Sexually Transmitted Diseases by both men and women. The reduction was significantly more for women. Nine months after their introduction, the fees were revoked and women's utilization rose to a greater level than before the fees were introduced.

Source: Nanda, 2002.

Nigeria, Zimbabwe, Tanzania: Introduction of user fees was associated with decrease in hospital admissions of pregnant women, decline in use of Maternal and Child Health services and an increase in maternal deaths.

Source: Mackintosh and Tibandebage, 2004.

South Africa: The post-apartheid government removed user fees for pregnant women and children under six. This led to a rise in attendance at most public sector health facilities, and an increase in the numbers of women booking for ante-natal care.

Box 43 Impact of user fees on women's use of health services in Africa
(Stevens, 1997.)

6.7.3 Water, sanitation and electricity

Affordable access to water, sanitation and electricity is vital for the achievement of substantive equality for women. Without these services, factors such as the social organization of the community, discriminatory patterns of resource distribution and distance from resources mean that women have to spend much of their time collecting fuel and water and dealing with the health hazards of lack of sanitation services. In recognition of these dangers, Article 14(h) of CEDAW specifically calls upon States to ensure that rural women enjoy 'adequate living conditions, particularly in relation to housing, *sanitation, electricity and water supply,* transport and communications' (emphasis added). The CESCR has also recognized that while the right to water is universal, States should give 'special attention' to those for whom the right has been traditionally difficult to exercise. It specifies women as being in this category and recommends that States Parties take steps to ensure that

---

Pregnant women are supposed to be exempt from paying fees in public hospitals, but while delivery of their babies is free, they have to pay admission charges. Moreover, they still have to make 'informal' payments to staff in the hospital as they have always done. Accounting for the fees is lax and the fees are easily misappropriated by officials, since the use of the funds cannot be traced.

The fees are not used to provide the materials necessary for a safe delivery. Women are told to come equipped with:
- two pairs of sterilized gloves
- two pairs of standard gloves
- two boxes of sanitary pads
- disinfectant solution
- two syringes
- the drug ergometrine (to stem excessive bleeding)
- catgut for stitches
- four pairs of bed sheets
- one pair of bedsheets for the baby

Men are not told to come with medical equipment for the treatment of conditions specific to men. The US$63,900 used by a Minister for treatment abroad could pay for services for about 12,500 pregnant women.

Box 44 Problems with administration of user fees for health services in Tanzania
(TGNP, 2004.)

women are included in decision-making processes and that their disproportionate burden in water collection be addressed (CESCR, General Comment 15, para. 16(a)).

Affordability of water, sanitation and electricity is often judged on the basis of per capita household income and rarely takes account of gender inequalities within households. The level assessed as affordable on a household basis can be higher than is affordable for poor women (see Box 45).

A water project in western Kenya found that cost recovery for water use was low despite high average household incomes. The cause was found to be the fact that it was women who were responsible for water payments, and they had much lower incomes than men.

Box 45 Gender and ability to pay for water in Kenya
(Vandemoortele, 2002: 58.)

Affordable access for poor women can be promoted through structures of charging in which there is cross-subsidy from better-off users to lower income users. This can be achieved by having higher per-unit charges for those who use larger amounts of the service than for those who use small amounts. Cross-subsidies can be used by public sector providers and can also be a requirement of the regulations governing the operation of operation of privately owned providers. This is the system in use in South Africa, known as a 'rising block tariff system'. It enables better-off users to subsidize poorer users (see Box 46).

Water

The Department of Water Affairs and Forestry set guidelines for water services charges made by municipalities as follows:

- basic human needs of 25 litres per person per day—lowest level of charges per litre
- 'normal consumption' (i.e. average consumption for the area)—higher level of charges per litre
- 'luxury consumption' (i.e. above average consumption for the area)—highest level of charges per litre

This framework was implemented in a variety of ways.

Capetown had a five block tariff in 2000:

- for the first 5 kl per month   R 0.50 per kl
- 5 kl to 15 kl per month   R 1.60 per kl
- 15 kl to 30 kl per month   R 2.70 per kl
- 30 kl to 50 kl per month   R 3.80 per kl
- over 50 kl per month   R 5.00 per kl

The Capetown city council reported that over half of all households used less than 23 kl per month, and that these households would pay less than under the previous system of charging.

Durban city council provided the first six kl free.

Electricity

The National Electricity Regulator, established in 1995, requires an equitable tariff structure, with a low tariff for poorer consumers. In some areas a flat rate tariff was introduced for a type of current (5 to 8 amps) which was suitable only for lighting, TV, radio and refrigeration, but not for cooking. The household pays a fixed amount a month regardless of how much is consumed. Households supplied with a current suitable for all uses are given meters, and pay a higher rate on the amount they actually use.

Box 46 Cross- subsidy in charging for water and electricity in South Africa
(Coopoo, 2000.)

This kind of system of user fees is not without problems. In South Africa the system of cross-subsidy in electricity charges was challenged as 'discriminatory' because it resulted in inhabitants of mainly 'white' districts (which don't have the flat rate) paying more per unit for their electricity than those of mainly 'African' districts which do have the flat rate). However, the Constitutional Court determined that this was not 'discriminatory' (Coopoo, 2000:28). A further problem is that many poor people cannot afford to pay even the lowest tariffs and are in arrears. Many have been disconnected from the supply of electricity.

In general it is difficult to set fees at a level which is affordable for poor households, if at the same time revenue from fees is the sole source of funding for the service. If the service is publicly owned, poor users can be subsidized using other sources of revenue. If the service is privatized, and the state merely regulates it, then cross-subsidy becomes much more difficult as profits have to be generated for shareholders. Privatization of public services is an important issue for gender equality, but further discussion of it is outside the scope of this report.

6.8 Conclusions

This section of the report has examined some key sources of revenue (income tax, VAT, excise tax, import duties and user fees) in the light of CEDAW obligations. All of these revenue measures have been found to run the risk of discriminating against women, either explicitly or implicitly. It is important to design revenue measures to minimize any adverse effects on the achievement of substantive equality between women and men, and to accelerate the achievement of equality.

Substantive equality in this context does NOT imply that 50% of tax revenue should be paid by women and 50% by men. It is a well-established principle in public finance that equality in taxation has to be related to ability to pay. Men on average have greater ability to pay than women, because on average their incomes are higher. This scope for differentiated taxing is generally consistent with the practice of the CEDAW Committee, which has recognized that meeting women's needs requires targeted reform of particular aspects of the tax system, for example through encouraging States to conduct a review of taxation legislation relating to small businesses to ensure 'gainful and secure' employment for women (Kyrgyzstan, CEDAW, A/54/38/Rev.1, part I (1999) 15 at para. 134).

Income tax is the only one of the five measures considered in which explicit and intentional discrimination against women may occur. This can happen in both joint tax filing systems and individual tax filing systems. The most obvious example is the allocation of tax exemptions and allowances for the support of dependents to husbands but not to wives. This is clearly in violation of CEDAW Article 13 (a) which obliges States to ensure equality between women and men in the right to family benefits. This kind of discrimination can be eliminated by reform of the tax law.

Revenue measures contain many other kinds of less overt obstacles to women's enjoyment of equal rights and their 'full development and advancement'. These arise because of the intersection of the tax laws with pre-existing gender inequality in incomes, employment and responsibility for unpaid domestic work and with the different decisions different women and men make about how to combine paid and unpaid work.

Personal income tax laws can be reformed so as to promote equal sharing of paid and unpaid work between women and men in households, and so as to be neutral between households with married, unmarried and same-sex partners. The great advantage of personal income tax is that its incidence is progressive, in the sense that those with higher incomes pay a higher proportion of their income in tax. Appropriately designed it can be an equality-promoting tax, reducing inequality in disposable income between men and women and between rich and poor women. It is, however, harder to administer than direct taxes.

VAT is regressive. The incidence of the tax on consumers is higher for poor consumers than for rich ones; since women's incomes tend to be lower than men's the incidence will tend to be higher on average on female consumers than on male consumers. The most important way to make VAT more equitable in gender terms is to exempt a wide range of basic necessities purchased by poor women form the tax. Care must be taken not to argue for exemptions simply on the basis of the goods in question being mainly purchased or used by women, without considering the merit of the goods and the income levels of the women who consume them. There is a strong case for exempting a good like paraffin, purchased by poor women for heating, cooking and lighting, but not for exempting a good like washing machines, used by better-off urban women. It must be recognized that every exemption reduces revenue, and this reduces resources that might otherwise have been spent of public programmes that promote substantive equality between women and men.

Excise taxes are likely to be less regressive, from a gender perspective, than VAT. This is because they tend to be levied on goods like alcohol and tobacco, which are consumed more by men than by women. However, it is possible that inequality within households may permit men to shift the incidence of the tax to women and children by reducing the amount of income that men devote to the needs of wives and children, so as to maintain their consumption of alcohol and tobacco. So there may be unintended negative side effects for gender equality from attempts to increase revenue by increasing excise taxes.

The effects of import duties on gender equality will depend on the particular structures of production and consumption of different types of economy. Exemptions from import duties for small quantities of goods may benefit small-scale women entrepreneurs, but the biggest exemptions (such as those conferred by Free Trade Zones) go to the biggest firms, often to foreign-owned firms.

User fees for basic education and heath services tend to restrict the access of poor people, but with even more adverse effects for women and girls than for men and boys. They produce outcomes that are in violation of CEDAW obligations. They can be made more gender-equitable through exemptions for the poorest people, but exemption schemes are difficult to administer and may in practice benefit better-off people more than poor people. CEDAW obligations on health and education are best served by not charging user fees for basic education and health services.

In the case of user fees for services such as water, sanitation and electricity, fee exemptions and block tariffs make the incidence of charges more equitable and reduce barriers to access. But is likely to be difficult to comply with the CEDAW obligation to ensure for rural women 'adequate living conditions, particularly in relation to housing, sanitation, electricity and water supply' if services have to be fully funded from cost recovery. Some element of subsidy is likely to be necessary if poor women are to get adequate access.

The revenue mix that is most suited to implementation of CEDAW would be one with:
- high reliance on income tax (reformed to remove provisions that hinder substantive equality between women and men);
- exemptions from VAT on a wide range of basic consumption items;
- excise taxes on non-necessities consumed mainly by men;
- no user fees for basic health and education services;
- fee exemptions and subsidized fees for water, sanitation and electricity supplied to poor households.

The practice of other treaty monitoring bodies confirms that taxation practices are required to ensure that the rights of vulnerable groups are protected. For example, the CESCR has noted that such appropriate measures include having a system that favours direct and progressive taxes (Morocco, CESCR, E/1995/22 (1994) 28 at para. 119).

The revenue measures must also seek to create the 'maximum available resources' for the 'progressive realization' of social, economic and cultural rights. This is further considered in the next section on the macroeconomics of the budget.

Section 7

Analysing the Macroeconomics of the Budget from a CEDAW Perspective

Analysing the Macroeconomics of the Budget from a CEDAW Perspective

So far the budget has been considered from the expenditure side, as a series of programmes; and from the revenue side, as a series of instruments. In this section both sides are brought together, and we consider total expenditure, total revenue and the budget deficit/surplus. We shall be particularly concerned with the macroeconomic impact of the budget as a whole on work, economic growth and inflation, issues which are critical for poverty reduction and realization of economic and social rights.

The budget is the embodiment of fiscal policy, which along with monetary policy are the two key components of macroeconomic policy. There is not agreement among economists on how macroeconomic policy should be designed to secure improvements in living standards, so some of these differences will be explored. In addition, most economists do not consider the implications of macroeconomic policy for women's unpaid work, including subsistence production and caring for others. This means they fail to recognize the ways in which macroeconomic impacts are not gender neutral. In this section we will highlight the gender dimensions of macroeconomic policy, examining the ways in which macroeconomic policy is related to the achievement of substantive gender equality, and showing how CEDAW principles may be applied. Particular attention will be paid to the implications of measures to reduce budget deficits and limit government debt.

7.1 Evaluating the macroeconomics of the budget: neo-liberal and alternative perspectives

As well as *primary* effects on people via public expenditures of which they are beneficiaries and via taxes that they pay, government budgets also have *secondary* effects on people, via their impact on the economy as a whole, especially on availability of paid employment, the extent of the unpaid work that has to be done to care for families and communities and the growth of output and the level of prices. These *secondary* effects work through the impact of the budget on the levels of aggregate market demand and market supply in an economy. This section will provide a brief, non-technical discussion of these impacts drawing on a recent discussion of 'budgeting as if people mattered' (Loxley, 2003, chapter 1). The scale and direction of the macroeconomic impacts depend on whether the budget is in deficit, in balance or in surplus (see Box 47).

- If expenditure exceeds revenue there will be a budget deficit.
- If expenditure is equal to revenue the budget will be balanced.
- If revenue exceeds expenditure there will be a budget surplus.

Box 47 The key budget aggregates

The expenditure side of the budget affects the level of aggregate demand in the economy because it puts money in people's hands through payments of wages and salaries; payments for materials and equipment; and income transfers, such as pensions or child benefits. This has a multiplier effect creating demand for goods and services from businesses, as government employees, suppliers and beneficiaries spend their money. At the same time the government takes money out of people's hands through taxation and other ways of raising revenue.

The net effect on aggregate demand in the markets depends on the relation between total expenditure and revenue:
- If there is a budget deficit, the effect on aggregate demand will be expansionary.
- If there is a budget surplus, the effect on aggregate demand will be contractionary.
- If the budget is balanced, the effect on aggregate demand will not be neutral. It will be expansionary. Even if expenditure is equal to revenue, there is still a positive multiplier effect on aggregate demand because the government will tend to spend all of its income, whereas many businesses and households will tend to save some of their income.

The budget also has an impact on the aggregate supply in an economy. Some of the spending creates physical and human resources (such as roads and a trained and healthy labour force) that increase the productive capacity of an economy. The revenue side of the budget may also have an impact on aggregate supply through the impact of taxation on incentives to produce. If high levels of income and profits tax discourage people from producing, aggregate supply will be reduced. However, this negative effect is likely to be small in relation to the positive effect that public investment has on aggregate supply.

The macroeconomic impacts of the budget take place over a longer period than the yearly budget cycle. They are therefore often referred to as the *dynamic* impacts of the budget. The impacts on aggregate demand are typically faster than the impacts on aggregate supply; but aggregate supply can also rise rapidly if there are unemployment and underutilized stocks of equipment and infrastructure.

The relation between aggregate demand and supply affects the general level of prices and the general level of unemployment. In countries that do not have unemployment benefit payments or other forms of social security, usually only better-off people can afford to be openly unemployed. Poor people in such countries have to find some way to survive through informal employment, even though this informal employment may be very poorly paid, insecure and lacking enjoyment of the right to work. The minimum elements of the human right to work include: non-discrimination in access to employment; equal pay for equal work; freedom of association; prohibition on arbitrary dismissal; adequate minimum wage; freedom from compulsory or forced labour; equal opportunity for promotion or advancement; and the right to rest and leisure (see further http://cesr.org/work). These rights are detailed in international instruments including the Universal Declaration of Human Rights (Article 23); ICESCR (Articles 6 to 8); ICCPR (Articles 8, 22); CEDAW (Article 11); Convention on the Rights of the Child (Article 32(1)); and the International Convention on the Elimination of All Forms of Racial Discrimination (Article 5). They are also set out in international labour standards such as the ILO Declaration on Fundamental Principles and Rights at Work (1998) (The Declaration covers four areas: freedom of association and the right to collective bargaining; elimination of forced and compulsory labour; abolition of child labour; and the elimination of discrimination in the workplace).

These elements of the right to work mean that it is necessary to consider the quality as well as the quantity of employment. The ILO has proposed that the creation of 'decent work' should be an objective. Decent work is defined as follows:

> 'Decent work sums up the aspirations of the people in their working lives. It involves opportunities for work that is productive and delivers a fair income, security in the workplace and social protection for families, better prospects for personal development and social integration, freedom for people to express their concerns, organize and participate in the decisions that affect their lives and equality of opportunity and treatment for all women and men' (http://www.ilo.org/public/english/decent.htm).

The lack of decent work, as well as the rate of unemployment, is an important indicator.
- If aggregate demand tends to move ahead of aggregate supply, then the general level of prices will tend to rise (inflation), unemployment will tend to be low and the availability of decent work will tend to grow.
- If aggregate supply tends to outstrip aggregate demand, then prices will tend to be stable or even fall, but there will tend to be insufficient demand for labour, and unemployment will tend to be high and a growing proportion of the population will be in employment that lacks the characteristics of decent work.

Different schools of thought in economics have opposing views about which problem, inflation or unemployment, should take priority (see Box 48). These different schools of thought evaluate the macroeconomics of budgets in very different ways.

Neo-liberal economists, whose views are dominant in the International Monetary Fund, the World Bank and the financial markets, argue that job creation and economic growth are best promoted via the achievement of a stable price level. They argue that inflation deters savings because it erodes the real value of the return that savers get on their financial assets. They suggest that this will in turn deter investment, as there will not be enough savings to finance investment in real assets, such as factories, mines, electricity generation, etc. Lack of investment will in turn mean low levels of job creation and economic growth. Stable prices will create 'confidence' in financial markets and enable a country to attract foreign savings as well as domestic savings. The budget should therefore be designed to ensure stable prices and this should be the number one priority. The policy target should be reducing inflation not job creation.

There are, however, substantial numbers of economists who do not share this view, including Nobel Prize-winners Amartya Sen and Joseph Stiglitz (formerly Chief Economic Advisor at the World Bank). They argue that investment in real assets is more likely to be constrained by lack of market demand than by lack of savings. Designing the budget so as to minimize inflation is likely to depress the level of demand so much that investment is discouraged, unemployment rises, there is not enough decent work and the level of output stagnates or falls. They recognize that very high and rising rates of inflation ('hyperinflation') will have negative effects. But they point to a lack of evidence that inflation rates of up to 40% have negative effects on economic growth (see for example Sen, 1998). They argue that stable prices should not be the number one priority, because this can only be achieved at the expense of other goals. Job creation and growth have to be given equal priority with inflation, and budgets should be designed with this in mind.

However, neither neo-liberal nor Keynesian economics recognizes that macroeconomic policy also has impacts on the unpaid work vital for the ongoing survival and well-being of families and communities. This issue is at the forefront of feminist macroeconomics (Elson (ed.) 2000, chap. 1; Elson, 2004) and is discussed further in Sections 7.2 and 7.3.

The macroeconomics of budgets also includes the issue of debt and the implications for the money supply and rate of interest. (Consideration of monetary policy is outside the scope of this report.) If there is a budget deficit, this has to be financed. Methods of financing include:
- Borrowing by selling government securities (such as bonds) denominated in the national currency: This results in 'internal debt', primarily to the citizens of a country;
- Borrowing by selling government securities denominated in foreign currency: This results in 'external debt', primarily to citizens of other countries;
- Paying for goods and services by putting more money into circulation via the banking system.

The pros and cons of each of these methods are subject to considerable debate:
- *Internal debt* can be serviced (i.e. the interest paid) in the national currency using the proceeds of the growth of national output; neo-liberal economists argue that borrowing by the government should nevertheless be limited because it reduces the ability of the local businesses to borrow and 'crowds out' efficient private investment, in favour of less efficient public investment, thus depressing aggregate supply below what could otherwise be achieved; economists from the alternative schools of thought argue that public investment encourages rather than displaces private investment by improving infrastructure, and the quality of the labour force, and by increasing markets.
- *External debt* has to be serviced (i.e. the interest paid) in foreign currency and therefore requires growth in earnings of foreign exchange; neo-liberal economists argue that foreign borrowing must be kept in line with the growth of foreign exchange earnings; economists from the alternative schools of thought urge caution on borrowing from abroad because of the volatility of international financial markets.
- *Increasing the money supply* will result in inflation if aggregate demand outstrips supply; neo-liberal economists tend to argue that this will automatically happen; economists from the alternative schools of thought argue that the degree to which this happens depends on the responsiveness of output to

an increase in demand: if there are unemployed resources there will be less tendency for prices to rise because aggregate supply will also rise.

It is widely accepted that some government borrowing will have to take place over the year of the budget cycle because typically the flows of expenditure and the flows of revenue within a year do not match exactly. Moreover, purchase of government securities provides a useful way of saving for households and businesses. What is controversial is the persistence of budget deficits beyond the budget cycle and the continued growth of government debt. The continued growth of government debt is regarded as a bad thing by the private sector financial organizations that give ratings to the securities issued by each government. Any reduction in the rating entails an increase in the rate of interest that the government has to pay. It appears that the organizations that give the ratings give a positive weight to governments that reduce deficits by cutting spending rather than raising taxes (Loxley, 2003:27).

If the rate of interest payable by the government rises, then the cost of servicing debt will rise. This additional cost can be met in the following ways:
- raise revenues (for example raise tax revenue);
- reduce expenditure on public services and income transfers;
- allow the budget surplus to fall/increase the budget deficit (implying additional borrowing and/or increases in the money supply).

In the early 1980s, interest rates in international financial markets rose steeply, and since then the dominant view has been that governments, particularly in developing countries, must prioritize action to reduce budget deficits and indebtedness, primarily through cutting expenditure (deflationary policies). This has been a condition of stabilization and structural adjustment programmes linked to loans from the IMF and World Bank. A key reason for the high levels of budget deficits in developing countries in the early 1980s was a rapid rise in the rate of interest they had to pay on their external debt. Governments have had to reduce expenditure on other items to be able to continue paying interest to holders of their external debt. In the Asian financial crisis of 1997, expenditure reduction was required of governments even if they did not have large deficits, supposedly in order to reassure foreign investors (Stiglitz, 2002).

A debt relief initiative for heavily indebted poor countries (HIPC Initiative) was introduced by the World Bank and IMF in 1996. As currently formulated, it allows a poor country to be eligible for debt relief if its debt is judged unsustainable, using the following benchmarks:
- a ratio of Net Present Value of debt to exports earnings above150%
- a ratio of Net Present Value of debt to budget revenue above 250%.

This has allowed the 42 eligible countries to increase spending on health and education, but it has not brought down debts to a level that is sustainable. Nongovernmental organizations argue that more needs to be done, and that these countries need total debt cancellation (Jubilee Debt Campaign, 2005).

In developed countries, a number of policy rules have been adopted which set limits to budget deficits and to government debt. These rules have been made into laws in some countries. These rules reduce the 'fiscal space' open to governments (see Box 49).

Balanced budgets:
Example: In Canada, six provinces have legislation requiring the provincial budget to be balanced.
Deficit to GDP and debt to GDP ratios:
Example: The Maastricht Treaty signed by most members of the European Union sets limits to the size of the budget deficit and the government debt in relation to national income (as measured by the Gross Domestic Product). The limits are
- deficit to GDP ratio 3%
- debt to GDP ratio 60%

Box 49 Policy rules on deficits and debt in developed countries

These policies have not been successful in promoting faster economic growth (see Box 50). In most regions, growth was higher in the period 1961-1980, in which interest rates were lower, than in the period 1981-2000, in which interest rates have been higher and deflationary policies have been adopted. The only region in which growth has been faster in the period 1981-2000 is Asia, and that is due to growth in countries like China, South Korea and India, which have not followed many of the neo-liberal policy prescriptions (UNRISD, 2005, chap. 2). By the end of the 1990s, the average rate of inflation (as measured by rises in consumer prices) was below 10% in every region except Africa (see Box 50).

Per capita GDP growth (annual average %)

Region	1961-1980	1981-2000
Developed economies	3.2	1.4
Africa	1.7	0.3
Asia	2.7	4.4
Latin America and Caribbean	3.0	0.6

Inflation (Consumer prices, ten year averages, %)

Region	1986-1995	1996-2005
Developed economies	3.6	1.8
Developing economies	8.0	8.8
Africa	27.4	12.2
Asia	11.2	4.0
Latin America and Caribbean	194.7	9.0

Box 50 Macroeconomic performance
(Adapted from UNRISD, 2005, tables 2.1 and 2.2.)

The slow growth in output has been accompanied by a rise in unemployment and there has been a rise in the proportion of the labour force that is in informal employment, with low pay, no job security and few or no rights to social security.

This outcome is seen by economists who are critical of neo-liberal policies as evidence of a 'deflationary bias' in budgetary policy, with an overemphasis on reducing deficits by cutting expenditure, pursuing inflation reduction at the expense of other important goals. The deflationary policies have prioritized the interests of foreign owners of external debt at the expense of poor people's livelihoods and well-being (Elson and Cagatay, 2000; Stiglitz, 2002).

There would also be less deflationary bias if more emphasis were put on reducing budget deficits (when this is necessary) by raising tax revenue than by cutting expenditure. This is because governments would be able to use some of the increased revenue to maintain employment and growth promoting public expenditure. In terms of the International Covenant on Economic, Social and Cultural Rights, they would be able to increase their 'maximum available resources'. Total government revenue as a share of GDP is much lower on average in developing countries than in developed countries (around 20% in developing countries and around 40% in developed countries). The ratio in some developing countries, including South Korea and the Caribbean, is higher, at around 30%. This suggests that more attention could be paid in many developing countries to ways of increasing the tax to GDP ratio (ECLAC, 1998:12).

Tax policy has been 'reformed' in many countries, but in ways that increase the role of indirect taxes, especially sales taxes and VAT, and reduce the role of direct taxes. Moreover, the top rates of direct taxes have been cut in many countries. These policies are supposed to reduce tax avoidance and evasion and increase revenues, but there is little evidence that this has happened (Huber, 2003; ECLAC, 1998). Liberalization of trade and investment has made it harder for developing countries to increase tax revenue, resulting in a 'fiscal squeeze' (Grunberg, 1998) (see Box 51). Slow growth and high levels of unemployment intensify these difficulties since tax revenues tend to fall in periods of slow growth, when companies make less profits and employment and earnings fall. There has been no increase in revenue from official development assistance to offset these problems. A short-run boost to revenue can be given by privatizing some public services, but this only increases revenue in the year that the assets are sold. Moreover, it tends to lead to loss of employment. As a result of the failure to increase government revenue on a permanent basis, most of the adjustment required to cut budget deficits has fallen on the expenditure side of the budget. The 'fiscal space' open to governments has been very small.

- Trade liberalization reduces revenue from import and export duties.

- Growth of tax havens enables multinational corporations and rich individuals to evade taxes.

- Competition to attract investment from multinational corporations leads to tax holidays, and lower rates of tax on profits and high income individuals.

- Growth of the informal economy makes tax administration more difficult.

Box 51 Components of the fiscal squeeze
(Grunberg, 1998.)

7.2 Evaluating the macroeconomics of the budget: CEDAW principles

Through their impact on the levels of unemployment, the growth of output and the level of prices, budgets clearly have implications for the realization of human rights.

The implications of subordinating the macroeconomics of the budget to the repayment of external debt has been examined by the UN Human Rights Commission, which in the late 1990s commissioned a number of reports by independent experts on debt, structural adjustment and human rights. The Commission passed a resolution in 2001 declaring that:

'the exercise of the basic rights of the people of the debtor countries to food, housing, clothing, employment, education, health services and a healthy environment cannot be subordinated to the implementation of structural adjustment policies and economic reforms arising from the debt' (UNO-HCHR, 2001, para. 7).

The CEDAW Committee has expressed its concern on a number of occasions about the impact of budget cuts on women, primarily in the context of structural adjustment and financial crisis (see Box 52). Such concerns were also expressed in the Beijing Platform for Action (para. 37) and the Beijing + 5 Outcome Document.

The Convention has a number of significant implications for the macroeconomics of the budget:

- Article 11 (relating to employment) requires States Parties to take 'all appropriate measures … to ensure, on the basis of equality of men and women, the same rights', in particular 'the right to work, as an inalienable right of all human beings'. CEDAW does not actually give women a substantive right to work. Instead, this right is provided to women by other international instruments, particularly Article 6 of ICESCR. The minimum elements of this right to work are set out above in 7.1. In addition to the requirements within these instruments that the right to work be recognized without discrimination between women and men (see e.g. Article 3 of ICESCR), Article 11 of CEDAW specifically requires States to ensure that women have the right to work on an equal basis with men. This means, for example, that in exercising its responsibility for reducing unemployment, the State must also assume responsibility for ensuring that gender disparities in unemployment rates are reduced. Moreover, it is clear from paragraphs (c), (d), (e) and (f) of Article 11 that 'work' should here be understood as paid

In the Concluding Comments on the Third Periodic Report by Uganda, the Committee states that it is concerned that:

'poverty is widespread among women, *inter alia,* as a consequence of gender-insensitive privatization and implementation of structural adjustment polices'.

(United Nations, Committee on the Elimination of Discrimination Against Women, A/57/38, para. 149.)

At its meeting in August 2002, at which it considered the combined fourth and fifth report for Argentina, the Committee expressed its concern at the impact of the financial crisis in Argentina and 'urged the government to take every precaution to ensure that women did not suffer disproportionately from job loss, interrupted or delayed payment of wages, shortages of food, medicines or health services' (Press Release WOM/1360). The Committee had heard from the President of the Women's National Council of Argentina that the Federal Plan for Women had suffered a 33% cut in its budget.

Box 52 Concerns of CEDAW Committee: some examples

employment with various rights attached, including rights to promotion, job security, training, social security, safe working conditions and conditions that allow parents to combine family obligations with work responsibilities (i.e. the kind of employment that the ILO calls 'decent work'). These rights are to be enjoyed by women on a basis of equality with men, not as dependents of men. Further clarification on the State obligations under Article 11 can be found in: CEDAW General Recommendation 13 (Eighth session, 1989): Equal Remuneration for Work of Equal Value; CEDAW General Recommendation 16 (Tenth session, 1991): Unpaid Women Workers in Rural and Urban Family Enterprises; CEDAW General Recommendation 17 (Tenth session, 1991): Measurement and Quantification of the Unremunerated Domestic Activities of Women and Their Recognition in the Gross National Product; CEDAW General Recommendation 19 (Eleventh session, 1992): Violence Against Women, at paras. 7(h), 17, 18 and 24 (j), (p) and (t) (i).

- Article 2 requires that States Parties 'refrain from engaging in any act or practice of discrimination against women'. This obliges governments to ensure that women should not suffer disproportionately from macroeconomic measures taken to manage their debts, such as reductions in budget deficits through cuts in public expenditure on public services.

- Article 3 requires that States Parties shall take 'all appropriate measures' to ensure the 'full development and advancement of women'. This obliges government to implement macroeconomic policies that promote gender equality and ensure women's well-being. In interpreting this obligation, it is useful to consider CEDAW General Recommendation No. 17. This refers to the measurement and quantification of the unremunerated domestic activities of women and their recognition in the gross national product (GNP), which is an indicator of fundamental importance in macroeconomic policy. General Recommendation 17 affirms that women's unpaid domestic work contributes to development in each country and states that 'such measurement and quantification offers a basis for the formulation of further policies related to the advancement of women'.

Further guidance on the human rights dimensions of macroeconomic policy has been provided by the Committee on Economic, Social and Cultural Rights, which has emphasized the principle of non-retrogression, which means that there is a strong presumption that expenditure cuts that hamper progressive realization of human rights are not permissible. Under this principle, the burden is put upon the state to justify why a particular set of cuts was made. It is not enough to say that the budget deficit had to be cut. An argument has to be made that there was no alternative policy that could have been pursued (CESCR, General Comment 3, para. 9; CESCR, General Comment 12, para. 45; CESCR, General Comment 14, para. 32; CESCR, General Comment 15, para. 19) (see Box 53). In addition, it is important to recall that any retrogressive measures that affect the equal right of men and women to the enjoyment of any economic, social and cultural rights violate Article 3 of ICESCR (CESCR, General Comment 16, para. 42).

'**As with all other rights in the Covenant, there is a strong presumption that retrogressive measures taken in relation to the right to health are not permissible**. If any deliberately retrogressive measures are taken, the State Party has the burden of proving that they have been introduced only after the most careful consideration of all alternatives and that they are duly justified by reference to the totality of rights provided for in the Covenant in the context of the full use of the State Party's maximum available resources'.

Box 53 The requirement to justify expenditure cuts
(General Comment 14, para. 47.)

The need to subject expenditure cuts to examination has been taken up in Ecuador by a human rights NGO, Centro de Derechos Economicos y Sociales (CDES), which has argued in a petition in 2000 to the Inter-American Commission on Human Rights that the Government of Ecuador breached its human rights obligations in its 1999 budget (CDES, 2000). CDES argues that in this budget, the allocation to the health sector was cut in real terms by 15%, while government revenues fell by only 2% in real terms. They argue that allocations to health have been cut back to make way for debt service payments. In 1999, debt service payments took 38% of expenditure, while health took only 3.8%. This is in the context of falling allocations to health and a crisis in the public health system, already criticized by the World Bank in its 1996 Ecuador Poverty report, and identified as a cause for concern by the Inter-American Commission on Human Rights (see Box 54).

'**The decreasing availability and quality of health care in the public sector has been identified as a source of increasing concern**. Spending on health has been cut from 8.6% of the general State budget in 1988 to 7.5% in 1992, to 4.9% in 1995. Pursuant to Executive Decree 114, public hospitals may now charge for services, which leaves the indigent with extremely limited access to care. A series of studies has identified the existence of substantial gaps in the provision of basic services and the "insufficient quality of health services due to maldistribution of services and underfunding" as core problems.'

Box 54 Budget Allocations to Health in Ecuador
(Inter-American Commission on Human Rights, 1997.)

As noted above, as well as strict examination of expenditure cuts, the Committee on Economic, Social and Cultural Rights has also emphasized the importance of 'the most careful consideration of all alternatives' (in General Comment 14). Consideration of all alternatives was, in effect, the approach adopted by Mr Fantu Cheru, one of the Independent Experts on Debt and Structural Adjustment, in his report to the Commission on Human Rights in 2001 (Cheru, 2001, para. 47c). Mr Cheru examined the policies of a number of poor countries covered by the HIPC Initiative and found that the conditions attached to eligibility for debt relief by the IMF and World Bank put in jeopardy the goal of sustainable reductions in poverty. He called for the cancellation of external debt for poor countries, an alternative policy that would have the immediate effect of increasing their 'maximum available resources'. The Commission on Human Rights has called upon governments, international financial institutions and the private sector to consider this possibility (UNOHCHR, 2001, para. 14).

The successor to Mr Cheru, Mr Bernardo Mudho, urged in his report in 2004 that 'States should intensify their respective commitments and increase support for the HIPC (Highly Indebted Poor Countries) Initiative to ensure its full implementation (Commission on Human Rights, 2004, para. 35 a). He also emphasized the importance of integrating human rights into the budget process, calling for human rights principles to be integrated into all stages of the budget cycle (para. 23).

Let us now summarize the implications of CEDAW, together with the International Covenant on Economic, Social and Cultural Rights, for the macroeconomics of the budget. The key requirements are that:
• Macroeconomic policy should support women's right to work, on equal terms with men.
• Women should not suffer disproportionately if a budget deficit is reduced by cutting the level of public expenditure; expenditure cuts should be closely examined to determine whether they violate the prin-

ciple of 'non-retrogression'. If these are retrogressive measures that affect the equal right of men and women to the enjoyment of any economic, social and cultural rights, then the State has failed to meet its obligation (under CEDAW and ICESCR) to achieve substantive equality.

- Macroeconomic policy should ensure the 'full development and advancement of women', taking into account women's unpaid work, as well as women's paid work.
- In the design of macroeconomic policy there should be 'the most careful consideration of all alternatives'.

In the next section, we consider how to apply these principles to the macroeconomic dimensions of the budget.

7.3 Applying CEDAW principles to the macroeconomics of the budget

There is no existing research that has specifically applied CEDAW principles to the macroeconomics of the budget. There is some analysis by Gender Budget Initiatives and feminist economists that examines macroeconomics policies from a gender equality perspective, and some analysis by heterodox economists that looks at macroeconomic policies form a social justice perspective. This section draws upon some of that analysis, together with reference to the CEDAW principles listed above.

7.3.1 Support for women's right to work on equal terms with men

The objectives of neo-liberal macroeconomic policy are typically growth of GNP and low rates of inflation. It appears that the IMF now tends to define a low rate of inflation as one below 10%. The conditions attached to Poverty Reduction and Growth Facility Loans attempt to drive down inflation rates if they are above 10% but not if they are in the 5-10% range (Independent Evaluation Office, IMF, 2004). To achieve these goals, the emphasis is on reducing budget deficits. This deflationary bias in turn depresses employment.

Economists from alternative schools of thinking argue that employment needs to be included as an equally important objective. The ILO agrees, arguing that:
> 'The ability to absorb the roughly 514 million additional people expected to enter into world labour markets between 2003 and 2015 depends on the efforts of policy makers to prioritize employment policies and to fully integrate them into macroeconomic policies' (ILO, 2004a: 2).

At the moment, macroeconomic policies are still prioritizing reduction of inflation, and not operating so as to provide decent work for all, and women tend to be more adversely affected than men. ILO data show that for the world as a whole, the female unemployment rate is somewhat higher than the male unemployment rate: in 2003, the global female unemployment rate was 6.4% while the global male unemployment rate was 6.1%. Both rates had risen over the 10 years since 1993, when the female rate was 5.8% and the male rate was 5.5% (ILO, 2004b: 2).

The gender gap in unemployment rates is largest in Latin America and the Caribbean (female rate 10.1%; male rate 6.7%) and in the Middle East and North Africa (female rate 16. 5%; male rate 10.6%). Unemployment rates are lower for women than for men in sub-Saharan Africa and East Asia (ILO, 2004b: 7).

Youth unemployment rates are higher than for the labour force as a whole. Sex-disaggregated rates by region for 1993 and 2003 are shown in Box 55. In six regions, the female youth unemployment was higher than male youth unemployment in 1993; in all these regions the gap between female and male youth unemployment rates widened in the 10 years to 2003, in a context of rising overall youth unemployment, except in the developed economies.

However, unemployment data often fail to capture the true extent of the impact of fiscal policy on women's employment. In many countries, definitions of unemployment exclude people who want a job but do not actively seek one because they feel none are available, or because they face a variety of physical or social barriers in obtaining a job. These so-called 'discouraged workers' are more likely to be women. If jobs are hard to find, women tend to drop out of the labour market altogether to a greater extent than men (ILO, 2004b: 7).

Region	1993		2003	
	M	F	M	F
Developed Economies	16.8	16.5	15.0	14.2
CIS	9.7	9.0	14.5	14.7
Northern Africa	27.1	32.7	25.5	39.1
Sub-Saharan Africa	23.7	19.5	23.0	18.6
Latin America & Caribbean	10.7	15.5	14.0	20.8
Eastern Asia	5.5	4.1	8.1	5.8
South Asia	12.7	14.6	13.5	17.1
South-eastern Asia	8.4	9.3	15.6	17.7
Western Asia	18.7	19.6	20.1	22.5
Oceania	7.3	7.8	8.4	9.2

Box 55 Male and female youth unemployment rates (%)
(ILO, 2004a, table 1.1.)

This happened as unemployment grew in several formerly centrally planned economies in their transition to the market and in some Asian countries after the financial crisis of 1997. Because of this it is also important to monitor male and female job losses and male and female labour market participation rates.

- In South Korea after the financial crisis, women lost their jobs at a rate twice that of men (Cho et al., 2003) but the unemployment data showed a higher rate for men than for women, while women's labour market participation rate fell (Lee, 2003).
- In Eastern Europe, female unemployment rates are higher than male unemployment rates in the Czech Republic and Poland, but not in Hungary. However, in the latter case, women's participation rate declined by much more than men's participation rates (Fodor, 2004).
- A study of the impact of contractionary inflation reduction in low- and middle-income countries found that in almost three quarters of cases, women's employment declined more than men's in the economic slowdown (Heintz, 2004).

In countries that do not have unemployment insurance, most people cannot afford to be unemployed if they lose their jobs, and so they have to find some kind of informal paid work. Informal employment, which tends to be low paid and insecure, and lacks social protection, is in fact growing throughout the world. Typically, a higher proportion of women's employment is in informal rather than formal employment. Men tend to be somewhat less concentrated in informal employment, and their informal employment tends to be somewhat better paid and less precarious (ILO, 2002). Most informal employment does not fulfill the requirements for 'decent work'. Ideally a country should monitor the male and female rates of employment in decent work, but the kind of survey necessary for this is still being piloted by the ILO.

The South African Women's Budget Initiative, in its third report, presented an instructive analysis of the macroeconomic implications of the budget for women's employment (Valodia, 1998). In 1996, the Government of South Africa launched a new macroeconomic strategy under the label 'Growth, Employment and Redistribution', usually referred to as GEAR. This aimed to cut the budget deficit in order to stimulate private investment. The deficit was to be cut from 5.4% of GDP in 1996 to 3% in 2000. The government believed that the jobs and growth that South Africa needed required higher levels of private investment. Their argument was that existing levels of government borrowing reduced the amount of savings available for the private sector to borrow, and thus reduced private investment. Valodia's analysis showed that the government did not plan to reduce the deficit by cutting expenditure but by increasing revenue at a faster rate than expenditure (see Box 56).

Valodia also scrutinized the assumptions underlying the projections made by the government. The growth in revenue was dependent on the economy growing by 3% a year and on improvements in the ability of the South African Revenue Service to reduce tax avoidance and evasion. If these rather optimistic assumptions were not

	2000/1	1998/9	1995/6	Av. yearly growth
Revenue	216,150	178,080	126,080	14.3%
Expenditure	241,480	202,050	154,525	11.3%
Deficit	25,330	23,970	28,444	-2.2%

Box 56 Plans for reducing the budget deficit in South Africa: government projections for revenue, expenditure and the budget deficit (Rand)
(Adapted from Valodia, 1998, Table 5.)

fulfilled, then the budget deficit could only be reduced by cutting expenditure. Thus the figures in Box 56 were shown to be of questionable validity. Valodia also discussed whether the GEAR employment targets were likely to be met, pointing to evidence that suggested that this was unlikely. The criticisms made of GEAR by a number of economists were discussed: They had pointed out that there was little empirical evidence that government borrowing reduced private investment. Such economists advocated a more expansionary strategy.

Valodia's analysis concluded with a careful analysis of the pros and cons of a more expansionary strategy. He recognized the problems that rising prices create for poor women managing the household budget. If their money incomes do not rise, then they will be worse off. Nevertheless, he concluded that an alternative, more expansionary, macroeconomic strategy 'could well be more advantageous to women than GEAR', because of its impact on employment opportunities. Valodia's scepticism about the employment targets proved justified. In fact, employment in the formal economy fell and unemployment rose, as did the numbers of people subsisting in the informal economy. The emphasis of government policy was changed in the 2001/02 budget, which was more expansionary.

To get a complete picture of the macroeconomic impact of a budget on women's work, it is necessary to go beyond an examination of paid work and take into account the non-market economy in which people do unpaid work to produce the goods and services required for the care and maintenance of their families and communities (Elson, ed., 2000, chap. 1). If aggregate demand in the labour market falls, so that people lose their jobs and move into unemployment or poorly paid informal work, then there will be a tendency to compensate, at least in part, for this fall in money income by producing more goods and services at home: for instance, producing homemade food and clothing rather than buying ready made. It is typically women and girls who are obliged by social norms to bear more of the burden of substituting domestically produced goods and services for those purchased on the market (Cagatay and Erturk, 1995; Elson, 1995).

A good example of what is likely to happen has been produced by a study of a community in Canada that suffered a heavy loss of employment in the mid 1990s (Mawhiney, 1997). Women were asked whether they done any of the following (most of which imply more unpaid work for women):
- cutting back on the amount and quality of food eaten
- engaging in bulk or group shopping
- making meals from scratch
- vegetable gardening
- canning or preserving
- hunting or fishing
- eating fewer snacks and junk food
- eating less often in restaurants
- using food banks.

More than three quarters of the women had used at least one of these methods, and 10% had used four or more.

So not only do government budgets fail in many countries to support women's equal right to decent paid jobs, they also intensify the burden of unpaid work on women and girls. This should be monitored using data on hours of unpaid work done by women and girls and men and boys, but only a minority of countries conducts the regular time-use surveys necessary for this. Unfortunately there are very few countries that publish regular data on the hours of unpaid work undertaken by men and women, boys and girls. Much more needs to be done to secure compliance with CEDAW General Recommendation 17, including to quantify unremunerated domestic activities (e.g. by research and experimental studies, such as including time-use surveys in national household surveys) and to incorporate these activities in government accounts (CEDAW General Recommendation 17). These steps are a necessary part of a State discharging its obligations under CEDAW; this data will show the *de facto* economic position of women and thereby direct attention to areas that need to be addressed to achieve substantive equality.

7.3.2 Ensuring that women do not suffer disproportionately from expenditure cuts

The burdens of unpaid work on women and girls are increased not only by the social obligation to produce substitutes for goods and service which might otherwise be purchased in the market, but also by the social obligation to produce substitutes for goods and services formerly provided by the state. This is one important reason why expenditure cuts may disproportionately affect women.

For instance, if expenditure on water and sanitation is cut, then women and girls have to spend more time collecting water from rivers and wells, and on taking care of family members who get sick as a result of drinking unsafe water.

An analysis by Elson (2002) based on data on access to services compiled by the Social Watch report shows that in the period 1990-1995, there was reduction in the proportion of the population with access to safe drinking water in 15 out of 62 countries for which data was available.

Women may be disproportionately affected because services that are targeted to women are reduced. In the period 1990-1996, there was a reduction in proportion of births attended by skilled personnel in just over one third of 132 countries providing this data (Elson, 2002).

Some gender budget initiatives, such as the one in Mexico, have given detailed scrutiny to the pattern of expenditure cuts, investigating whether the cuts have fallen more heavily on services of particular importance to women (Colinas, 2003). In 1998-2000, the Ministry of Finance announced that there would have to be expenditure cuts and that these would fall on the National Electricity Commission, the state-owned oil company (PEMEX) and the Department of Communication and Transport. Gender budget analysts showed that the cuts actually fell on the Ministry of Social Affairs, the Ministry of Health and the Ministry of Education. In 2002, further cuts were made. Although programmes specifically targeted to women were not cut, there were cuts in anti-poverty programmes of which women were the main beneficiaries. The budgets of the Ministries of Health and Education were cut, and that of the Social Security Institute. The budgets of the Ministry of National Defence, the Ministry of the Navy and the Ministry of Public Security were not cut. In response, the Commission on Gender Equality of the Chamber of Deputies became active in negotiations on the 2003 budget and succeeded in getting larger appropriations than the ones proposed by the government for programmes for reproductive health, reduction of maternal mortality, women in agriculture and immigrant women (Colinas, 2003).

Scrutiny of expenditure trends was also part of the Gender Budget Audit for Nepal, carried out by a team from the Institute for Integrated Development Studies, led by Dr Meena Acharya. The Audit recognized that in the early 1980s a huge fiscal deficit had created major economic problems, including high rates of inflation (Acharya, 2003:118). A Structural Adjustment Programme was introduced in 1985 and lasted until 1988; a further Programme took place in 1993-95. The Audit examined trends in social expenditure compared to total expenditure. The analysis was done in terms of current prices, not in real terms adjusted for inflation. This means that, in a situation of inflation, such as prevailed in Nepal, a cut in real terms shows as a deceleration of the rate of growth in money terms (or nominal terms, as economists usually say) (see Box 57).

The first phase of structural adjustment in the mid-1980s resulted in a deceleration of growth in public expenditure in current prices, and this was faster for social expenditure (defined here as education, health, drinking water and local development) than for total expenditure. In real terms, allowing for inflation, expenditure was cut, and the cuts fell more heavily on social sector expenditure than on total expenditure. This was not the case during the second Programme in the early 1990s. In that period, although total expenditure decelerated even faster, social expenditure did not. In fact, in current prices, social sector expenditure grew faster than in the second half of the 1980s, mainly as a result of a large expansion of decentralized expenditure for local develop-

Nominal growth in public expenditure, annual average % changes, in current prices

Expenditure	1981-85	1986-88	1993-95	1996-2000
Total	19.7	18.9	14.0	11.2
Social	27.3	16.2	22.1	14.4

Source: adapted from table 8.1, Acharya 2003:119.

Box 57 Trends in public expenditure in Nepal

ment. However, the Audit revealed that the local development expenditure was not very effective in addressing gender equality and the empowerment of women. In 1996-2000, the deceleration of nominal growth in expenditure continued, and continued to be faster for total expenditure than social expenditure. The share of social expenditure increased from 18.3% in 1991 to 31.3% in 2000 (Acharya, 2003:139).

However, social expenditure is not the only kind of expenditure of importance to women. The Audit also looked at expenditure on subsidies of various kinds. Subsidies are very often cut as part of deficit reduction programmes. The Audit found that in Nepal subsidies of importance to poor women had been cut while other subsidies, of importance to politicians, had been maintained. For instance, in 2001, food and fertilizer subsidies were withdrawn, crippling the food security system. Other subsidies, like those extended to bio-gas, small irrigation projects, livestock insurance and credit for small farmers, were either withdrawn or reduced. But subsidies to the media continued. The Audit commented, 'Subsidization of the media is purely a political action perpetuated by the politicians for their own propaganda' (Acharya, 2003:125).

It is important to consider not only cuts in the expenditure appropriated in the budget, but also cuts that take place in the budget cycle after the budget has been approved. This is the lesson of a study (Prescod, 2002) on how expenditure cutbacks took place within the budget cycle in Jamaica, based on data for 11 years comparing the initial appropriations which appear in the Budget document with the 'Final Supplementary Estimates' presented at the end of the financial year. The study shows that the government prioritized debt service and payment of wages and salaries, so that all the cutbacks fell on the capital account rather than the current account of the budget. Within the capital account, the cuts fell most heavily on the capital expenditure on social and community services, whereas capital expenditure on infrastructure beneficial to business (economic services) suffered far smaller cuts. The Budget Division believed that the costs of postponing capital expenditure on economic services were more than the costs of postponing capital expenditure on social and community services; and the Ministries dealing with economic services were more powerful than those dealing with social and community services, which are likely to be particularly important for poor women.

7.3.3 Macroeconomic policy which ensures 'the full development and advancement of women', taking into account women's unpaid work as well as women's paid work

There is emerging evidence that macroeconomic policies that are based on high tax revenue and high public expenditure are more conducive to 'the full development and advancement of women'.

For instance, a recent study of 15 countries in Western Europe and North America investigated the determinants of women's relative economic position, both inside and outside marriage (Huber, et al., 2001). The investigation focused on the extent of relative poverty among single mothers and the earnings of women relative to their husbands. Among the influences it investigated were the levels of taxation and expenditure (measured in relation to GDP). It found that the ratio of tax revenue to GDP and expenditure on social security income transfers as a percentage of GDP, were significant positive factors in reducing poverty among single mothers. There was less poverty among single mothers in countries with higher levels of taxation and higher levels of social security income transfers.

These factors were also significantly associated with the levels of married women's earnings compared to their husbands. The higher the levels of taxation and social security income transfers, the higher was the share of married women in the combined earnings of husband and wife. In this case the causal mechanism is more complex. Countries with higher levels of taxation and expenditure are likely to have higher levels of provision of the public services that facilitate the labour market participation of married women and higher levels of civilian public sector employment offering relatively well-paid jobs for women. Overall, it was in the high-taxing, high-spending states that rates of poverty among single mothers were lowest and that married women's earnings (in relation to those of their husbands) were highest.

Differences in economic and social structures and in data availability mean that the relationship between gender equality and macroeconomic policies needs to be investigated in a different way in other regions of the world. A study of gender equality in Latin America and the Caribbean from 1970 to 2000 included aggregate public expenditure on government programmes and debt service among the factors that might influence gender equality (Seguino, 2003). Gender equality was measured in three ways: the female to male population ratio; the ratio of female to male secondary school enrolment ratios; and relative male to female mortality rates. Public expenditure was measured as the ratio of government consumption (i.e. programme expenditure) to GDP; and the debt burden as the ratio of debt service payments to export earnings. The study found that the share of public expenditure in GDP was significant and positively related to the first two of the measures of gender equality. It also found that the debt burden was significant and negatively related to these dimensions of gender equality.

An important reason why high levels of taxation and expenditure in relation to GDP may be associated with greater gender equality is that this may facilitate investment in public services that reduce the amount of unpaid domestic work that women and girls have to do in families and communities. This makes it easier for girls to go to school and to complete their schooling and for adult women to participate in the labour market and to obtain more of the better-paying jobs with social rights.

7.3.4 Designing macroeconomic policy with 'careful consideration of all alternatives'

Many countries have adopted very restrictive policy rules that make it difficult to consider alternatives that would be better able to comply with CEDAW. These rules include balanced budget rules and specific limits on the debt to GDP ratio and the budget deficit to GDP ratio (for examples see Box 49 above).

These rules prevent governments from acting to counter the ups and downs of the economic cycle to which all market economies are subject. If a household spends beyond its means, it cannot create more income and employment for members of that household. But if a government runs a budget deficit at a time when private sector output is falling, private sector investment is falling and unemployment is rising, then by increasing the level of demand in the economy, it can create more employment for the people in the country and avoid a recession. Balanced budget rules prevent this, and leave a government with no possibility of counteracting recessions.

Governments would have more possibility of complying with CEDAW if budget rules allowed governments to balance their budgets over the economic cycle (which is generally from four to eight years), not each year. This means that the government would:
- run a deficit in the downswing of the cycle, when job losses in the private sector tend to rise;
- offset this with a budget surplus in the upswing of the cycle, when more jobs are being created by the private sector.

This is known as an anti-cyclical fiscal policy. Some governments do have fiscal policy rules that permit an anti-cyclical fiscal policy. An example is the UK (see Box 58).

More flexible rules on managing the budget are recommended by the UN Economic Commission for Latin America and the Caribbean as an important component of the fiscal covenant that should be developed in that region (ECLAC, 1998:18). One suggestion is that growth of current expenditure should be kept at a stable level, not exceeding the trend rate of growth of the economy, and tax revenue should be used to stabilize the economy. In the upswing of the economy, increases in tax revenue should be saved in a stabilization fund. This fund would then be used to avoid cutbacks in expenditure in the downswing.

A more radical approach to alternatives has been adopted by a group of about 50 Canadian civil society organizations that have produced an Alternative Federal Budget (AFB) for Canada each year since 1995. The AFB is coordinated by a social justice coalition called Cho!ces and the Canadian Center for Policy Alternatives, in consultation with a wide-ranging group of civil society organizations, including women's organizations (Loxley 2003).

The objectives of the Canadian Alternative Federal Budget Project are:
- full employment
- a more equitable distribution of income
- eradication of poverty
- economic equality between women and men
- protection of political, economic, social and cultural rights
- improvement in the environment
- strengthening of social programmes and public services
- creation of a more just, sustainable and peaceful world.

The AFB agreed with the Canadian Government that the budget deficit was too high in the mid-1990s, but it disagreed with the view that the only way to reduce this was by cutting expenditure. Instead, it proposed a strategy of directing the Bank of Canada to take measures to cut the Canadian interest rate, which would lower the costs of debt service on internal debt and at the same time stimulate private sector investment and thus create more jobs. This would reduce the costs of public expenditure on programmes for the unemployed, and this would also contribute to reducing the deficit (Loxley, 2003:81). This strategy was possible because the Canadian Government maintained control over monetary policy, and could use capital controls to prevent holders of Canadian Government debt from rapidly liquidating their holdings. The Canadian Government preferred, however, to cut expenditure and maintain a high level of returns for the financial institutions and well-off individuals from whom it had borrowed.

In the late 1990s, the economic situation improved and the budget deficit turned into a budget surplus, as more tax revenue flowed in. The policy of the Canadian Government was to reduce the outstanding debt and to cut tax rates rather than to restore the social programmes which had been cut. The AFB argued against tax cuts (except for those targeted to the very poor) and cuts in the outstanding debt, and for restoring social programmes. It presented analysis showing that it would be quite possible to do this without risking macro-economic instability. Among the objectives that this would make possible would be increased economic equality between women and men, through measures such as provision for pay equity in public sector employment and child care programmes (Loxley, 2003:93).

Feminist economics would suggest a modification of one key element of the AFB. The goal of 'full employment', which is the first objective of the AFB, is based on a model of the economy that ignores unpaid work and informal work. It assumes a norm of employment that is based on the working lives of men working in the formal sector: a standard working week of 35-45 hours (varying by country), with paid holidays of two-three weeks, and typically with a wife to look after them and their children.

Lower-income women in poor countries cannot afford to be unemployed. They have to find some kind of work, and in addition have to bear a heavy load of unpaid work fetching fuel and water, caring for kitchen gardens, producing meals and cleaning clothes. They have very long working days when we take both unpaid and paid work into account. Their problem is 'overfull employment' in terms of demands on their time and energy.

Lower-income women in better-off countries can turn on the tap for water and press a switch for electricity, but there is still a lot of pressure on their time, as they still have major responsibility for the work involved in caring for children and for family members who are sick and old. Their job choices are constrained by what will fit in with their family responsibilities, and these are frequently part-time jobs that do not enjoy the same social rights as full-time jobs.

It is also important not to lose sight of the problems that rising prices cause for women who have to manage household budgets. This is particularly difficult for women who depend on incomes whose level is fixed by the government, such as pensions, and income transfers directed to poor mothers. It is important that all income transfers from the state be raised in line with inflation. This can be done by indexing such transfers to the retail price index.

In the light of CEDAW's standard of substantive equality, macroeconomic policy objectives should include:
- availability of decent paid work for all who want it, women equally with men;
- high enough level of taxation and expenditure to provide enough public services to significantly reduce the burdens of unpaid domestic work;
- creation of incentives for equal sharing of remaining unpaid domestic work between women and men;
- increasing availability of the marketed goods and services people need;
- moderate level of inflation, taking into account the particular circumstances of the country and the trade-off between creating more jobs and reducing the level of inflation;
- indexing of income transfers, such as basic pensions and grants to poor mothers, to the retail price index.

Of course, such objectives cannot be achieved overnight, and have not yet been achieved anywhere, but the full realization of substantive gender equality requires objectives like these.

It is important to have the 'fiscal space' to consider alternatives because there is no simple rule that can validly be applied everywhere at all times. As one of the leaders of the Canadian Alternative Federal Budget puts it, 'There is, however, no magic number representing the point at which the running of deficits or increases in debt should cease' (Loxley, 2003:25). There is always an alternative macroeconomic strategy which is *economically* feasible; but different strategies imply different distributions of the costs and benefits This makes it very important that there should be widespread dialogue about the macroeconomic strategy implemented through the budget, rather that reserving macroeconomic policy to a small group of technocrats (Elson and Cagatay, 2000).

7.4 Conclusions

In this section we have considered the macroeconomics of the budget, distinguishing between neoliberal and alternative schools of economic analysis. We have seen that neoliberal macroeconomic policies have been successful in bringing down inflation to below 10% in most regions of the world in the years since the early 1980s, but not in combining this with adequate levels of economic growth and job creation. Budgets in most countries have been marked by deflationary bias. Tax revenue has not been raised; instead, reduction of budget deficits has taken place through expenditure cuts. In developing countries these policies have been related to stabilization loans from the IMF and structural adjustment loans from the World Bank. There has been some debt relief for Highly Indebted Poor Countries, but this has been inadequate.

The UN Human Rights Commission passed a resolution in 2001 declaring that the human rights of people in debtor countries cannot be subordinated to economic policy.

The CEDAW Committee has expressed its concern on a number of occasions about women's unemployment and the impact of expenditure cuts on women. The question of expenditure cuts has also been addressed by the Committee on Economic, Social and Cultural Rights, which has advised that there is a requirement for the State to justify expenditure cuts, including by explaining that they took place after 'the most careful consideration of all alternatives'.

The implications of CEDAW, together with the International Covenant on Economic, Social and Cultural Rights, for the macroeconomic of the budget can be summarized as follows:

- Macroeconomic policy should support women's right to work, on equal terms with men.
- Women should not suffer disproportionately if a budget deficit is reduced by cutting the level of public expenditure; expenditure cuts should be closely examined to see whether they violate the principle of 'non-retrogression'. If these are retrogressive measures that affect the equal right of men and women to the enjoyment of any economic, social and cultural rights, then the State has failed to achieve substantive equality.
- Macroeconomic policy should ensure the 'full development and advancement of women', taking into account women's unpaid work, as well as women's paid work.
- In the design of macroeconomic policy there should be 'the most careful consideration of all alternatives'.

Evidence has been discussed on some of the ways in which macroeconomic policy is not conforming to these principles, especially higher female than male unemployment rates, and budget cuts which disproportionately affect women. It would be easier to conform to CEDAW obligations if budgets incorporated alternative macro-economic policies which focus not only on lower inflation and higher growth, but also on greater availability of decent paid work and a reduction of unpaid domestic work, in ways that result in substantive equality between women and men.

Section 8

Monitoring Budget Decision Processes
from a CEDAW Perspective

Monitoring Budget Decision Processes from a CEDAW Perspective

This section first briefly outlines the main characteristics of budget decision processes and the roles played by different actors. Then the public sector management perspective on budget decision processes is discussed. This is followed by an elaboration of the implications of CEDAW for budget decision processes. Examples of ways of monitoring the relative roles of women and men in budget decisions are presented. Finally, some ways of promoting women's full equality in participation in budget decisions are discussed.

8.1 Key features of budget decision processes

Budget decision processes can best be understood in terms of the annual budget cycle. The cycle has four phases:
- formulation
- approval and enactment into law
- implementation
- audit and evaluation.

Each tier of government has its own budget cycle, at national, regional and local levels, in which there is ongoing interaction between the executive and legislative arms of government. The law of each country prescribes the framework for budget decision-making, with some significant variations between countries. Nevertheless there are some important common features.

We will first consider the roles of government bodies. In the formulation phase the budget is prepared by the responsible executive bodies, led by the Budget Office of the Ministry of Finance (or comparable body), which stipulates the framework in which all the other Ministries must prepare draft budgets for their departments. In many countries a Planning Commission is also involved in determining the framework, especially in budgeting for new capital expenditure. But it is the Ministry of Finance that is responsible for looking at the overall budget, bringing the revenue and the expenditure sides together and setting the ceiling for overall government expenditure.

Of course the budget is not formulated completely afresh each year. There is a large degree of continuity from year to year. Nevertheless, policy decisions have to be taken on what to continue and what to change. On the revenue side, decisions have to be made about whether to change the structure of tax rates and whether to sell any government assets. On the expenditure side, a large amount is generally already pre-committed to meet statutory obligations, including debt service obligations. (For an analysis of the amount of finance which is pre-committed in the national budget of Bolivia, see Box 59.)

Type of expenditure	% of total expenditure
Amortization of foreign public debt	2.7
Interest on foreign public debt	1.9
Amortization of domestic public debt	4.2
Interest on domestic public debt	1.8
Payment of other financial liabilities	10.3
Other current expenses (including payment of interest for public financial institutions)	26.1
Transfers to the private sector	4.0
Total	51.0

Box 59 Pre-committed finance in the national budget of Bolivia, 1998
(Gutierrez 2004, table 3.)

Nevertheless, decisions have to be made about whether total expenditure should be increased, maintained at the same level or reduced, and about the distribution of expenditure across different uses. The simplest approach is incremental budgeting, in which Ministries are allocated the same funds as last year, plus a percentage increase which may vary depending on economic, social and political priorities. But this does not relate budget appropriations to performance, so many countries are moving to more complex systems of decision-making in which additional funding is related to plans for achievement of agreed targets (Sharp, 2003).

Elected representatives can influence budget formulation through drawing the attention of Ministers to the needs of the people they represent through the regular processes of the parliament/congress/council (questions, motions, hearings, reports of committees, etc.) and through making submissions to Ministers.

In the approval and enactment phase, typically the budget is presented to the relevant elected assembly for scrutiny and the Budget Act is passed. Different countries have somewhat different scrutiny procedures, in terms of the time allowed for scrutiny, the role of committees of the assembly, the extent to which Ministers are questioned about the budget and the powers of the legislative body to change the budget, etc. (IPU, 2001). In some cases there is a separate vote to approve the appropriation for each department (for example, in the South African national parliament), whereas in other cases there is one vote to accept or reject the total appropriation for all public expenditure (for example in the Ghanaian national parliament). Perhaps the most important difference is the extent to which members of the elected assembly may modify the proposed budget. In some countries, the elected assembly can only vote to either accept or reject the budget (as a whole, or in relation to particular appropriations). A rejection of the budget is often treated as a vote of no confidence in the government, and as such might lead to major political changes. It is therefore very rare. In other countries, elected representatives can make some changes to the budget (usually within stipulated limits). An example of the latter is Botswana, where the national parliament can decide to change the distribution of appropriations between Ministries, but not to change the total amount appropriated (IPU, 2001:68). In these countries, parliamentary rejection of part of the budget proposals is not treated as a vote of no confidence, and does not lead to major political changes.

Implementation is the joint responsibility of the Ministers, administrators and all the other public sector employees. Implementation begins with decisions by budget offices (or similar authorities) to authorize of release of funds, followed by decisions in each department about how to use the funds. These decisions involve a degree of discretion but are structured by rules, norms and financial incentives. Decentralization sometimes leads to long and complex chains of decision-making, in which funds disbursed from central government may not reach frontline service delivery because they are retained at provincial or local level budget offices. Members of elected assemblies can play a part in monitoring implementation on behalf of their constituents by asking questions in the assembly and holding public hearings.

Audits are undertaken by publicly funded, but independent, units, such as the Office of the Auditor-General, which investigate financial and other records to see whether money has been spent as authorized by the Budget Act and decide whether to approve the government accounts. Audits have traditionally focused on the question of misappropriation and corruption. Increasingly, there is also evaluation to assess whether the money was spent not only as appropriated in the budget, but also effectively, to achieve policy objectives. Elected assemblies also play a role in auditing and evaluation, since the auditors and evaluators must frequently make their reports to the elected assembly, often to a specialized Public Accounts Committee, which has powers of investigation. Ideally, the results of audit and evaluation inform the formulation of subsequent budgets, but generally the budget for the next year has to be prepared before the audit of the current budget is completed.

At each level, final responsibility for budget decisions rests with the relevant executive body, with the Ministry of Finance having overall responsibility; but there are also a variety of ways in which other powerful actors regularly participate in budget decision-making. For instance, in the budget formulation process:
- The IMF and World Bank regularly stipulate the total amount of expenditure and the structure of taxation and expenditure, as conditions for access to loans.
- The IMF often insists that in highly indebted poor countries, disbursement of funds is limited by the amount of cash which the government has in its account with the central bank, so that spending cannot take place until tax revenues, grants and loans have actually been received by the government.
- Bilateral donors increasingly supply aid in the form of budget support, and require that allocations across programmes address their priorities.

- Big companies, trade associations and chambers of commerce frequently lobby Ministers for tax concessions, subsidies and contracts, perhaps indicating that if their wishes are met, they will contribute funds to the Ministers' election campaigns.

In the last decade, there has been growing emphasis on the participation of civil society ('civic engagement'). For example, the World Bank has made civil society participation in the production of Poverty Reduction Strategy Papers (which are important inputs into budget formulation in many poor countries) a condition for receipt of loans. In Brazil, individual citizens have been enabled to participate in setting priorities for new expenditure and monitoring implementation in the participatory budget process developed by the Partido dos Trabalhadores (PT: (Workers' Party)) in Porto Alegre and other Brazilian cities. In Rajasthan in India, the Mazdoor Kisan Shakthi Sangathan (MKSS: Workers and Peasants Power Association) has developed participatory audits in villages (Goetz and Jenkins, 2004).

8.2 Evaluating budget decision processes from a public sector management perspective

Budget decision processes have come under close scrutiny by experts on public sector management. A public sector management perspective evaluates budget decision processes using criteria of economy, efficiency and effectiveness (Sharp, 2003; Norton and Elson, 2002), rather than human rights norms. However, both a public sector management perspective and a human rights perspective refer to requirements of transparency, accountability and participation. Human rights law gives a particular content to both how these requirements should be executed and their significance. In terms of how these processes should be executed, at a minimum, human rights law requires that the systems be non-discriminatory and that they advance substantive equality. It requires that systems for transparency, accountability and participation be organized in ways that effectively support the realization of human rights, especially for those who least enjoy them. This latter point means that in design of these systems, States must provide extra guarantees for vulnerable groups or individuals. In relation to participation, for example, this would mean a State has to undertake activities (including temporary special measures under Article 4(1)) to ensure that all persons are able to equally partake in decision-making processes that affect their enjoyment of human rights. In terms of the significance of these systems, human rights bodies, such as the Committee on Economic, Social and Cultural Rights, have identified that the requirements of transparency, accountability and participation are key elements of a rights-based approach because they create the good governance that is needed to implement human rights (CESCR, General Comment 14, para. 55; General Comment 15, para. 49).

Until recently, transparency in budget decision-making mainly referred to the production of sufficiently detailed financial documents for submission to elected assemblies and government auditors. The concern was that the decisions of the executive should be transparent to the legislature. Budget documents typically contain tabulations of proposed expenditure, covering debt-servicing charges and expenditure on government activities. The latter can be tabulated in a number of ways. For example:
- by function (e.g. defence, education, health, agriculture, etc.);
- by economic category (e.g. in a Capital (or Development) Account, covering investment in new infrastructure and equipment; a Current Account, covering wages, salaries, transfer payments, supplies and materials);
- by administrative agency (e.g. Ministry, Department, Board, etc.);
- by programme and sub-programme (e.g. primary, secondary and tertiary education).

Documents presented to auditors purport to show how the money had been spent, so that auditors can check that it had not been misappropriated, and contain tabulations of payments made to employees, suppliers of equipment and contractors for construction projects.

However, the production of big documents with lots of figures does not necessarily guarantee transparency. Transparency requires that information be presented in ways that clearly show all the income a government has received and for what activities its has been appropriated, in formats that can be understood by non-specialist users.

There are additional problems. For instance, the budget may fail to cover all receipts and all expenditure, especially in countries where there are significant inflows of foreign aid. Moreover, the tabulations may fail to link expenditure clearly to specific programmes. For example it may be possible to see how much has been appropriated for education, but not how much for different types of education (e.g. primary, secondary, tertiary, etc.). Or it may be possible to see how much has been appropriated for health services in total, but not how much for different types of service (e.g. clinics and hospitals).

Ordinary members of elected assemblies testify to their difficulties in interpreting the meaning of the data in budget documents (IPU, 2001). In checking how money has been spent, auditors may be thwarted by collusion between officials and private sector suppliers and contractors to falsify records. Moreover, conventional methods of auditing cannot check the quantity and quality of the outputs that have been produced. The money may not have been misappropriated but it may still have been misspent (see Box 60).

'In Africa, our audit services are developed to the stage where we can catch out a civil servant who has stolen a bit of money on his travel claim. That is very easy to do. But the greater losses are in those contractors who are building with sand and not cement. Those can run into much more money ... we need to develop very rapidly, a capability for auditing value for money'.

Box 60 Limitations of conventional auditing
(J. H. Mensah, Ghana, IPU, 2001:29.)

The public sector management approach is intended to remedy the lack of transparency by introducing new techniques. New formats are developed for presenting the budget, showing the programmes for which money is to be appropriated and the outputs and outcomes it is meant to achieve. New forms of evaluation are developed which attempt to measure value for money (Sharp, 2003). As yet there has been little focus on including in budget documentation data on the value of tax concessions (sometimes called 'tax expenditures' since they are equivalent to the government collecting taxes and spending part of the revenue on a subsidy equal to the value of the concession). Nor has the management approach focused on including information on the distributional implications of the budget.

As well as transparency, the public sector management perspective seeks to promote accountability. Until recently, accountability of budget decisions referred to the accountability of the executive branch of government to elected representatives. But elected representatives face many problems in holding the executive to account. African parliamentarians, at a workshop on budget decision-making processes, identified the following (IPU, 2001):
- lack of time for scrutiny of the budget bill and of the audited accounts
- lack of expertise and facilities (such as computers, research assistants, libraries)
- complexity of the implementation process
- delays in submission of reports of the Auditor-General
- weakness of the powers of the elected assembly
- constraints of party discipline, which undermine the separation of powers in government.

The public sector management approach is intended to strengthen the Auditor-General's office; reform procedures in elected assemblies and improve resources and capacities of elected representatives; and increase accountability of public sector employees to Ministers and elected assemblies through devices like performance agreements (Sharp, 2003; IPU, 2001).This managerial reform approach does not, however, ensure that attention will be paid to the representation of the interests of those most deprived of enjoyment of human rights (Norton and Elson, 2002).

A fundamental problem is that elected representatives may pursue their own interests, or those of their most powerful constituents, or those of commercial interests to whom they act as consultants, and they may use budgets to reward their relatives and political supporters. Periodic elections are insufficient to ensure the accountability of elected representatives to socially excluded groups (Goetz and Jenkins, 2004).

The limitations of accountability were amply revealed in an investigation of gender dimensions of budgets in three cities in the Philippines (Budlender et al., 2001). The Philippines has a law, passed in 1992, requiring every government agency to allocate at least 5% of their budgets to gender and development (GAD) programmes that promote gender equality. Studies of three cities in 2000 found there was considerable confusion about how this was meant to apply at the local level. Budget officials, when asked to produce information on expenditure on GAD programmes included many expenditure items that had no clear gender equality focus. None of the cities had a GAD plan to guide appropriations and their execution. Moreover, the absence of a system for monitoring actual local government expenditures meant it was extremely difficult to track where money had gone. The research revealed a big gap between what was supposed to happen and what did happen. In one city, a specific allocation was made to a GAD budget, but this served as a 'cookie jar' for funding a variety of diverse activities by the local budget officer, who had complete control and discretion over its use. In another city, one third of the budget (accounting for two thirds of the finance available for non-office expenditures) was controlled by the Mayor's office, under the oversight of an unaccountable official whose tenure was co-terminus with that of the Mayor. Officials produced a list of projects, funded by the Mayor's office, which were supposed to be related to gender equality, but the researchers found that many were not. Expenditure on the employment of casual workers was centralized in the Mayor's office; it had grown rapidly and workers were employed unnecessarily and without proper qualifications. In the third city, the GAD budget was under the control of the Mayor, and 70% of it was spent on equipping and staffing a GAD office employing 33 people. However, appropriations made for grants to women's organizations had not been received by those organizations, despite the fact that budget documentation showed the funds as having been disbursed.

Some of the proponents of managerial reforms have recognized some of the limitations of this approach and now promote wider civic engagement with budgets. This extends to organizations like the World Bank and other donors, which have been making improved public sector management a condition of increased aid. The Participation and Civic Engagement Group at the World Bank has endorsed a number of strategies for civil society participation in budget decision processes, under the title of 'social accountability' (see Box 61).

The World Bank has identified the following strategies for 'social accountability':

Participatory policy and budget formulation. This involves direct citizen/CSO participation in formulating public policy and budgets (i.e. in proposing projects and allocating funds). Participatory policy formulation has become an increasingly common trend, particularly with the introduction of the PRSPs at the national level and community-driven development initiatives at the local level. Participatory budget formation is less common and usually occurs at the local level (as in over 100 municipalities in Brazil) but is also theoretically applicable at higher levels.

Participatory budget review/analysis. Here, CSOs review budgets in order to assess whether allocations match the government's announced social commitments. This may involve analysing the impact and implications of budget allocations, demystifying the technical content of the budget, raising awareness about budget-related issues and undertaking public education campaigns to improve budget literacy.

Participatory public expenditure/input tracking. This involves citizen groups tracking how the government actually spends funds, with the aim of identifying leakages and/or bottlenecks in the flow of financial resources or inputs. Typically, these groups employ the actual users or beneficiaries of government services (assisted by CSOs) to collect and publicly disseminate data on inputs and expenditures.... The participatory tracking of primary education expenditures in Uganda and the social audit techniques used under Bolivia's social monitoring initiative are examples of such an approach.

Participatory performance monitoring and evaluation. This entails citizens' groups or communities monitoring and evaluating the implementation and performance of public services or projects, according to indicators they themselves have selected. This is achieved through the use of participatory monitoring and evaluation tolls (e.g. community scorecards) and at a more macro level, through the use of public opinion surveys, citizens' juries or citizens' report cards, for example, as carried out in India and the Philippines. The findings of participatory M&E exercises are presented at interface meetings (where users and service providers come together to discuss the evidence and seek solutions) or, as in the case of citizen report cards, are publicly disseminated and presented to government officials to demand accountability and lobby for change.

Box 61 Social Accountability
(Participation and Civic Engagement Group, World Bank, 2003:6.)

In considering this, it is important to distinguish joint decision-making by citizens and government from other kinds of citizen participation (Norton and Elson, 2002). Of the examples cited in Box 59, only one entails joint decision-making: the participatory budgeting in Porto Alegre and other Brazilian municipalities. Civil society participation in the production of a PRSP is a form of consultation, not of joint decision-making. The other examples in Box 61 are of participation in alternative forms of audit and evaluation to produce a range of information different from that produced by conventional financial audits. The ability to do this depends on access to government data and officials. The impact of the reports produced depends on the availability of effective mechanisms to enable civil society to hold governments accountable. Based on detailed research in a number of countries, political scientist Anne Marie Goetz argues that it is vital that citizens have 'concrete rights to a response from public actors' (Goetz, 2003:6). (For further details see Box 62.)

Anne Marie Goetz argues that for accountability practices to be meaningful and productive for citizens, to produce both answers and the hope of seeing complaints addressed and misdemeanours redressed, some of the following conditions should be fulfilled:
1. Legal standing or formal recognition for nongovernmental observers within policy-making arenas or institutions of public sector oversight;
2. A continuous presence for these observers throughout the process of the agencies' work;
3. Structured access to the flow of official documentary information;
4. The right of observers to issue a dissenting report directly to legislative bodies; or
5. The right of service users to demand a formal investigation or seek legal redress for poor or non-delivery of services.

Box 62 Accountability rights for effective participation in budget decisions
(Goetz, 2003.)

Moreover, mechanisms for effective participation, including joint decision-making, tend to be strongest at the local level. But the scope of decisions at local level is very constrained, since revenue-raising powers are very limited at the local level. Even at the national level, the scope of decisions is very limited in countries that are highly indebted and dependent on loans from the World Bank and IMF. Countries that are not so dependent have more room for maneuver but in them, budget decisions are constrained by the views that prevail in international financial markets (Elson, 2004).

8.3 Evaluating budget decision processes from a CEDAW perspective: key principles

CEDAW obliges governments to take all appropriate measures to ensure that women participate on equal terms with men in budget decision processes. This stems in particular from Article 7, which obliges States Parties to ensure to women, on equal terms with men, the following rights:
(a) To vote in all elections and public referenda and to be eligible for election to all publicly elected bodies;
(b) To participate in the formulation of government policy and the implementation thereof and to hold public office and perform public functions at all levels of government;
(c) To participate in nongovernmental organizations and associations concerned with the public and political life of the country.

In relation to Article 7, point (a), States Parties are not only obliged to remove formal barriers, such as laws which disbar women from voting or standing as candidates for elected office, but also obliged to take measures to ensure *de facto* equality, as clarified in CEDAW General Recommendation 23 (1997). It is clear that *de facto* equality requires the presence of women themselves in public bodies, not merely women's right to vote for representatives (GR23, para. 13); and that CEDAW encourages the use of temporary special measures to achieve this (GR 23, para. 15). The CEDAW Committee endorses the interim goal of 30-35% of positions to be held by women in order to achieve a 'critical mass' that will have a transformative impact on the style and content of political decision-making, making it more responsive to the realization of women's rights (GR23, para. 16), and also commends the adoption of a rule that that neither sex should constitute less than 40% of the members of public bodies (GR23, para. 29). Read as a whole, GR23 makes it clear that the ultimate goal is 'full equality' (*cf* para. 17).

In relation to women's participation in the formulation and implementation of public policy (Article 7, point (b)), States Parties have a responsibility both to appoint women to senior positions and 'to consult and incorporate the advice of groups which are broadly representative of women's views and interests' (GR23, para. 26).

Non-state actors also have obligations. For instance:
> 'Other organizations such as trade unions and political parties have an obligation to demonstrate their commitment to the principle of gender equality in their constitutions, in the application of those rules and in the composition of their memberships with gender-balanced representation on their executive boards so that these bodies may benefit from the full and equal participation of all sectors of society and from contributions made by both sexes' (GR23, para. 34).

States have the obligation to 'encourage non-governmental organizations and public and political associations to adopt strategies that encourage women's representation and participation in their work' (GR23, para. 47 (b)).

International human rights treaties, taken together, provide a normative framework for further clarifying what kind of participation women, equally with men, should enjoy. For instance, this has been spelled out in relation to decisions on poverty eradication policies by the Committee on Economic, Social and Cultural Rights (CESCR, 2001). The Committee stresses 'the right of those affected by key decisions to participate in the relevant decision-making processes', referring to 'active and informed participation'. It also emphasizes that people must be able to hold governments to account for their decisions:
> 'Critically, rights and obligations demand accountability: unless supported by a system of accountability, they can become no more than window dressing ... whatever the mechanisms of accountability, they must be accessible, transparent and effective' (CESCR, 2001, para. 14).

The specific obligation of governments to ensure that budget decision processes comply with human rights norms has been clearly articulated by Mr Bernard Mudho, the Independent Expert on the Effects of Structural Adjustment Policies and Foreign Debt, appointed by the Commission on Human Rights:
> 23. It is therefore pertinent and necessary that considerations of human rights principles such as non-discrimination, equality and participation are integrated into all stages of the public budgeting cycles, which typically consist of formulation, legislative review, execution and auditing. In formulating the budget, the executive branch of the government should ensure effective participation by stakeholders and constituencies in setting priorities, through wide consultative processes. The preparation of a participatory PRSP is a right step towards this direction, although more explicit linkages could be made to human rights dimensions of poverty, including economic, social and cultural rights.
> 24. Equal attention needs to be made to the capacity of the legislature to play its constitutional role effectively in budget oversight. It is encouraging to note that many legislatures in developing countries are starting to play a more effective role in budgetary matters ...
> 27. ... more efforts are needed to strengthen the capacities of national institutions in public expenditure management, monitoring and review. From the independent expert's perspective, the integration of human rights considerations into these processes can help make them more open, participatory and transparent ... (Mudho, 2004).

Human rights norms also provide an important framework to guide the execution of budgets. In the delivery of public services, users of the services must be treated with respect, as citizens who are holders of rights, not as supplicants for handouts. This is made clear in the CEDAW Committee's General Recommendation 24 (1999) on women and health, which stipulates:
> '... Acceptable services are those which are delivered in a way that ensures that a women gives her fully informed consent, respects her dignity, guarantees her confidentiality and is sensitive to her needs and perspectives ...' (GR24, para. 22).

Measures to improve the effectiveness and efficiency of public service delivery tend to put the emphasis on treating users as consumers, rather than citizens with rights. Incentive systems reward staff that deliver services at lowest cost, and performance measures emphasize quantity over quality, often failing to allow enough time for staff to deliver services in ways that respect the dignity of users. CEDAW General Recommendation 24 prohibits this.

8.4 Monitoring the position of women and men in budget decision processes

It is useful to distinguish between the positions of women and men in budget decision-making processes as Ministers, elected representatives, officials and other public sector employees, and as members of civil society. To monitor compliance with CEDAW, a first step is ascertaining the numbers of women and men occupying positions at key points in the decision-making process.

8.4.1 Positions within government

For national-level decisions, the first question would be the numbers of women and men in national parliaments. Information is provided by the databases maintained by the Inter-Parliamentary Union and the UN Statistical Division. These show that in the period 1987-2004 there has been a slow increase in the average share of seats in the national parliament held by women in all regions, except in Central and Eastern Europe and Eastern Asia. But no national parliament has full equality in number of seats of held by women and men. The country nearest to full equality is Rwanda, where women held 48.8 per cent of the seats after the election in 2004. In 15 other countries (in Africa, Latin America and Western Europe), where, like Rwanda, special measures of various kinds have been adopted (by governments or by political parties), women held at least 30% of the seats in April 2004 (Goetz, 2004). Parity of representation in all elected assemblies is the goal of the 50/50 campaign launched by the Women's Environmental and Development Organisation (WEDO) in 2000. This goal has been adopted by at least 154 organizations in at least 45 countries (Elson and Keklik, 2002:46). But in most countries that have not adopted special measures, women only hold between 5 and 20% of seats. If women are only present in national parliaments in small proportions, they are unlikely to be able to participate in budget decisions on equal terms with men. This is exacerbated by the way in which women tend to be assigned to the parliamentary committees that deal with 'social' issues rather than those centrally concerned with budget scrutiny (variously called Appropriations, Ways and Means, Finance, Public Accounts) (Goetz, 2004).

Turning to the executive arm of government, on average, women's share of ministerial and sub-ministerial positions is more or less in line with their share of seats in parliament, leaving women in a small minority in most countries. But the role of women Ministers in the budget decision process is limited by the portfolios that women Ministers tend to hold and the parliamentary committees to which they tend to be assigned. The positions in Ministry of Finance and other 'economic' Ministries are still primarily held by men, while women are more often appointed to the 'social' Ministries, such as Health, Education, Welfare, Family Affairs, Women's Affairs, etc. (Goetz, 2004). This means that female Ministers tend not play as big a role as male Ministers in budget formulation. Women also tend to be scarce among the top officials in the Ministries that play the biggest role in budget formulation. As part of their gender budget initiative, the Tanzania Gender Networking Programme produced a detailed analysis of the role of women and men in the formulation and enactment of the national budget in 1999. Their findings are shown in Box 63.

There is no comprehensive global database that would throw light on the relative position of women and men elected representatives in the formulation and legislative enactment of budgets at lower tiers of government. However, a global survey was conducted in 2003 by United Cities and Local Governments (a global network supporting social inclusion in local government). The results for the 52 countries that replied indicate that in Latin America, women tend to hold a higher proportion of seats in local councils than in national parliaments; but that this is not the case in other developing regions, except in countries where quotas or other affirmative action measures have been applied at the local level, but not the national level (Goetz, 2004). Examples of developing countries that have introduced affirmative action measures are Uganda and India. In Uganda, the 1997 Local Government Act reserves 30% of local council seats for women. In India, a constitutional amendment was introduced in 1992 that reserved one third of all seats in local councils for women.

The presence of women elected representatives at local level does not necessarily mean that they will play much role in budget decisions, since they may still be under-represented in key decision-making positions. In Uganda, the GBI organized by FOWODE (Forum for Women in Democracy) has analysed the position of women and men in the budget process. Their findings for Pallisa District in 2000 are shown in Box 64. It is noteworthy that they have included the District Tender Board, which makes decisions about which private sector businesses should get contracts for implementation of the Capital Account.

The Committee for Plan and Budget Guidelines draws up guidelines for all government ministries, indicating how much money they will get in the next year, and what government priorities are for their areas of work. It is made up of the Permanent Secretary and two Deputy Permanent Secretaries from the Ministry of Finance, the Deputy Permanent Secretary of the Planning Commission, the Director of Public Investments and the Commissioner for the Budget. None of these are women.

The Interministerial Technical Committee examines the spending plans produced by each ministry and gives advice to the Cabinet. It includes the Permanent Secretaries of all ministries. Out of twenty, only two are women.

The Cabinet discusses the advice from the Interministerial Technical Committee and agrees the budget proposals. Only 3 of the 23 full ministers are women, and 4 of the 14 deputy ministers.

The Finance and Economic Committee of parliament discusses the proposals and questions ministers. It sends its recommendation to the parliament. Only 3 of the 30 members are women.

The National Parliament discusses the recommendations, and sends their decision to the President. Only 45 of the 275 members are women.

Box 63 Women and men in the national budget decision process, Tanzania, 1999
(TGNP, 1999:16-18.)

Category	%females	%males
Civil servants	34	66
District Service Commission	14	86
Public Accounts Committee	17	83
District Tender Board	20	80
District Council	33	67

Box 64 Women and men in the budget decision process, Pallisa District, Uganda, 2000
(FOWODE, 2002.)

In many parts of India, newly elected women councilors have been routinely denied access to accounts and budget documents, and have not been informed about meetings of the council (Goetz, 2004). In the state of Karnataka, an action research project on the role of elected women representatives (EWRs) in the determination of the budgets of two village councils and two municipal councils was carried out by the Karnataka Women's Information and Resource Centre (Bhat, 2003). It found that EWRs lacked detailed information about the budget and were unable to participate effectively in its formulation and implementation. 'EWRs were kept in the dark as far as budget making was concerned' (Bhat, 2003:46). This was partly due to their own perceptions: many felt that if they had little formal education, they lacked the capacity to engage with the budget. But it was also due to barriers erected by men and by cultural norms (see Box 65).

In India, local government administrators, like accountants and land registration officials, tend to resist transfer of authority from their line ministries to elected representatives whom they may consider to be their social inferiors. In some cases, these officials undermine the authority of women councilors by refusing to cooperate with them (Goetz, 2004).

Where women councilors have been able to play an effective role in budget decisions, there is evidence that they have introduced shifts in local spending patterns to meet women's priorities. Two studies of the spending patterns of councils headed by women in West Bengal and Rajasthan found that there was a strong link between women's stated spending priorities and changed levels of spending (Chattopadhyay and Duflo, 2004). Evidence from a few all-women councils in Maharashtra, Karnataka, Madhya Pradesh and West Bengal shows

'One of the EWRs said that she knows about the budget and has attended the meetings but she never spoke in the meeting. The reason being men never allow their female colleagues to speak. If they speak by chance, men snub them' (Bhat, 2003:31).

'One of the EWRs said "In a village if a woman takes the lead and speaks loudly to get the work done, people would call her aggressive. On the other hand, if a woman is quiet, people would say how mild and godly she is" ' (Baht, 2003:47).

Box 65 Barriers facing women elected representatives in local councils in Karnataka, India

that there have been changes in expenditure patterns, giving greater priority to land transfers to women and water and sanitation (Kaushik, 1996:93-96).

8.4.2 Women's role in civil society engagement with budgets

No international surveys have been conducted on women's role in civil society engagement with budgets, but some information is available on some of the leading examples of civic engagement with government budgets.

Perhaps the most well-known of these are the participatory budget processes in Brazilian cities, which give citizens a direct say in how local funds for new capital investments are spent and institutionalizes their role in monitoring the execution of public works and in reviewing actual spending. In Porto Alegre, this is a complex annual exercise involving city residents in public assemblies (open to all) which establish spending priorities for their own neighbourhoods and elect representatives to a Budget Area Forum for their district and to the city-wide Participatory Budget Council, alongside senior municipal officers. This Council is responsible for compiling the municipal budget. The agreed investment plan is widely disseminated, so that citizens can monitor its implementation and the information on outputs are presented to public assemblies.

The NGO Centro de Assessoria e Estudos Urbanos (CIDADE) has made a study of women's participation in the participatory budget in Porto Alegre. It found that women have always been present in large numbers in the neighbourhood public assemblies, typically constituting over half the participants. However, they were in a minority among representatives elected to the Area Forums and the Participatory Budget Council. Over time their share has risen, and in 2000, half of the members of the Budget Council were women. Women's involvement in participatory budget processes in Porto Alegre is considerably higher than in electoral politics (Sugiyama, 2002:14).

Participatory budgeting has also been introduced in some other Latin American countries, including the municipality of Villa El Salvador in Peru. It includes district committees and thematic commissions that deal with particular issues. A study of gender and the Villa El Salvador budget (Andia-Perez and Beltran-Barco, 2004) found that to date the priorities are chosen by community leaders who are almost all male and focus mainly on expenditure on public works. Women report that they would like support for other activities, such as micro-enterprise development.

The Indian state of Kerala has also introduced measures to facilitate citizen participation in setting budget priorities and in the implementation of budgets (Goetz and Jenkins, 2004). Annual village assemblies (*gram sabhas*) formulate local development plans. Beneficiary committees are formed for any development project. These committees can implement projects themselves with their own labour or subcontract them to local businesses. The selection of beneficiaries for anti-poverty schemes is done on a points scale and the criteria are supposed to be widely published. Neighbourhood committees and the *gram sabhas* make selections of beneficiaries on the basis of these criteria, and objections are invited before the list is finalized. The poorest women in local communities have been assigned responsibility for monitoring inclusion in the list of households below the poverty line.

Women comprise almost one third of the participants in the annual *gram sabha* meetings that identify local needs. All-women groups are convened in annual *gram sabhas* to set priorities for the allocation of the Women's Development Fund, for which 10% of the budget is earmarked. There are examples of women trying to monitor the spending of the Women's Development Fund. But there are also accounts of resistance to this, and of malpractice in the use of these funds (Goetz and Jenkins, 1999). There are also worries that these arrangements create a female ghetto, with women being excluded from decisions about how to use the other 90% of the budget (Jain, 2004).

An innovation in limiting malpractice is the strategy of participatory auditing, developed in the Indian state of Rajasthan by the grass-roots organization MKSS (Goetz and Jenkins, 1999). This is done through public hearings, in which detailed accounts and other documents are read aloud to independently organized informal assemblies of villagers. The villagers can then identify any discrepancies between the official record and their own experiences of employment on public works projects and applicants to means-tested anti-poverty schemes.

Around 60% of the members of the MKSS are women, reflecting male out-migration from the region and the preponderance of women among employees of public works projects. They have been able to uncover the methods being used to cheat women of the payment due to them and which has been siphoned off to local politicians, officials and contractors (methods include names of non-existent 'ghost workers' on the employment rosters; failing to record fully the amount of work done by women; falsifying signatures on receipts for wages paid). However, although women are enthusiastic about participating in hearings, they are often the targets of threats of violence from those who have been benefiting from corruption, and this may deter women from participating (Goetz and Jenkins, 1999).

Budget review and analysis is now undertaken by many civil society groups in a wide range of countries (Norton and Elson, 2002). Women are almost certainly in the majority in groups carrying out review and analysis as part of a GBI, though men also play a significant role in some of these groups (such as in South Africa, the United Republic of Tanzania and Uganda). Equally, women are almost certainly in a minority in groups carrying out review and analysis that is not specifically linked with a GBI. Some of these groups have taken specific steps to include women. For instance, the two groups that produce the Canadian Alternative Federal Budget (AFB) have sought to increase the representation of women in the AFB steering committee and policy groups and to have women leading some of their 'budget schools', in which people in different communities learn about budget processes and identify their priorities for taxation and expenditure in the AFB (Loxley, 2004:93).

8.5 Promoting women's full equality in participation in budget decision-making

To achieve full equality for women in budget decision-making requires:
- increasing the presence of women
- increasing the capacity of women
- reforming budget decision-making processes.

There is now considerable evidence to show that the achievement of a critical mass of women in elected assemblies requires special measures (Goetz, 2004). As noted earlier, a variety of special measures have been introduced in at least 16 countries, depending on the type of electoral system, and have been effective in achieving at least 30% of seats in the hands of women (Goetz, 2004).

Special measures may also be introduced to increase the presence of women in community assemblies that engage with budgets. For instance, in India, some states have introduced special measures to increase women's presence in the village assembles in which citizens can inform their elected representatives of their needs and priorities. In Madhya Pradesh, rules for the quorum of people who must be present for a valid meeting to take place include the requirement that at least one third of those present must be women. In Rajasthan, a similar provision requires that women must be present in the same proportions as they are in the local population, which could imply 50% or even more in areas of male out-migration. Based on their study of Villa el Salvador in Peru, Andia-Perez and Beltran-Barco (2004) recommend the establishment of a minimum quota for women's participation in the various decision-making bodies of the participatory budget process in that city.

However, increased presence in an assembly does not necessarily mean increased influence of women in budget decisions. That requires increasing the capacity of women to understand and engage with budget matters and reforming the budget process to give elected representatives and members of civil society more rights: to information; to a voice in deliberations; and to redress if money is not spent as authorized and services are not properly delivered.

These have been important objectives of a number of GBIs (especially those in Uganda, the United Republic of Tanzania, South Africa, Mexico and Karnataka in India). For instance, in Uganda, the GBI organized by the Forum for Women in Democracy (FOWODE) and a number of women parliamentarians has increased the capacity of women parliamentarians to engage with the budget by producing short briefing papers specifically for parliamentarians to enable them to scrutinize the budget from a gender equality perspective. These papers also enabled the women to get male parliamentarians to take gender issues more seriously. (For the views of a leading Uganda parliamentarian, see Box 66.)

'Representing women is a special challenge. Articulating issues of gender inequality, oppression and discrimination and obtaining results in a legislature where the majority is men requires a different set of skills from the usual ones. Gender budget analysis is a tool that can be used to expose gender inequalities and biases in the distribution of public resources. It can be used to move the debate on gender issues away form mere sentimental or moral exhortations to concrete demands supported by economic arguments'.

Box 66 Gender and the budget: views of a leading Ugandan parliamentarian
(Winnie Byanyima, 2002:132.)

The research on which the issue papers are based was conducted as a partnership between university researchers, gender activists and government officials. Initially officials questioned the right of civil society to access government information, but after working together for some time, they became convinced of the value of the work and began to facilitate access to government documents, overcoming a long tradition of official secrecy (Byanyima, 2002:131-2). The GBI has also contributed to making the national budget process more participatory. The advocacy of FOWODE and other civil society groups has been important in improving the legal framework through a new Budget Act, establishing a Budget Office and a Budget Committee of parliament. Sector Working Groups, with civil society representation, have been created to set priorities and performance indicators for the different areas of expenditure. FOWODE is a member of the Poverty Eradication Working Group, whose mandate is to ensure that all national sector budgets address the concerns of the poor and also of the working groups on the education, health and agriculture sectors. FOWODE has also conducted training workshops with members of district councils and local government officials (FOWODE, 2003).

Some GBIs, such as those in Chile and the Philippines, have emphasized enhancing the role of the national women's machinery in budget decision processes, in both those cases, in the evaluation phase. For example in Chile, the national women's machinery, SERNAM (Servicio Nacional de la Mujer), worked with the Budget Office in the Ministry of Finance to mainstream gender into the management of public expenditure from 2002 onwards. Gender equality considerations must be mainstreamed into the ongoing programme for the improvement of the management of public services and gender impact assessment must be included as part of the evidence that must be provided with any bid by a department for additional funding for the extension of its existing programmes or for new programmes. SERNAM has responsibility for training officials how to do this and for evaluating their performance in practice and certifying that gender has been properly taken into account. If departments fail to be validated by SERNAM, the employees of the department do not get their 2% salary bonus (Sugiyama, 2002; Direccion de Presupestos, Minisiterio de Hacienda, Gobierno de Chile, 2001).

Civil society groups that participate in auditing and evaluation of budgets are generally hampered by lack of information. There are two problems:
  • lack of access by citizens to data in the hands of officials
  • failure of officials to produce sex-disaggregated data even for their own use.

The first problem has been tackled by the civil society organization MKSS in Rajasthan (India) by a successful campaign for Right to Information legislation. The second problem has been tackled by the Institute for Oaxacan Women (Mexico) by persuading the Governor of the State of Oaxaca to pass law that makes it compulsory for officials to produce sex-disaggregated data (Cos-Montiel, 2004:19).

Even when information is available, there need to be rights to use this to hold governments to account. The MKSS has won an amendment to Rajasthan's local government act that legally empowers village assemblies to conduct 'social audits' of the development projects initiated by local elected representatives and local officials. The assemblies have the right to take cases of mis-use of funds to higher-level officials.

But even when such rights exist, the challenge still remains of getting redress when analysis of the information reveals that poor women have been cheated out of services or payments to which they are entitled. It is difficult to get police to investigate or higher-level officials to mount an investigation (Goetz and Jenkins, 1999). For poor women to claim and make practical use of these rights requires a high level of social mobilization.

8.6 Conclusions

CEDAW requires that governments take steps to ensure that women participate on equal terms with men in decision-making about the budget. This is specifically provided for in Article 7(a) (the right of women to equally participate in the formulation of government policy and its implementation and to hold public office and perform all public functions) and Article 7(b) (the right of women to equally participate in nongovernmental organizations and associations which address the State's public and political life). These Articles require *de facto* equality (CEDAW General Recommendation 23, para. 13) and States are encouraged to adopt temporary special measures in this area to accelerate achievement of this requirement (CEDAW General Recommendation 23, para. 15).

On the whole, women do not appear to be participating on equal terms with men in budget decision processes, either as members of government bodies or of civil society assemblies and budget decision processes are frequently structured in ways that make this difficult. Indeed these processes are often structured in ways that make effective participation in key decisions difficult for more than a few powerful men (Ministers of Finance, chairs of Budget Committees, leaders of missions from the World Bank and IMF, etc.). Monitoring the comparative participation of women and men has been undertaken by some GBIs. The absence of women matters because there is accumulating evidence that a critical mass of women does make a difference to the content of public decisions.

Some positives can be noted: a growing number of countries have used temporary special measures to increase women's presence in public decision-making processes. Many GBIs have as one of their aims strengthening the capacity of women to engage with budgets and are achieving some important successes. Some also focus on reforms of budget processes, to secure changes in legislation and procedures that strengthen accountability rights, including the right to information, the right to a voice in deliberations and the right to redress. Actually exercising those rights very often requires social mobilization.

Section 9

Conclusions and Recommendations

Conclusions and Recommendations

1. Women's human rights and government budgets: basic principles

The report aims to clarify:
- how the Convention on the Elimination of All Discrimination Against Women (CEDAW) can help to set criteria for what constitutes gender equality in budgetary matters and provide guidance for Gender Budget Initiatives (GBIs);
- how GBIs can help in monitoring compliance with CEDAW.

The report draws upon the Convention and documentation on the CEDAW reporting process, including reference to selected General Recommendations, States Parties' Periodic Reports and Concluding Comments. Reference is also made to relevant aspects of the International Covenant on Economic, Social and Cultural Rights and the Convention on the Rights of the Child. The report also presents an accessible explanation of the main aspects of government budgets and presents examples of the work of GBIs in all regions of the world.

Government budgets affect people in multiple ways:
- Their *primary* impact is through distributing resources to people via expenditure to provide services, infrastructure and income transfers; and though claiming resources from them via tax and other measures, such as charges for use of public services.
- They also have *secondary, macroeconomic* impacts via their impacts on job creation, economic growth and inflation.

GBIs use gender budget analysis to show how budgets affect women and girls, as compared to men and boys. There are examples of such analysis in at least 50 countries, undertaken by GBIs organized both by civil society organizations and by governments. However, many GBIs are not yet institutionalized on an ongoing basis. Most GBIs have not yet made an explicit link with CEDAW obligations.

The report clarifies that CEDAW requires that all government measures must be non-discriminatory and ensure the achievement of *substantive* equality between women and men, as autonomous possessors of all human rights, civil and political, and economic, social and cultural. Achievement of substantive equality goes well beyond formal legal equality. It requires the state to actively work towards ensuring equality in families, communities, markets and businesses, as well as in the public sector and throughout the operations of the state. This may entail, for example, the use of 'temporary special measures' (Article 4(1)) and requires 'modification of social and cultural patterns of conduct' based on 'stereotyped roles for men and women' (Article 5).

The report clarifies that government budgets (like any other activity carried out by the State) should be constructed and implemented in ways that *respect, protect and fulfil* human rights. In turn, it is clear that government budgets are indispensable for the realization of human rights, which cannot be realized without public expenditure and the revenue required to finance this.

This report discusses the status of CEDAW as part of a broader human rights framework. It identifies how CEDAW clearly sets out a number of general principles (e.g. non-discrimination and equality) that are binding on States in the decisions they make about gender and budgets. The fact that the exact meaning of these principles in specific contexts is not detailed in the Convention does not mean that States can act without regard to human rights standards. CEDAW is a *non-discrimination* treaty and its requirements extend to ensuring the realization of women's rights in all spheres. Its provisions thereby affect the implementation of substantive rights guaranteed in other treaties (e.g. ICESCR) regarding resource allocation. In this regard, relevant principles on resource allocation that emerge from the ICESCR include: the principle of 'progressive realization'; immediate obligations; minimum-core; and non-retrogression. From a gender perspective, it is important to stress that even though human rights law allows for progressive realization of economic, social and cultural rights over time, there is an immediate obligation of a State not to discriminate in striving for the achievement of human rights. It is also important that retrogressive measures (e.g. spending cuts) that infringe the guarantee of substantive equality between men and women can never be justified by a State Party to the ICESCR.

Some human rights advocates and civil society budget analysts are beginning to work together to analyse whether budgets are being designed and implemented in ways that realize the human rights of children, poor people and indigenous people. This report aims to promote comparable collaboration between advocates of women's human rights and GBIs.

Use of the human rights framework in general, and CEDAW in particular, will not change government budgets overnight. There are frequently institutional or behavioural practices that will frustrate compliance with the legal framework which human rights provides. For example, Ministers of Finance may tend to give priority to financial obligations, especially to creditors, rather than to human rights obligations, which they tend to regard as the responsibility of other Ministers. Moreover, compliance can be sometimes difficult to achieve because courts are not the major vehicle for shaping the ways governments raise and spend money and there is sometimes limited judicial use of international human rights standards on budgets. However, this report makes it clear that CEDAW does impose binding legal standards on States, although the exact nature of obligations for a particular State will vary according to whether, and under what conditions, CEDAW forms part of its domestic law.

In addition to the legal force of human rights regarding budgets, there is also the moral authority conveyed by the discourse of human rights. Budgets are never the outcomes of a purely technical process based only on financial analysis. In the words of Pregs Govender, former chair of the South African Parliamentary Committee on the Improvement of the Quality of Life and Status of Women:

'The budget reflects the values of a country—who it values, whose work it values and who it rewards … and who and what and whose work it doesn't'.

Reference to CEDAW enables us to reposition women who are under-valued, who suffer discrimination, disadvantage and exclusion, as active agents. Human rights must always take precedence over financial expediency, though this does not mean ignoring financial constraints. To have a stronger practical impact on budgets, human rights advocacy needs to be backed by detailed analysis of budgets, relating finance to human rights norms.

2. Analysing public expenditure programmes from a human rights perspective

This report discusses some of the above issues by analysing public expenditure programmes (in particular the Human Development Expenditure Ratios; public expenditure on health in Mexico; and the child support grant programme in South Africa) from a general human rights perspective.

3. Conclusions and recommendations on general approach to setting standards for CEDAW-compliant budgets and CEDAW reporting

The report concludes that it is not possible to sum up the total comparative impact of the budget on males and on females in just *one* indicator and use this to judge whether the budget is non-discriminatory and advances the achievement of substantive gender equality.

This report recommends a *step-by-step approach, examining particular dimensions of the budget separately, taking into account their interactions where appropriate and possible.* The key dimensions considered in this report are:
- public expenditure
- public revenue, especially taxation and user fees
- macroeconomics of the budget (secondary impacts on inflation, jobs and economic growth)
- budget decision-making processes.

In relation to CEDAW reporting and government budgets, the report notes that the CEDAW Committee has begun to make more specific reference to the role of government budgets in relation to women's human rights. One example is *General Recommendation 24 on Women and Heath,* issued in 1999. Other examples can be found in some recent Concluding Comments issued by the Committee after the consideration of reports by States Parties:
- In reference to Luxembourg in 2000, the Committee 'welcome[d] the [Women's] Ministry's interest in, and support for, proposals to conduct a gender analysis of the entire State budget. This will contribute

to a better understanding of the way in which women and men benefit from governmental expenditures in all areas'.

- In 2002, when reviewing Fiji's report, the Committee 'commend[ed] the efforts of the State Party to strengthen gender mainstreaming and monitoring through the gender budget initiative, and a gender audit project'.
- The Committee has, on at least one occasion, asked a State to conduct a gender analysis of its budget and to report on the results. In its concluding comments concerning Austria in 2000, the Committee 'request[ed] the Government to ensure, on a regular basis, the evaluation and assessment of the gender impact of the federal budget as well as governmental policies and programmes affecting women'.

Moreover, some States Parties have made references to Gender Budget Initiatives in their reports. The first was South Africa in its initial report to the CEDAW Committee in 1997. France also recently mentioned gender analysis of its government budget in its report to the CEDAW Committee.

This report provides many examples of how analysis conducted by GBIs is useful for monitoring the extent to which budgets comply with CEDAW. The report also shows how CEDAW provides standards that can be used to evaluate the results of analysis conducted by GBIs, to judge whether any particular aspect of the budget is or is not consistent with the achievement of substantive gender equality.

The report recommends:
- greater efforts to institutionalize capacity for gender budget analysis in both governments and civil society;
- greater efforts to build links between the CEDAW reporting process and GBIs;
- development of some guidelines for what governments should report to CEDAW about their budgets;
- development of some guidelines for how NGOs can incorporate gender analysis of budgets into their shadow reports.

4. Conclusions and recommendations for assessing Gender Budget Initiatives

As this report indicates, GBIs are very diverse and of varying scope and effectiveness. Given the diversity of GBIs, it is important to seek more information from states that report that there is, or is planned to be, a GBI operative within their country. This report concludes that the mere presence of some kind of GBI is not sufficient to ensure that the budget complies with CEDAW.

It is recommended that as a starting point for determining whether the design and implementation of GBIs conform with CEDAW requirements, the following questions be asked:
- What kind of GBI is planned or is operative in the country?
- What are the roles of the government, parliament and civil society?
- What is the role of the Ministry of Finance and the Office of the Budget?
- Is the GBI institutionalized in ongoing, regular, transparent procedures?
- Do women enjoy equal participation in budget decision-making?
- In what ways has it made women and girls visible in the budget?
- What impact is it expected to have, or has had, on women's substantive enjoyment of equality?
- What benchmarks or standards are used to assess the budget?
- How do the results of gender budget analysis influence the formulation and implementation of budgets?

Debbie Budlender, a leading researcher for the South African GBI, summarizes good practice in the organization of GBIs by referring to 'the triangle of players':
- progressive elected politicians
- effective government institutions staffed with well-trained officials
- active and well-informed coalitions of NGOs.

Effective and sustainable GBIs are generally based on the interaction of all three.

Rhonda Sharp, adviser to the south Australian GBI, points to a different triangle, a *'triangle of goals'*:
- Raise awareness and understanding of gender issues and the impacts of budgets and policies.
- Make governments accountable for their budgetary and policy commitments.
- Change and refine government budgets and policies to promote gender equality.

No guidelines have yet been suggested for the specific indicators or benchmarks that should be used to evaluate and assess government budgets from a CEDAW perspective. This report is a contribution to the formulation of such standards, recognizing that the general and overriding requirement of substantive equality has to be interpreted in light of specific circumstances.

5. Conclusions and recommendations on public expenditure

The report concludes that it is not possible to summarize the implications of public expenditure for gender equality in one single indicator. It is recommended that consideration should be given to the following issues:
- priority given to gender equality and the advancement of women in distribution of public expenditure between programmes:
- elimination of discrimination (in both policy and effect) against women in the distribution of public expenditure;
- adequacy of public expenditure for realization of the obligation to achieve *de facto* gender equality;
- gender equality in the impact of public expenditure;
- gender equality and public expenditure reform.

5.1 Monitoring public expenditure for compliance with CEDAW: starting points

This report recalls that the monitoring of public expenditure applies to both gender-specific programming and programming which on the face of it appears to be gender-neutral, because it is not specifically targeted to either sex. This scrutiny is necessary because not all gender-specific programming will necessarily result in *de facto* equality and not all apparently gender-neutral programming will be equally beneficial to males and females. In making decisions about expenditure by programme, it is also necessary to bear in mind the three different types of measures for which CEDAW provides: general measures; temporary special measures (Article 4(1)); and permanent special measures (Article 4(2)). Each of these measures has different criteria against which particular government expenditure will need to be assessed to determine if it complies with CEDAW.

5.2 Priority given to gender equality and the advancement of women in distribution of public expenditure between programmes

The report confirms that expenditure targeted specifically to women and girls is generally a very small percentage of total programme expenditure (typically between 0.5 and 1%). The report concludes that it is not possible to draw a general conclusion that compliance with CEDAW requires an *increase* in expenditures specifically targeted to women and girls, since such programmes may serve to reinforce traditional unequal gender roles.

The report recognizes that many programmes not specifically targeted to women and girls have benefits for women and girls. It considers the possibility of constructing an internationally agreed benchmark for the priority that should be given to expenditure that promotes gender equality and the full development and advancement of women, comparable to the 20/20 benchmark. The latter benchmark was agreed at the World Summit for Social Development in 1995. (It suggests that 20% of expenditure on public programmes should be allocated to basic services, as should 20% of foreign aid.) Compliance with this benchmark would undoubtedly have many benefits for women, especially poor women, but expenditure on basic services does not necessarily directly promote gender equality and the advancement of women.

However, examination of the analysis done by GBIs suggests there are many complexities in identifying which programmes promote gender equality and the advancement of women, since many programmes which have benefits for women nevertheless serve to reinforce traditional unequal gender roles. These complexities suggest that it is not possible to identify *a priori* which programmes promote gender equality and the advancement of women. It is necessary to investigate the content and impact of programmes in a particular social context. This means it is difficult to construct meaningful *a priori* benchmarks comparable to the 20/20 benchmarks. A simple, quantitative, internationally applicable benchmark for a gender equality expenditure ratio does not seem feasible.

Some governments have found it useful to require a minimum proportion of the expenditure of all public agencies to be devoted to the promotion of gender equality. For instance, the Government of the Philippines requires that 5% of the finance allocated to each public agency be allocated 'to address gender issues'. This may be a useful tool for persuading every part of the public sector to address gender equality issues, not just the national women's machinery. But experience in the Philippines shows that public agencies do not automatically spend this allocation in ways that do in fact promote gender equality and the advancement of women.

5.3 Presence of discrimination against women and girls in the distribution of public expenditure

The report clarifies that CEDAW is concerned not only with *de jure* discrimination but also with *de facto* discrimination. *De facto* discrimination does not require any intention to discriminate on the part of the State; instead, it encompasses all actions and inactions that have a disproportionately negative impact on women. To overcome both *formal* and *de facto* inequality, CEDAW requires States to use a model of substantive equality. CEDAW also distinguishes between *de jure* discrimination and temporary special measures, allowing—and in some cases requiring—the use of specially targeted measures to overcome gender discrimination. For these reasons, the report concludes that a general benchmark of numerically equal shares of expenditure for males and females cannot be used as a test for the absence of discrimination.

Where separate public services are provided for men and women (e.g. schools or hospitals or sports facilities), the purpose in separating the sexes must be scrutinized to ensure that women's equality is not diminished by the division. Once this hurdle is passed, in general, the standards of provision should be equal for the separate programmes. The recommended benchmark is that:

- *With respect to equality-respecting separate programmes, per capita expenditures on comparable services provided separately to males and to females should be equal.*

However, departures from this may be required to achieve substantive equality for women, including to cater for differing sex-specific needs (provided that the measures respect women's equality instead of reinforcing discriminatory gender roles).

For programmes providing services to both males and females, and delivering them on an individual basis, the recommended general benchmark is that:

- *The share of expenditure going to females should be at least equal to their share of the relevant population, and should be more where equal expenditure is inadequate to overcome discrimination.*

In some programmes, such as education, this will generally imply *numerically equal shares of expenditure for boys and girls,* because there are equal numbers of boys and girls in the school-age population. If girls receive less than 50%, this does not imply that the government is *intentionally* discriminating against girls, but it does mean that the government is failing to take measures to persuade and enable families to enrol girls in school at the same rate as boys. CEDAW requires that the State adopt such measures.

In some cases, equating women's share of expenditure to their share of the intended beneficiary population may run the risk of preserving the traditional roles of women and men, to the disadvantage of women. So consideration would need to be given to designing programming in such ways that traditional roles are not reinforced, and to additional expenditure on measures to promote greater equality in the sex-composition of the beneficiary population.

Some governments have tried to promote greater equality in the gender distribution of expenditure on poverty alleviation and rural development programmes through the use of quotas. For instance:
- Indian 9th plan (1995-2000) has a women's component requiring 30% of expenditure of a variety of poverty alleviation programmes to go to women.
- In Mexico in the late 1990s, the Ministry of Social Development had a policy that 50% of beneficiaries of poverty alleviation programmes should be women.
- In South Africa, the code of conduct for special public works programmes states that 60% of the beneficiaries should be women. In the skills development programmes, 54% of the beneficiaries are meant to be women and 85% black South Africans.

If this method is adopted, the rationale for the choice of the stipulated percentages requires clarification. The quotas in South Africa are chosen to reflect the needs of different groups, and relate to the percentage of women (and black people) in the target group (poor people and people who need skills development).

There are many important public services whose use cannot be broken down into individual units, consumed exclusively by this or that person. For example, street lighting, paved roads, sanitation systems, defence and policing. These services are described by economists as 'public goods'. Here the appropriate benchmark for non-discrimination cannot be constructed in terms of male and female shares of expenditure. However, men and women often have different priorities for expenditure on 'public goods'. The recommended benchmark is:

- *Equal weight to women's and men's priorities, with an emphasis on priorities that are in fact equality-enhancing.*

Some governments, such as that in the Indian state of Kerala, have found it useful to reserve a certain proportion of expenditure for meeting women's priorities (10% of the development expenditure budget, in the case of Kerala). However, this runs the risk of excluding women's priorities from consideration in allocation of the rest of the budget. Further, women's priorities might not always be equality-enhancing, so additional scrutiny is always required.

5.4 Adequacy of public expenditure for realization of obligations to gender equality

The report clarifies that compliance with CEDAW requires consideration of the adequacy of funding. This is because it would be possible to have a non-discriminatory distribution of funding, but nevertheless insufficient funds to carry out the measures that are vital for the 'full development and advancement of women'. For instance, girls and boys could enjoy equal shares of government expenditure on education, without the level of that expenditure being sufficient to provide education for all girls and boys.

To develop benchmarks for adequacy of expenditure requires going beyond financial inputs to look at required *activities, outputs and outcomes*. It requires:
- agreement on the outcomes to be achieved
- investigation of the activities and outputs required to achieve the agreed outcomes
- investigation of the costs of providing these activities, and
- comparison of the costs with the finance allocated in the budget.

Developing such benchmarks also requires that account be taken of the important finding from several GBIs that poor women's unpaid work often represents a hidden subsidy to public programmes.

If using the benchmark developed, funding is found to be inadequate, it is also important to consider how more resources can be found, in ways that are in compliance with CEDAW. This might imply:
- redistribution of funding between programmes
- measures to increase tax revenue
- increased foreign aid flows, and
- extension of debt relief.

The report recommends that reference be made to the UN Millennium Project, which has developed methods for estimating the costs of the services required to achieve the Millennium Development Goals, including Goal 3, *Gender Equality and Women's Empowerment.* These include services that protect women's rights and enable women to claim their rights (e.g. Gender Equality Commissions, counseling services, legal services, media campaigns).

5.5 Gender equality in the impact of public expenditure

The report clarifies that it is possible to monitor the extent to which a State Party has met its *obligations of conduct* by looking at the allocation of expenditure. But to monitor how far *obligations of result* have been met requires an investigation of the impact of public expenditure.

This means that monitoring for compliance with CEDAW must *follow the money* from the budget appropriations to the activities and outputs it funds, and investigate the substantive outcomes in terms of gender equality and the advancement of women. The report recommends the use of:
- *expenditure-tracking studies, to see if money gets through to the point of service delivery;*
- *beneficiary assessments, to see if the intended beneficiaries are satisfied with the services;*
- *quantitative studies of the links between public expenditure and gender equality and women's well-being.*

To fully comply with CEDAW, a State Party needs to show that:
- the money did reach the point of service delivery as intended
- the intended beneficiaries were satisfied
- there were improvements in gender equality and women's well-being.

5.6 Gender equality and public expenditure reform

The report notes that in many countries measures are being introduced to reform the management of public expenditure, with the aim of making it more efficient. Some of these changes may make it easier to introduce gender equality criteria into public finance, but there is also potential for the introduction of measures that will create obstacles to gender equality. Among the reforms are:
- performance-oriented budgeting
- decentralization of expenditure and services
- narrower targeting of public expenditure
- privatization of public services.

Rebecca Grynspan, former Vice-President of Costa Rica, argues that women need to take a critical look at these reforms, as they may have 'perverse effects on women in terms of their access to quality services and of the increasing and unpaid workload implicit in many reforms'.

The report recommends that:

- *Governments be asked to show that they have designed reforms in ways that further gender equality and the advancement of women.*

6. Conclusions and recommendations on taxation and user fees

The report examines the following key sources of revenue in the light of CEDAW obligations:
- personal income tax
- value added tax
- excise tax
- import duties
- user fees.

CEDAW does not contain any explicit reference to taxation. However, CEDAW's general principles (such as non-discrimination and substantive equality) apply to taxation measures. Further, in view of the fact that the distributional effects of taxation are generally discussed in terms of the impact on households, rather than individuals, it is relevant that Article 1 of CEDAW specifies that marital status is not an acceptable basis for any 'distinctions, exclusions or restrictions' which impair women's equality with men in the enjoyment of human rights. CEDAW requires that families be based on 'principles of equity, justice and individual fulfilment for each member' (General Recommendation 21, para. 4).

The report clarifies that CEDAW requires that women must be treated as equal to men in tax laws; as individual, autonomous citizens, rather than as dependents of men. Moreover, the impact of tax laws (in terms of tax burden/incidence and incentives for particular kinds of behaviour) should promote substantive, and not merely formal, equality between women and men, including egalitarian family relations.

The report concludes that substantive equality *does not* imply that 50% of tax revenue should be paid by women and 50% by men. It is a well-established principle in public finance that equality in taxation has to be related to ability to pay. Men on average have greater ability to pay than women, because on average their incomes are higher. The report recommends the following benchmark:

- *Men's share of aggregate tax payments should be at least equal to their share of income.*

Income tax is the only one of the five revenue measures considered in which *explicit* and *intentional discrimination* against women may occur. This can happen in both joint tax filing systems and individual tax filing systems. The most obvious example is the allocation of tax exemptions and allowances for the support of dependents to husbands but not to wives. This is clearly in violation of CEDAW Article 13(a) which obliges States to ensure equality between women and men in the right to family benefits. The report recommends that:

- *Explicit discrimination should be eliminated by reform of the tax law.*

The report explains that income tax rules may also contain implicit discrimination because of their implications for the different incidence of tax on women's and men's earnings when they live in the same family. These arise because of the intersection of the tax laws with pre-existing gender inequality in incomes, employment and responsibility for unpaid domestic work; with the different decisions women and men make about how to combine paid and unpaid work; and with different forms of family (such as whether partners are married, unmarried, heterosexual or same sex).

The report finds that it is a complex matter to judge whether or not particular distributions of income tax burden discriminate against particular types of family and particular categories of women. Many gender equality advocates would argue that the tax system should not differentiate between couples who are married, unmarried or same sex, or result in a lower tax burden for families with breadwinner husbands and financially dependent housewives who do not engage in paid employment. They argue that the tax code should result in a lower tax burden for more egalitarian families in which both partners undertake some unpaid domestic work and some paid employment. However, some women argue that this would fail to give equal treatment to women who have chosen to be exclusively homemakers compared to those women who have chosen to do paid work and unpaid work.

The report concludes that while CEDAW does imply that all that women should be equally free to choose how to live their lives, they must be able to make and realize these choices in conditions of substantive equality. The recommended benchmarks are that:

- *The income tax system should be neutral in the burden of taxation on different types of family irrespective of the marital status and sex of the partners.*
- *The income tax system should not perpetuate gender stereotypes in which men are expected to be the breadwinners and women the homemakers, but should support the modification of social and cultural patterns of conduct in ways that promote substantive equality.*

The great advantage of personal income tax is that its incidence is progressive, in the sense that those with higher incomes pay a higher proportion of their income in tax. Appropriately designed, it can be an equality-promoting tax, reducing inequality in disposable income between men and women and between rich and poor women. It is, however, harder to administer than direct taxes, for political as well as technical reasons.

Value added tax (VAT) is levied on what people spend rather than on their income. The report clarifies that while VAT does not explicitly discriminate against women, it tends to *implicitly discriminate* against women. This is because the incidence of the tax on consumers is higher for poor consumers than for rich ones and since women's incomes tend to be lower than men's, the incidence will tend to be higher on average on female consumers than on male consumers. VAT can be made more equitable in gender terms by exempting goods mainly purchased by women from the tax. However, this will reduce the finance available to government and may mean that programmes important for the advancement of women are not financed. So exemptions need to be carefully considered. There is a strong case for exempting a good like paraffin, purchased by poor women for heating, cooking and lighting, but not for exempting a good like washing machines, used by better-off urban women. The report recommends that:

- *The VAT system should exempt basic necessities.*

As the report explains, excise taxes are likely to be less regressive from a gender perspective than VAT. This is because they tend to be levied on goods like alcohol and tobacco, which are consumed more by men than by women. At first sight this would suggest that higher excise taxes should be recommended to raise revenue to finance gender equality-promoting programmes. However, it is possible that inequality within households may permit men to shift the incidence of the tax to women and children by reducing the amount of income that men devote to the needs of wives and children, so as to maintain their consumption of items like alcohol and tobacco. More research is required on this.

The report concludes that the effects of import duties on gender equality in employment depend on the particular structures of production and consumption of different types of economy. Exemptions from import duties for small quantities of goods may benefit small-scale women entrepreneurs, but the biggest exemptions (such as those conferred by Free Trade Zones) go to the biggest firms, often to foreign-owned firms. The most important gender equality implication of trade liberalization is loss of revenue, leading to declines in investment in social and physical infrastructure.

With respect to user fees, the report concludes that user fees for basic health and education services tend to restrict the access of poor people, but with even more adverse effects for women and girls than men and boys. User fees for basic education and health services produce outcomes that are in violation of CEDAW obligations (especially Articles 10 and 12). The report recommends:

- *No user fees for basic education and health services.*

In relation to water, sanitation and electricity, user fees will be in violation of CEDAW (especially Article 14) if they deny poor women access to adequate basic levels of the service. The report recommends:

- *The structure of fees for water, sanitation and electricity must ensure poor women have adequate access to basic amounts.*
- *This implies low fees, with fee exemptions where necessary, for basic amounts supplied to poor households.*
- *Higher fees for those who consume more.*

The structure of taxation has been reformed in many countries, to reduce direct taxation of incomes of high-earning individuals and corporations and increase indirect taxation, especially taxes like VAT. However, the revenue mix that is most suited to implementation of CEDAW would be one with:

- *high reliance on income tax (reformed to remove provisions that hinder substantive equality between women and men);*
- *exemptions from VAT on a wide range of basic consumption items;*
- *excise taxes on non-necessities consumed mainly by men;*
- *no user fees for basic health and education services;*
- *low fees, with exemptions where necessary, for basic amounts of water, sanitation and electricity supplied to poor households.*

7. Conclusions and recommendations on the macroeconomics of the budget

The report finds that the main implications of CEDAW for the macroeconomics of the budget are as follows:

- Macroeconomic policy should support women's right to equality in (paid) work, on equal terms with men (CEDAW Article 11); the work should conform to human rights standards concerning work and the ILO definition of 'decent work'.
- Women should not suffer disproportionately if a budget deficit is reduced by cutting the level of public expenditure (CEDAW Article 2).
- Macroeconomic policy should ensure the 'full development and advancement of women', taking into account women's unpaid work, as well as women's paid work (CEDAW Article 2; CEDAW General Recommendation 17).

The dominant form of macroeconomic policy today is the neo-liberal form that aims to achieve growth of GNP and very low rates of inflation via reduction of budget deficits, primarily through cutting expenditure. These polices have been described as marked by deflationary bias. The report shows that such policies have not been capable of providing decent paid work for all and that women tend to be more adversely affected than men.

ILO data show that for the world as a whole, the female unemployment rate is somewhat higher than the male unemployment rate; in 2003, the global female unemployment rate was 6.4% while the global male unemployment rate was 6.1%. Both rates had risen over the 10 years since 1993, when the female rate was 5.8% and the male rate was 5.5%.

In countries that do not have unemployment insurance, most people cannot afford to be unemployed if they lose their jobs, and so they have to find some kind of informal paid work. Informal employment, which tends to be low paid and insecure and lacks social protection, is a persistent feature of global capitalism. Typically, a higher proportion of women's employment is in informal rather than formal employment. Men tend to be somewhat less concentrated in informal employment and their informal employment tends to be somewhat better paid and less precarious.

The report recommends that:

- *Creation of decent work should be a target of macroeconomic policy, with specific targets for reduction of female unemployment, and increase in proportion of employed women who enjoy decent work.*

The report discusses the pressure to cut public expenditure. Examples are provided of how expenditure on services most crucial to the well-being of poor women has been cut more than other expenditures. The report recommends that:

- *Expenditure cuts should be closely examined to determine whether they violate the principle of 'non-retrogression'. If these are retrogressive measures that affect equality, then the State has failed to meet its obligation.*
- *Debt should be cancelled so that highly indebted poor countries can increase expenditure critical to the well-being of women.*

The report discusses emerging evidence that macroeconomic policies that are based on high levels of *both* tax revenue *and* public expenditure are more conducive to gender equality and advancement of women. The report recommends that:

- *Governments should not be pressured to aim for low ratios of tax and expenditure to GNP.*
- *Benchmarks for appropriate ratios of tax and expenditure to GNP should be derived from countries with high levels of gender equality and advancement of women.*

The report concludes that many governments have adopted, or had imposed on them, very restrictive policy rules that make it difficult to consider alternatives that would be better able to comply with CEDAW. These rules include balanced budget rules and specific limits on the debt to GDP ratio and the budget deficit to GDP ratio. The report recommends:

- *More flexible rules for macroeconomic policy.*

The report concludes that it is vital to consider alternative macroeconomic policies because there is no simple rule that can validly be applied everywhere at all times. As John Loxley, one of the leaders of the Canadian Alternative Federal Budget, puts it, 'There is, however, no magic number representing the point at which the running of deficits or increases in debt should cease'. There is always an alternative macroeconomic strategy that is *economically* feasible; but different strategies imply different distributions of the costs and benefits. The report recommends:

- *Extensive and inclusive public dialogue about the macroeconomic strategy implemented through the budget, rather than reserving macroeconomic policy to a small group of officials.*

8. Conclusions and recommendations on budget decision-making processes

The report clarifies that CEDAW (especially Article 7) obliges governments to take all appropriate measures to ensure that women participate on equal terms with men in budget decision processes.

The report considers the four phases on budget decision-making:
- formulation
- approval and enactment into law
- implementation
- audit and evaluation.

The report concludes that nowhere are women yet playing an equal role with men. However, special measures and/or reforms of the decision-making process have increased women's participation, especially at the local level, in some countries, including India and Brazil. Where this has happened there is emerging evidence of changes in spending patterns to better address women's priorities (e.g. more expenditure on water and sanitation).

Links are also being built in some countries between GBIs and women elected representatives, and GBIs are building the capacity of women elected representatives, through training and through production of Briefing Notes. There are also examples of successful grass-roots mobilization of women to hold governments to account for their allocation and use of public expenditure. However, such efforts are hampered by lack of information, especially sex-disaggregated information, and lack of means of redress if money is misspent.

The report concludes that to achieve full equality for women in budget decision-making requires:
- increasing the presence of women
- increasing the capacity of women
- reforming budget decision-making processes to make them more transparent and participatory.

The report recommends special measures to increase women's presence in:

- *national parliaments, and in parliamentary committees that scrutinize budgets*
- *local councils, and in council committees responsible for budgets*
- *participatory planning and budget processes.*

The report recommends:

- *ongoing support for existing efforts to build links between women elected representatives and GBIs*
- *support for new efforts to build links between women elected representatives and GBIs.*

The report recommends that men and women, as full participants in the life of their country, must have:

- *a right to information, including sex-disaggregated information*
- *a right to demand a formal investigation or seek legal redress for misappropriation of funds and poor delivery of services.*

The collective mobilization of women to actively use CEDAW and to actively use GBIs will be needed to bring about real changes and the full implementation of the vision of gender equality and the advancement of women that is set out in the Convention.

ARTICLES, BOOKS, REPORTS AND RESEARCH PAPERS

Abbo, E. & Reinikka, R. (1998) *Do Budgets Really Matter? Evidence from Public Spending on Education and Health in Uganda,* World Bank Policy Research Working Paper, 1926.

Acharya, M. (2003) *Gender Budget Audit in Nepal,* 'Follow the Money' Series 2, United Nations Development Fund for Women (UNIFEM), New Delhi.

Adelzadeh, A. (2001) *NIEP Social Policy Model: a policy tool for fighting poverty in South Africa,* National Institute for Economic Policy (NIEP), Johannesburg.

Anderson, D. M. (1999) 'Tax Policy' in Peterson, J. & Lewis, M. (eds.) (1999) *The Elgar Companion to Feminist Economics,* Edward Elgar, Cheltenham.

Andia-Perez, B. & Beltran-Barco, A. (2004) 'Analysis of the Public Budget with a Gender Approach: Villa El Salvador, Lima, Peru' in UNIFEM (ed.) *Toward Transparency and Governance with Gender Equity: Gender-sensitive Budgets in the Andean Region,* UNIFEM, New York.

Appleberry, R. (2001) 'Breaking the Camel's Back: Bringing Women's Human Rights to Bear on Tobacco Control', *Yale Journal of Law and Feminism* 13:71, 84.

Banerjee, N. (2003) *What is Gender Budgeting? Public Policies from Women's Perspective in the Indian Context,* 'Follow the Money' Series 1, United Nations Development Fund for Women (UNIFEM), New Delhi.

Banerjee, N. & Sen, J. (2003) *Swarnajayanti Gram Swarojgar Yojana. A Budgetary Policy in Working,* 'Follow the Money' Series 6, United Nations Development Fund for Women, (UNIFEM), New Delhi.

Barnett, K. & Grown, C. (2004) *Gender Impacts of Government Revenue Collection: The Case of Taxation*, Economic Paper 62, Commonwealth Secretariat, London.

Budlender, D. (ed.) (1996) *The Women's Budget*, Institute for Democracy in South Africa (IDASA), Cape Town.

Budlender, D. (2000) 'The Political Economy of Women's Budgets in the South',*World Development,* 28(7):1365-1378.

Budlender, D. (2003) *Budgeting to Fulfill International Gender Commitments,* United Nations Development Fund for Women (UNIFEM), Southern African Regional Office (SARO), Zimbabwe.

Budlender, D., Buenaobra, M., Rood, S. & Sadorra, M. (eds.) (2001) *Gender Budget Trail: The Philippine Experience,* Asia Foundation, Makati City.

Budlender, D., Elson, D., Hewitt, G. & Mukhopadhyay, T. (2002) *Gender Budgets Make Cents,* Commonwealth Secretariat, London.

Budlender, D. & Hewitt, G. (2002) *Gender Budgets Make More Cents. Country Studies and Good Practice,* Commonwealth Secretariat, London.

Budlender, D. & Sharp, R. (1998) *How to do a gender-sensitive budget analysis: Contemporary research and practice,* Commonwealth Secretariat, London.

Byanyima, W. (2002) 'Parliamentary Governance and Gender Budgeting: The Uganda Experience' in United Nations Development Fund for Women (UNIFEM), *Gender Budget Initiatives. Strategies, Concepts and Experiences,* UNIFEM, New York.

Byrnes, A. (1996) 'Human Rights Instruments Relating Specifically to Women, with Particular Emphasis on the Convention on the Elimination of all Forms of Discrimination Against Women, Advancing the Human Rights of Women: Using International Human Rights Standards in Domestic Litigation' (Papers and Statements from the Asia/South Pacific Regional Judicial Colloquium, Hong Kong, 20-22 May 1996), http://www.law-lib.utoronto.ca/Diana/fulltext/byrne.htm

Byrnes, A. (2003) 'The Use of International Human Rights Instruments in Domestic Litigation' (draft) (copy on file with International Women's Rights Action Watch (IWRAW)—Asia Pacific).

Caharian, M. & Lampauog, C. (2001) 'Gender Budgeting in the Philippines: A Review of the GAD Budget Policy Experience', in Budlender, D., Buenaobra, M., Rood, S. & Sadorra, M. (eds.) (2001) *Gender Budget Trail: The Philippine Experience*, Asia Foundation, Makati City.

Centro de Derchos Economicos y Sociales (CDES) (2000) Peticion ante la Comision Interamericana de Derechos Humanos en lo referente a violaciones de la Convencion de la OEA con respecto a los ajustes economicos en el Ecuador, http://cdes.org.ec/a-promo.htm

Chang, H-J., (2002) *Kicking Away the Ladder: Development Strategy in Historical Perspective,* Anthem Press, London.

Chattopadhyay, R. & Duflo, E. (2004) 'Impact of reservations in Panchayati Raj: Evidence from a nationwide randomized experiment', *Economic and Political Weekly,* 39 (9):979-986.

Cho, H., Zammit, A., Chung, J. & Kang, I. (2004) 'Korea's Miracle and Crisis: What Was In It For Women?' in Razavi, S., Pearson, R., & Danloy, C. (eds.) *Globalization, Export-Oriented Employment and Social Policy: Gendered Connections,* Palgrave, Houndmills.

Clark, W. (2000) 'Economic Gender Equality Indicators 2000', Status of Women Canada. Online document accessed at http://www.sws-cfc.gc.ca/publish/egei/layout.pdf

Colinas, M. (2003) 'Gender Budgets and Development Planning in Mexico', MA Thesis, University of Essex.

Coopoo, S. (2000) 'Women and local government revenue', in *The Women's Budget Series,* IDASA, Community Agency for Social Enquiry and the Parliamentary Committee on the Quality of Life and Status of Women, Cape Town.

Cos-Montiel, F. (2004) 'Macro or Microstreaming Gender Economics? Engendering Economic Policy in Mexico', paper presented at conference on Engendering Macroeconomics and International Economics, June, University of Utah, Salt Lake City.

Creamer, K. (2002) *The impact of South Africa's evolving jurisprudence on children's socio-economic rights on budget analysis,* IDASA, Cape Town.

Crow, M. E. (2004) 'Smokescreens and state responsibility: using human rights strategies to promote global tobacco control', *Yale Journal of International Law* 29:209.

Day, S. & Brodsky, G. (1998) *Women and the Equality Deficit: The Impact of Restructuring Canada's Social Programs,* Status of Women Canada, Ottawa.

Demery, L. (2002) 'Gender and Public Spending: Insights from Benefit Incidence' in United Nations Development Fund for Women (UNIFEM) *Gender Budget Initiatives. Strategies, Concepts and Experiences,* UNIFEM, New York.

Department of National Planning, Ministry of Finance and Planning, Government of Sri Lanka (2000) *Engendering the National Budget of Sri Lanka,* Centre for Women's Research (CENWOR), Colombo.

Dhooge, L. (1998) 'Smoke Across the Waters: Tobacco Production and Exportation as International Human Rights Violations', *Fordham International Law Journal* 22:355, 414

Diokno, M. (1999) *A Rights-Based Approach Towards Budget Analysis,* International Human Rights Internship Program, Washington, D.C.

Economic Commission for Latin America and the Caribbean (ECLAC) (1998) *The Fiscal Covenant. Strengths, Weaknesses, Challenges,* ECLAC, United Nations, Santiago, Chile.

Elson, D. (1995) 'Gender Awareness in Modeling Structural Adjustment', *World Development,* 23 (11):1851-1868.

Elson, D. (1997) 'Tools for gender integration into macroeconomic policy', in *Link in to Gender and Development, 2,* Summer: 13, Commonwealth Secretariat, London.

Elson, D. (2002) 'Gender Justice, Human Rights and Neoliberal Economic Policies' in M. Molyneux and S. Razavi (eds.) *Gender Justice, Development, and Rights*, Oxford University Press, Oxford.

Elson, D. (ed.) (2000) *Progress of the World's Women*, United Nations Development Fund for Women (UNIFEM), New York.

Elson, D. (2004a) 'Feminist Economics Challenges Mainstream Macroeconomics', *IAFFE Newsletter*,14 (3):6-9.

Elson, D. (2004b) 'Engendering Government Budgets in the Context of Globalization(s)', *International Feminist Journal of Politics,* 6 (4):623-642.

Elson, D. & Cagatay, N. (2000) 'The Social Content of Macroeconomic Policies', *World Development,* 28(7): 1347-1364.

Elson, D. & Keklik, H. (2002) *Progress of the world's women 2002.* Volume 2, United Nations Development Fund for Women (UNIFEM), New York.

Erturk, K. & Cagatay, N. (1995) 'Macroeconomic Consequences of Cyclical and Secular Changes in Feminization: An Experiment at Gendered Macromodeling', *World Development,* 23(11): 1969-1977.

Esim, S. (2000) *Impact of government budgets on poverty and gender equality*, Paper prepared for the Inter-Agency Workshop on Improving the Effectiveness of Integrating Gender Into Government Budgets, April 26-27, Commonwealth Secretariat, London.

Fontana, M. (2003) 'Modeling the effects of trade on women, at work and at home: A comparative perspective', *TMD Discussion Paper No. 110*, Trade and Macroeconomics Division, International Food Policy Research Institute, Washington, D.C.

Fodor, E. (2004) 'Women at Work. The Status of Women in the Labour Markets of Czech Republic, Hungary and Poland', Background Paper for UNRISD report, *Gender Equality: Striving for Justice in an Unequal World.*

Forum for Women In Democracy (FOWODE) (2002) *Pallisa District 2000/2001 Gender Budget Analysis Issues Brief,* FOWODE, Kampala.

Forum for Women In Democracy (FOWODE) (2003) *Speak,* Issue No. 5, Kampala.

Freiler, C., Stairs, F. & Kitchen, B. (2001) 'Mothers as Earners, Mothers as Carers: Responsibility for Children, Social Policy and the Tax System', Status of Women, Canada. Online document accessed at http://www.swc-cfc.gc.ca/pubs/

Gobierno de Chile, Ministerio de Hacienda, Direccion de Presupuestos (2001) *Enfoque de Genero,* Santiago, Chile.

Goetz, A-M. (2003) 'Reinventing Accountability—Making Democracy Work for the Poor', Paper presented to World Bank Community of Practice on Social Accountability Launch, Washington, D.C.

Goetz, A-M. & Jenkins, R. (1999) 'Accountability to Women in Development Spending—Experiments in Service-Delivery Audits at the Local Level', Paper presented at UNDP conference on Gender, Poverty and Environment-Sensitive Budget Analysis, New York.

Goetz, A-M. & Jenkins, R. (2004) *Reinventing Accountability: Making Democracy Work for the Poor,* Palgrave, London.

Goldman, T. (2000) 'Customs and excise paper', in *The Women's Budget Series,* 2000 Issue, IDASA, Community Agency for Social Enquiry and the Parliamentary Committee on the Quality of Life and Status of Women, Cape Town.

Goldman, T. & Budlender, D. (1999) *Making the Act Work, A Research Study into the Budget Allocations for the Implementation of the Domestic Violence Act,* Gender Advocacy Project, Cape Town.

Gore, R. & Minujin, A. (2003) *Budget Initiative for Children,* Global Policy Section, United Nations Children's Fund (UNICEF), United Nations, New York.

Govender, P. (2002) 'Lesson from Practice: The Role of Parliament in South Africa's Women's Budget' in United Nations Development Fund for Women (UNIFEM), *Gender Budget Initiatives. Strategies, Concepts and Experiences,* UNIFEM, New York.

Grown, C., Gupta, G. R. & Kes, A. (2005) *Taking Action: Achieving Gender Equality and Empowering Women,* Taskforce on Education and Gender Equality, UN Millennium Project, Earthscan, London.

Grunberg, I. (1998) 'Double Jeopardy: Globalization, Liberalization, and the Fiscal Squeeze', *World Development,* 26(4):591-605.

Grynspan, R. (2003) 'Economic Policies, Public Spending and Gender-differentiated Effects' in Gutierrez, M. (ed.) *Macro-economics: Making Gender Matter,* Zed Books, London.

Gutierrez, M. (2004) 'Public Budgets with a Gender Approach: A Look at the National Budget of Bolivia and the Municipal Budget of La Paz' in UNIFEM (ed.) *Toward Transparency and Governance with Gender Equity: Gender-sensitive Budgets in the Andean Region,* UNIFEM, New York.

Hartzenberg, T. (1996) 'Taxation' in Budlender, D. (ed.) (1996) *The Women's Budget,* Institute for Democracy in South Africa (IDASA), Cape Town.

Heintz, J. (2004) 'Inflation Reduction and Women's Formal Employment', Mimeo, Political Economy Research Institute, University of Massachusetts, Amherst.

Hewitt, G. (2002) 'The Commonwealth Secretariat: The role of external agencies', in Budlender, D. & Hewitt, G. (2002) *Gender Budgets Make More Cents. Country Studies and Good Practice,* Commonwealth Secretariat, London.

Himmelweit, S. (2002) 'Making Visible the Hidden Economy: The Case for Gender-Impact analysis of Economic Policy', *Feminist Economics,* 8(1): 49-70.

Hirschl, R. (2000) ' "Negative" Rights vs. "Positive" Entitlements: A Comparative Study of Judicial Interpretations of Rights in an Emerging Neo-liberal Economic Order', *Human Rights Quarterly,* 22(4):1060-1098.

Hofbauer, H. (2000) *Women, Human Rights and Budget Analysis,* FUNDAR, Center for Analysis and Research, Cuernavaca and Women's Economic Equality Project, Cape Town.

Hofbauer, H. (2002) 'Mexico: Collaborating with a wide range of actors' in Budlender, D. & Hewitt, G. (2002) *Gender Budgets Make More Cents. Country Studies and Good Practice,* Commonwealth Secretariat, London.

Hofbauer, H. (2003) *Overview Report. Gender and Budgets,* Cutting Edge Pack,   BRIDGE, Institute of Development Studies, University of Sussex.

Hofbauer, H., Lara, G. & Martinez, B. (2002) *Health Care: A Question of Human Rights, Not Charity,* FUNDAR, Center for Analysis and Research, Cuernavaca.

Huber, E. (2003) 'Gendered Implications of Tax Reform in Latin America: Argentina, Chile, Costa Rica and Jamaica', Working Paper, UNRISD project on Gender and Social Policy.

Huber, E., Bradley D., Moller, S., Nielson, F. & Stephens, J. (2001) 'The Welfare State and Gender Equality', Luxembourg Income Study, Working Paper No. 279.

Independent Evaluation Office (IEO), International Monetary Fund (IMF) (2004) *Report on the Evaluation of Poverty Reduction Strategy Papers (PRSPs) and the Poverty Reduction and Growth Facility (PRGF),* www.imf.org/External/NP/ieo/2004/prspprgf/eng/index.htm

Inter-American Commission on Human Rights (1997) Report of the Situation of Human Rights in Ecuador, http://www.cidh.org/countryrep/ecuador-eng/index

International Bureau of Fiscal Documentation (1995) 'Taxation and Investment in Asia and the Pacific', Singapore, March 1995.

International Center for Research on Women (ICRW) (2003) *How to Make the Law Work? Budgetary Implications of Domestic Violence Policies in Latin America,* ICRW, Washington, D.C.

International Labour Office (ILO) (1998) *Declaration on Fundamental Principles and Rights at Work,* www.ilo.org/dyn/declaris/DECLARATIONWEB.INDEXPAGE

International Labour Office (ILO) (2002) *Women and Men in the Informal Economy. A Statistical Picture.* Employment Sector, ILO, Geneva.

International Labour Office (ILO) (2004a) *World and Regional Trends in Youth Employment*, Paper prepared for the Expert Group Meeting on the Monitoring of the Millennium Development Goals, Employment Trends Team, Employment Strategy Department, Geneva.

International Labour Office (ILO) (2004b) *Global Employment Trends for Women 2004,* http://www.ilo.org/public/english/employment

International Monetary Fund (2000) Debt Initiative for the Highly Indebted Poor Countries, www.imf.org/external

Inter-Parliamentary Union (IPU) (2001) *Parliament and the Budgetary Process, Including from a Gender Perspective,* Report of Regional Seminar for English-Speaking African Parliamentarians, IPU, Geneva.

Jain, D. (2004) 'Localising the Global: the double challenge of decentralization and the inclusion of women', Paper presented to International Meeting on Local Level Gender Budgeting, India International Centre, New Delhi.

James, B. & Simmonds, G. (1997) 'Energy' in Budlender (ed.) (1997) *The Second Women's Budget,* Institute for Democracy in South Africa (IDASA), Cape Town.

Jubilee Research (2005) Jubilee Debt Campaign Briefing, http://www.jubilee2000uk.org/hipc/progress_report/briefing070103.htm

Karnataka Women's Information and Resource Centre (2002) *Building Budgets From Below,* Karnataka Women's Information and Resource Centre, Bangalore.

Kaushik, P. D. (ed.) (1996) *New Dimensions of Government and Politics of Nepal,* South Asian Publishers, New Delhi.

Lee, J-K. (2003) *The Impact of the East Asian Crisis on Korean Women's Employment,* Research paper, Department of Sociology, University of Essex.

Loxley, J. (2003) *Alternative Budgets. Budgeting as if People Mattered*, Fernwood Publishing, Winnipeg.

Mackintosh, M. & Tibandebage, P. (2004) 'Gender and Health Sector Reform: Analytical Perspectives on African Experience', Background paper for UNRISD report, *Gender Equality: Striving for Justice in an Unequal World.*

Mawhiney, A-M. (1997) 'Social and Institutional Costs Sub-Project Analytic Paper' Elliot Lake Tracking Study, Mimeo.

Mehrotra, S. & Delamonica, E. (forthcoming) *Public Spending for the Poor: Getting the Fundamentals Right on Macro-*

economic and Social Policy.

Ministry of Rural Development (2000) *Annual Report 1999-2000,* Ministry of Rural Development, Government of India, New Delhi.

Nanda, P. (2002) 'Gender dimensions of user fees: implications for women's utilization of health care', *Reproductive Health Matters,* 10(20): 127-134.

National Institute of Public Finance and Policy (NIPFP) (2003) *Gender Budgeting in India, 'Follow the Money' Series 3,* United Nations Development Fund for Women (UNIFEM), New Delhi.

National Commission on the Role of Filipino Women (NCRFW) (1999) *Planning and Budgeting for Gender Equality: The Philippine Experience,* NCRFW, Manila.

Nelson, J. A. (1996) 'Tax reform and feminist theory in the USA: incorporating human connection', *Journal of Economic Studies,* 18 (5/6): 11-29.

Norton, A. & Elson, D. (2002) *What's Behind the Budget? Politics, Rights and Accountability in the Budget Process,* Overseas Development Institute, London.

Pearl, R. (2002) 'The Andean Region: A multi-country programme', in Budlender, D. & Hewitt, G. (2002) *Gender Budgets Make More Cents. Country Studies and Good Practice,* Commonwealth Secretariat, London.

Philippe-Raynaud, F. (2001) 'The Yellow Budget Paper and Gender Equality in France', in United Nations Development Fund for Women (UNIFEM), *Gender Budget Initiatives. Strategies, Concepts and Experiences,* UNIFEM, New York.

Philipps, L. (2002) 'Tax Law and Social Reproduction: The Gender of Fiscal Policy in an Age of Privatization', in Cossman, B. & Fudge, J. (eds.), *Privatization, Law, and the Challenge to Feminism,* University of Toronto Press.

Pillay, K., Manjou, R. & Paulus, E. (2002) *Rights, Roles and Resources: An Analysis of Women's Housing Rights – Implications of the Grootboom case,* Women's Budget Initiative, Cape Town.

Prescod, M. (2002) 'Budget Implementation Practices in Jamaica: A Review with Emphasis on the Consequences for Social Sector Spending', Background study for Jamaica Social Policy Evaluation Project.

Reed, B., Coates, C., Parry-Jones, S. & Smout I. (forthcoming) *Infrastructure for All: a practical guide for engineers, technicians and project managers on how they can meet the needs of both men and women in development projects,* Water, Engineering and Development Centre, University of Loughborough.

Republic of South Africa (1998) *Budget Review,* Pretoria: Department of Finance.

Reyes, C. (2002) 'Institutionalizing a Gender and Development Initiative in the Philippines', in United Nations Development Fund for Women (UNIFEM) *Gender Budget Initiatives. Strategies, Concepts and Experiences,* UNIFEM, New York.

Robinson, S. & Biersteker, L. (1997) *First Call: The South African Children's Budget,* Institute for Democracy in South Africa (IDASA), Cape Town.

Rusimbi, M. (2002) 'Mainstreaming Gender into Policy, Planning and Budgeting in Tanzania', in United Nations Development Fund for Women (UNIFEM), *Gender Budget Initiatives. Strategies, Concepts and Experiences,* UNIFEM, New York.

Sawer, M. (2002) 'Australia: The mandarin approach to gender budgets', in Budlender, D. & Hewitt, G. (2002) *Gender Budgets Make More Cents. Country Studies and Good Practice,* Commonwealth Secretariat, London.

Seguino, S. (2003) 'Is Economic Growth Good for Well-being? Evidence of Gender Effects in Latin America and the Caribbean 1970-2000', Background paper, United Nations Millennium Project, Taskforce on Education and Gender Equality.

Sen, A. K. (1998) 'Human development and financial conservatism', *World Development,* 26(4).

Senapaty, M. (1997) 'Gender Dimensions of Structural Adjustment and Macroeconomic Strategies in India', PhD Thesis, University of Manchester.

Senapaty, M. (2000a) *Government of India Budget 2000-2001 and Gender,* report for the Inter-Agency Workshop on Improving the Effectiveness of Integrating Gender into Government Budgets, Marlborough House, London (26-27 April 2000).

Senapaty, M. (2000b) 'Report of the Workshop on Gender Budgets', United Nations Development Fund for Women (UNIFEM), New Delhi.

Sharp, R. (2002) 'Moving Forward: Multiple Strategies and Guiding Goals' in United Nations Development Fund for Women (UNIFEM), *Gender Budget Initiatives. Strategies, Concepts and Experiences,* UNIFEM, New York.

Sharp, R. (2003) *Budgeting for Equity. Gender budget initiatives within a framework of performance oriented budgeting*, United Nations Development Fund for Women (UNIFEM), United Nations, New York.

Sharp, R. & Broomhill, R. (2002) 'Budgeting for Equality: The Australian Experience', *Feminist Economics,* 8(1):25-47.

Shultz, J. (2002) *Promises to Keep. Using Public Budgets as a Tool to Advance Economic, Social and Cultural Rights,* FUNDAR, Center for Analysis and Research, Cuernavaca.

Smith, T. (2000) 'Women and Tax in South Africa', in *The Women's Budget Series*, Institute for Democracy in South Africa (IDASA), Community Agency for Social Enquiry (CASE) and the Parliamentary Committee on the Quality of Life and Status of Women, Cape Town.

St. Hill, D. (2000) *Gender Analysis of the National Budget: 1998-1999: Barbados Pilot.* (Draft, April, 2000), Commonwealth Secretariat, London.

Stevens, M. (1997) 'Health', in Budlender, D. (ed.) (1997) *The Second Women's Budget,* Joint Standing Committee on Finance (Gender and Economic Policy Group), the Community Agency for Social Enquiry (CASE), the Law Race & Gender Project (University of Cape Town), & the Institute for Democracy in South Africa (IDASA), Cape Town.

Stiglitz, J. (2002) *Globalization and its discontents,* Penguin Books, London.

Stotsky, J. (1996) *Gender Bias in Tax Systems,* International Monetary Fund (IMF) Working Paper/96/99.

Strategic Analysis for Gender Equality & San Francisco Commission on the Status of Women (1999) *Guidelines for a Gender Analysis of City Departments in the City and County of San Francisco,* Commission on Status of Women, San Francisco.

Streak, J. & Wehner, J. (2002) *Budgeting for socio-economic rights in South Africa: The case of the child support grant programme,* Institute for Democracy in South Africa (IDASA), Cape Town.

Sugiyama, N. (2002) 'Gendered Budget Work in the Americas: Selected Country Experiences', Mimeo, Department of Government, University of Texas, Austin.

Sutherland, H. (2000) 'Gender accounting of Budget changes with illustrations from the 2000 Budget', Mimeo, University of Cambridge.

TGNP (2004) *Gender Budget Analysis in Tanzania,1997 - 2000,* Tanzania Gender Networking Programme (TGNP), Dar es Salaam.

Toynbee, P. (2001) 'Better than men. Special Report: New Labour in power', *The Guardian,* March 16.

United Nations Development Programme (UNDP) (1991) *Human Development Report 1991,* Oxford University Press, New York.

United Nations Development Programme (UNDP) (2000) *Human Development Report 2000,* Oxford University Press, New York.

UNDP, UNESCO,UNFPA, UNICEF, WHO and WORLD BANK (1998) *Implementing the 20/20 Initiative: Achieving Universal Access to Basic Social Services,* UNICEF, New York.

United Nations Development Fund for Women UNIFEM (1998) *En-gendering the ninth five-year plan of India (1997-2002),* UNIFEM, New Delhi.

United Nations Development Fund for Women (UNIFEM) (2002) *Gender Budget Initiatives. Strategies, Concepts and Experiences,* UNIFEM, New York.

United Nations Research Institute for Social Development (UNRISD) (2005) *Gender Equality: Striving for Justice in an Unequal World,* UNRISD, Geneva.

Valodia, I. (1998) 'Finance, State Expenditure, SA Revenue Service and Central Statistical Service' in D. Budlender (ed.) *The Third Women's Budget*, Institute for Democracy in South Africa (IDASA), Cape Town.

Van Staveren, I. & Akram-Lodhi, A. H. (2003) 'A Gender Analysis of the Impact of Indirect Taxes on Small and Medium Enterprises in Vietnam', Paper presented at Conference of International Association for Feminist Economics, 27-29 June, University of the West Indies, Barbados.

Vandemoortele, J. (2002) 'Shortcuts to Public Service Provision? User Fees and Narrow Targeting', in United Nations Development Fund for Women (UNIFEM), *Gender Budget Initiatives. Strategies, Concepts and Experiences,* UNIFEM, New York.

Vargas-Valente, V. (2002) 'Municipal Budgets and Democratic Governance in the Andean Region', in United Nations Development Fund for Women (UNIFEM), *Gender Budget Initiatives. Strategies, Concepts and Experiences,* UNIFEM, New York.

Villota, P. de & Ferrari, I. (2001) 'The Impact of the Tax/Benefit System on Women's Work', Mimeo, Universidad Complutense de Madrid.

Wanyaka, S. H., Sulait, K. & Francis, K. (2003) *Report on gender budget analysis of taxation in Uganda,* Mimeo, United Nations Development Fund for Women (UNIFEM), Nairobi.

World Bank, Participation and Civic Engagement Group (2003) *Social Accountability: A Concept Note Based on Emerging Practice,* Mimeo, World Bank, Washington, D.C.

Young, C. (1999) 'Taxing Times for Women: Feminism Confronts Tax Policy', Dunhill Madden Butler Lecture, Faculty of Law, University of Sydney. Online document accessed at http://80-web.lexis-nexis.com.osiyou.cc

Young, C. (2000) 'Women, Tax and Social Programs; The Gendered Impact of Funding Social Programs Through the Tax System', Status of Women, Canada. Online document accessed at http://www.sws-cfc.gc.ca/pubs/

INTERNATIONAL HUMAN RIGHTS INSTRUMENTS

Convention on the Elimination of All Forms of Discrimination against Women, GA Res. A/RES/39/46, UN GAOR, 39th Session, (Supp. No.51), UN Doc. A/39/51 (1986), Can. T.S. 1987 No.36.

International Covenant on Economic, Social and Cultural Rights, GA Res. 2200A (XXI), 21 UN GAOR, (Supp. No. 16) 59, UN Doc. A6316 (1966), 999 U.N.T.S. 302, Can. T.S. 1976 No. 47.

Convention on the Rights of the Child, GA Res. 44/25, UN GAOR, 44th Session, (Supp. No. 49), UN Doc. A/44/49 (1989).

UNITED NATIONS HUMAN RIGHTS DOCUMENTS

Commission on Human Rights

Cheru, F. (2001) 'The Highly Indebted Poor Countries (HIPC) Initiative: a human rights assessment of the Poverty Reduction Strategy papers', UN Commission on Human Rights, E/CN.4/2001/56.

Mudho, B. (2004) ' Effects of structural adjustment policies and foreign debt on the full enjoyment of human rights, particularly economic, social and cultural rights', UN Commission on Human Rights, E/CN.4/2004/47.

United Nations Office of the High Commission on Human Rights (UNOHCHR) (2001) Effects of structural adjustment policies and foreign debt on the full enjoyment of all human rights, particularly economic, social and cultural rights. Commission on Human Rights Resolution 2001/27.

Committee on the Elimination of Discrimination Against Women

United Nations, Committee on the Elimination of Discrimination Against Women (1989)
General Recommendation No. 13: Equal Remuneration for Work of Equal Value
http://www.un.org/womenwatch/daw/cedaw/recomm.htm

United Nations, Committee on the Elimination of Discrimination Against Women (1991)
General Recommendation No. 16: Unpaid Women Workers in Rural and Urban Family Enterprises
http://www.un.org/womenwatch/daw/cedaw/recomm.htm

United Nations, Committee on the Elimination of Discrimination Against Women (1991)
General Recommendation No.17: Measurement and quantification of the unremunerated domestic activities of women and their recognition in the gross national product
http://www.un.org/womenwatch/daw/cedaw/recomm.htm

United Nations, Committee on the Elimination of Discrimination Against Women (1992)
General Recommendation No. 19: Violence Against Women
http://www.un.org/womenwatch/daw/cedaw/recomm.htm

United Nations, Committee on the Elimination of Discrimination Against Women (1994)
General Recommendation No. 21: Equality in Marriage and Family Relations

http://www.un.org/womenwatch/daw/cedaw/recomm.htm

United Nations, Committee on the Elimination of Discrimination Against Women (1996)
Concluding Comments of the Committee on the Elimination of Discrimination Against Women: Belgium,
UN Doc. A/51/38 22 at para. 191 (2 February 1996)

United Nations, Committee on the Elimination of Discrimination Against Women (1997)
General Recommendation No. 23: Political and Public Life
http://www.un.org/womenwatch/daw/cedaw/recomm.htm

United Nations, Committee on the Elimination of Discrimination Against Women (1997)
Initial Periodic Reports of States Parties: South Africa.

United Nations, Committee on the Elimination of Discrimination Against Women (1999)
General Recommendation No. 24: Women and Health
http://www.un.org/womenwatch/daw/cedaw/recomm.htm

United Nations, Committee on the Elimination of Discrimination Against Women (1999)
Concluding Comments of the Committee on the Elimination of Discrimination Against Women: Kyrgyzstan.
UN Doc. A/54/38/Rev.1.part I 15 at para. 134 (5 February 1999).

United Nations, Committee on the Elimination of Discrimination Against Women (1999)
Second Periodic Reports of States Parties: Jordan.
UN Document CEDAW/C/JOR/2 (26 October 1999).

United Nations, Committee on the Elimination of Discrimination Against Women (2000)
Concluding Comments of the Committee on the Elimination of Discrimination Against Women: Luxembourg.
UN Doc. A/55/38, paras. 379-416 (21 January 2000).

United Nations, Committee on the Elimination of Discrimination Against Women (2000)
Concluding Comments of the Committee on the Elimination of Discrimination Against Women: Germany.
UN Doc. A/55/38 part I 29 at para. 314 (4 February 2002).

United Nations, Committee on the Elimination of Discrimination Against Women (2000)
Concluding Comments of the Committee on the Elimination of Discrimination Against Women: Austria, UN
Doc. A/55/38, paras. 211-243 (15 June 2000).

United Nations, Committee on the Elimination of Discrimination Against Women (2002)
Concluding Comments of the Committee on the Elimination of Discrimination Against Women: Fiji,
UN Doc. A/57/38 (Part I), paras. 24-70 (7 May 2002).

United Nations, Committee on the Elimination of Discrimination Against Women (2002)
Concluding Comments of the Committee on the Elimination of Discrimination Against Women: Argentina,
UN Doc. A/57/38 part III 196, paras. 356 and 357 (23 August 2002).

United Nations, Committee on the Elimination of Discrimination Against Women (2002)
Fifth Periodic Reports of States Parties: France, UN Doc. CEDAW/C/FRA/5 (26 September 2002).

United Nations, Committee on the Elimination of Discrimination Against Women (2003)
Concluding Comments of the Committee on the Elimination of Discrimination Against Women: Brazil,
UN Doc. A/58/38 part II 93 (18 July 2003).

Committee on Economic, Social and Cultural Rights

United Nations, Committee on Economic, Social and Cultural Rights (1990)
General comment 3: The nature of States Parties obligations (Art.2, para. 1) (14 December 1990).

United Nations, Committee on Economic, Social and Cultural Rights (1991)
General comment 4: The right to adequate housing (Art.11(1)) (13 December1991).

United Nations, Committee on Economic, Social and Cultural Rights (1994)
Concluding Observations of the Committee on Economic, Social and Cultural Rights: Morocco, UN Doc.
E/1995/22 (1994) 28 at para. 119 (19 May 1994).

'The Maastricht Guidelines on Violations of Economic, Social and Cultural Rights', *Human Rights Quarterly*, Vol. 20
(1998): 691-705.

United Nations, Committee on Economic, Social and Cultural Rights (1998)

Concluding Observations of the Committee on Economic, Social and Cultural Rights: Canada, UN Doc. E/C.12/1/Add.31 (10 December 1998).

United Nations, Committee on Economic, Social and Cultural Rights (1999)
General comment 11: plans of action for primary education (Art. 14), UN Doc. E/C.12/1999/4 (10 May 1999).

United Nations, Committee on Economic, Social and Cultural Rights (1999)
General comment 12: The right to adequate food (Art.11) (12 May 1999)

United Nations, Committee on Economic, Social and Cultural Rights (1999)
General comment 13: The right to education (Art. 13), UN Document E/C.12/1999/10 (8 December 1999).

United Nations, Committee on Economic, Social and Cultural Rights (2000)
General comment 14: The right to the highest attainable standard of health (Art. 12), UN Doc. E/C.12/2000/4 (11 August, 2000).

United Nations, Committee on Economic, Social and Cultural Rights (2001)
Poverty and the International Covenant on Economic, Social and Cultural Rights, UN Doc. E/C.12/2001/10 (10 May 2001).

United Nations, Committee on Economic, Social and Cultural Rights (2003)
General comment 15: The right to water (Arts. 11 and 12), UN Doc. E/C.12/2002/11 (20 January 2003).

United Nations, Committee on Economic, Social and Cultural Rights (2005)
General comment 16: Article 3: the equal right of men and women to the enjoyment of all economic, social and cultural rights (13 May 2005) (unedited version).

Committee on the Rights of the Child

United Nations, Committee on the Rights of the Child (1996) *General Guidelines for periodic reports,* UN Doc. CRC/C/58 (20 November 1996).

United Nations, Committee on the Rights of the Child (2002) *Concluding observations of the Committee on the Rights of the Child: Israel,* UN Doc. CRC/C/15/Add.195 (10 October 2002).

United Nations, Committee on the Rights of the Child (2003) *General comment 5: General measures of implementation for the Convention on the Rights of the Child,* UN Doc. CRC/GC/2003/5 (3 October 2003).

United Nations, Committee on the Rights of the Child, *Concluding observations of the Committee on the Rights of the Child: Sri Lanka,* UN Doc. CRC/C/15/Add. 207 (2 July 2003).

Committee on the Elimination of Racial Discrimination

United Nations, Committee on the Elimination of Racial Discrimination (2000)
General comment 25: Gender-related dimensions of racial discrimination (20 March 2000).

OTHER UNITED NATIONS DOCUMENTS

United Nations, *Beijing Declaration and Platform for Action,* Fourth World Conference on Women, UN Doc. A/CONF.177/20 (15 September 1995) and A/CONF.177/20/Add.1 (15 September 1995).

United Nations, General Assembly, *Further actions and initiative to implement the Beijing Declaration and Platform for Action,* UN GA, 23rd Special Sess., UN Doc. A/RES/S-23/3 (16 November 2000).

WEBSITES

www.ohchr.org

www.un.org/womenwatch/daw/cedaw

www.gender-budgets.org

www.internationalbudget.org

Convention on the Elimination of All Forms of Discrimination Against Women

The States Parties to the present Convention,

Noting that the Charter of the United Nations reaffirms faith in fundamental human rights, in the dignity and worth of the human person and in the equal rights of men and women,

Noting that the Universal Declaration of Human Rights affirms the principle of the inadmissibility of discrimination and proclaims that all human beings are born free and equal in dignity and rights and that everyone is entitled to all the rights and freedoms set forth therein, without distinction of any kind, including distinction based on sex,

Noting that the States Parties to the International Covenants on Human Rights have the obligation to ensure the equal rights of men and women to enjoy all economic, social, cultural, civil and political rights,

Considering the international conventions concluded under the auspices of the United Nations and the specialized agencies promoting equality of rights of men and women,

Noting also the resolutions, declarations and recommendations adopted by the United Nations and the specialized agencies promoting equality of rights of men and women,

Concerned, however, that despite these various instruments extensive discrimination against women continues to exist,

Recalling that discrimination against women violates the principles of equality of rights and respect for human dignity, is an obstacle to the participation of women, on equal terms with men, in the political, social, economic and cultural life of their countries, hampers the growth of the prosperity of society and the family and makes more difficult the full development of the potentialities of women in the service of their countries and of humanity,

Concerned that in situations of poverty women have the least access to food, health, education, training and opportunities for employment and other needs,

Convinced that the establishment of the new international economic order based on equity and justice will contribute significantly towards the promotion of equality between men and women,

Emphasizing that the eradication of apartheid, all forms of racism, racial discrimination, colonialism, neo-colonialism, aggression, foreign occupation and domination and interference in the internal affairs of States is essential to the full enjoyment of the rights of men and women,

Affirming that the strengthening of international peace and security, the relaxation of international tension, mutual co-operation among all States irrespective of their social and economic systems, general and complete disarmament, in particular nuclear disarmament under strict and effective international control, the affirmation of the principles of justice, equality and mutual benefit in relations among countries and the realization of the right of peoples under alien and colonial domination and foreign occupation to self-determination and independence, as well as respect for national sovereignty and territorial integrity, will promote social progress and development and as a consequence will contribute to the attainment of full equality between men and women,

Convinced that the full and complete development of a country, the welfare of the world and the cause of peace require the maximum participation of women on equal terms with men in all fields,

Bearing in mind the great contribution of women to the welfare of the family and to the development of society, so far not fully recognized, the social significance of maternity and the role of both parents in the family and in the upbringing of children, and aware that the role of women in procreation should not be a basis for discrimination but that the upbringing of children requires a sharing of responsibility between men and women and society as a whole,

Aware that a change in the traditional role of men as well as the role of women in society and in the family is needed to achieve full equality between men and women,

Determined to implement the principles set forth in the Declaration on the Elimination of Discrimination against Women and, for that purpose, to adopt the measures required for the elimination of such discrimination in all its forms and manifestations,

Have agreed on the following:

PART I

Article 1

For the purposes of the present Convention, the term "discrimination against women" shall mean any distinction, exclusion or restriction made on the basis of sex which has the effect or purpose of impairing or nullifying the recognition, enjoyment or exercise by women, irrespective of their marital status, on a basis of equality of men and women, of human rights and fundamental freedoms in the political, economic, social, cultural, civil or any other field.

Article 2

States Parties condemn discrimination against women in all its forms, agree to pursue by all appropriate means and without delay a policy of eliminating discrimination against women and, to this end, undertake:

(a) To embody the principle of the equality of men and women in their national constitutions or other appropriate legislation if not yet incorporated therein and to ensure, through law and other appropriate means, the practical realization of this principle;

(b) To adopt appropriate legislative and other measures, including sanctions where appropriate, prohibiting all discrimination against women;

(c) To establish legal protection of the rights of women on an equal basis with men and to ensure through competent national tribunals and other public institutions the effective protection of women against any act of discrimination;

(d) To refrain from engaging in any act or practice of discrimination against women and to ensure that public authorities and institutions shall act in conformity with this obligation;

(e) To take all appropriate measures to eliminate discrimination against women by any person, organization or enterprise;

(f) To take all appropriate measures, including legislation, to modify or abolish existing laws, regulations, customs and practices which constitute discrimination against women;

(g) To repeal all national penal provisions which constitute discrimination against women.

Article 3

States Parties shall take in all fields, in particular in the political, social, economic and cultural fields, all appropriate measures, including legislation, to ensure the full development and advancement of women, for the purpose of guaranteeing them the exercise and enjoyment of human rights and fundamental freedoms on a basis of equality with men.

Article 4

1. Adoption by States Parties of temporary special measures aimed at accelerating *de facto* equality between men and women shall not be considered discrimination as defined in the present Convention, but shall in no way entail as a consequence the maintenance of unequal or separate standards; these measures shall be discontinued when the objectives of equality of opportunity and treatment have been achieved.

2. Adoption by States Parties of special measures, including those measures contained in the present Convention, aimed at protecting maternity shall not be considered discriminatory.

Article 5

States Parties shall take all appropriate measures:

(a) To modify the social and cultural patterns of conduct of men and women, with a view to achieving the elimination of prejudices and customary and all other practices which are based on the idea of the inferiority or the superiority of either of the sexes or on stereotyped roles for men and women;

(b) To ensure that family education includes a proper understanding of maternity as a social function and the recognition of the common responsibility of men and women in the upbringing and development of their children, it being understood that the interest of the children is the primordial consideration in all cases.

Article 6

States Parties shall take all appropriate measures, including legislation, to suppress all forms of traffic in women and exploitation of prostitution of women.

PART II

Article 7

States Parties shall take all appropriate measures to eliminate discrimination against women in the political and public life of the country and, in particular, shall ensure to women, on equal terms with men, the right:

(a) To vote in all elections and public referenda and to be eligible for election to all publicly elected bodies;

(b) To participate in the formulation of government policy and the implementation thereof and to hold public office and perform all public functions at all levels of government;

(c) To participate in non-governmental organizations and associations concerned with the public and political life of the country.

Article 8

States Parties shall take all appropriate measures to ensure to women, on equal terms with men and without any discrimination, the opportunity to represent their Governments at the international level and to participate in the work of international organizations.

Article 9

1. States Parties shall grant women equal rights with men to acquire, change or retain their nationality. They shall ensure in particular that neither marriage to an alien nor change of nationality by the husband during marriage shall automatically change the nationality of the wife, render her stateless or force upon her the nationality of the husband.

2. States Parties shall grant women equal rights with men with respect to the nationality of their children.

PART III

Article 10

States Parties shall take all appropriate measures to eliminate discrimination against women in order to ensure to them equal rights with men in the field of education and in particular to ensure, on a basis of equality of men and women:

(a) The same conditions for career and vocational guidance, for access to studies and for the achievement of diplomas in educational establishments of all categories in rural as well as in urban areas; this equality shall be ensured in pre-school, general, technical, professional and higher technical education, as well as in all types of vocational training;

(b) Access to the same curricula, the same examinations, teaching staff with qualifications of the same standard and school premises and equipment of the same quality;

(c) The elimination of any stereotyped concept of the roles of men and women at all levels and in all forms of education by encouraging coeducation and other types of education which will help to achieve this aim and, in particular, by the revision of textbooks and school programmes and the adaptation of teaching methods;

(d) The same opportunities to benefit from scholarships and other study grants;

(e) The same opportunities for access to programmes of continuing education, including adult and functional literacy programmes, particularly those aimed at reducing, at the earliest possible time, any gap in education existing between men and women;

(f) The reduction of female student drop-out rates and the organization of programmes for girls and women who have left school prematurely;

(g) The same opportunities to participate actively in sports and physical education;

(h) Access to specific educational information to help to ensure the health and well-being of families, including information and advice on family planning.

Article 11

1. States Parties shall take all appropriate measures to eliminate discrimination against women in the field of employment in order to ensure, on a basis of equality of men and women, the same rights, in particular:

(a) The right to work as an inalienable right of all human beings;

(b) The right to the same employment opportunities, including the application of the same criteria for selection in matters of employment;

(c) The right to free choice of profession and employment, the right to promotion, job security and all benefits and conditions of service and the right to receive vocational training and retraining, including apprenticeships, advanced vocational training and recurrent training;

(d) The right to equal remuneration, including benefits, and to equal treatment in respect of work of equal value, as well as equality of treatment in the evaluation of the quality of work;

(e) The right to social security, particularly in cases of retirement, unemployment, sickness, invalidity and old age and other incapacity to work, as well as the right to paid leave;

(f) The right to protection of health and to safety in working conditions, including the safeguarding of the function of reproduction.

2. In order to prevent discrimination against women on the grounds of marriage or maternity and to ensure their effective right to work, States Parties shall take appropriate measures:

(a) To prohibit, subject to the imposition of sanctions, dismissal on the grounds of pregnancy or of maternity leave and discrimination in dismissals on the basis of marital status;

(b) To introduce maternity leave with pay or with comparable social benefits without loss of former employment, seniority or social allowances;

(c) To encourage the provision of the necessary supporting social services to enable parents to combine family obligations with work responsibilities and participation in public life, in particular through promoting the establishment and development of a network of child-care facilities;

(d) To provide special protection to women during pregnancy in types of work proved to be harmful to them.

3. Protective legislation relating to matters covered in this article shall be reviewed periodically in the light of scientific and technological knowledge and shall be revised, repealed or extended as necessary.

Article 12

1. States Parties shall take all appropriate measures to eliminate discrimination against women in the field of health care in order to ensure, on a basis of equality of men and women, access to health care services, including those related to family planning.

2. Notwithstanding the provisions of paragraph I of this article, States Parties shall ensure to women appropriate services in connection with pregnancy, confinement and the post-natal period, granting free services where necessary, as well as adequate nutrition during pregnancy and lactation.

Article 13

States Parties shall take all appropriate measures to eliminate discrimination against women in other areas of economic and social life in order to ensure, on a basis of equality of men and women, the same rights, in particular:

(a) The right to family benefits;

(b) The right to bank loans, mortgages and other forms of financial credit;

(c) The right to participate in recreational activities, sports and all aspects of cultural life.

Article 14

1. States Parties shall take into account the particular problems faced by rural women and the significant roles which rural women play in the economic survival of their families, including their work in the non-monetized sectors of the economy, and shall take all appropriate measures to ensure the application of the provisions of the present Convention to women in rural areas.

2. States Parties shall take all appropriate measures to eliminate discrimination against women in rural areas in order to ensure, on a basis of equality of men and women, that they participate in and benefit from rural development and, in particular, shall ensure to such women the right:

(a) To participate in the elaboration and implementation of development planning at all levels;

(b) To have access to adequate health care facilities, including information, counseling and services in family planning;

(c) To benefit directly from social security programmes;

(d) To obtain all types of training and education, formal and non-formal, including that relating to functional literacy, as well as, *inter alia*, the benefit of all community and extension services, in order to increase their technical proficiency;

(e) To organize self-help groups and co-operatives in order to obtain equal access to economic opportunities through employment or self employment;

(f) To participate in all community activities;

(g) To have access to agricultural credit and loans, marketing facilities, appropriate technology and equal treatment in land and agrarian reform as well as in land resettlement schemes;

(h) To enjoy adequate living conditions, particularly in relation to housing, sanitation, electricity and water supply, transport and communications.

PART IV

Article 15

1. States Parties shall accord to women equality with men before the law.

2. States Parties shall accord to women, in civil matters, a legal capacity identical to that of men and the same opportunities to exercise that capacity. In particular, they shall give women equal rights to conclude contracts and to administer property and shall treat them equally in all stages of procedure in courts and tribunals.

3. States Parties agree that all contracts and all other private instruments of any kind with a legal effect which is directed at restricting the legal capacity of women shall be deemed null and void.

4. States Parties shall accord to men and women the same rights with regard to the law relating to the movement of persons and the freedom to choose their residence and domicile.

Article 16

1. States Parties shall take all appropriate measures to eliminate discrimination against women in all matters relating to marriage and family relations and in particular shall ensure, on a basis of equality of men and women:
(a) The same right to enter into marriage;

(b) The same right freely to choose a spouse and to enter into marriage only with their free and full consent;

(c) The same rights and responsibilities during marriage and at its dissolution;

(d) The same rights and responsibilities as parents, irrespective of their marital status, in matters relating to their children; in all cases the interests of the children shall be paramount;

(e) The same rights to decide freely and responsibly on the number and spacing of their children and to have access to the information, education and means to enable them to exercise these rights;

(f) The same rights and responsibilities with regard to guardianship, wardship, trusteeship and adoption of children, or similar institutions where these concepts exist in national legislation; in all cases the interests of the children shall be paramount;

(g) The same personal rights as husband and wife, including the right to choose a family name, a profession and an occupation;

(h) The same rights for both spouses in respect of the ownership, acquisition, management, administration, enjoyment and disposition of property, whether free of charge or for a valuable consideration.
2. The betrothal and the marriage of a child shall have no legal effect, and all necessary action, including legislation, shall be taken to specify a minimum age for marriage and to make the registration of marriages in an official registry compulsory.

PART V

Article 17

1. For the purpose of considering the progress made in the implementation of the present Convention, there shall be established a Committee on the Elimination of Discrimination against Women (hereinafter referred to as the Committee) consisting, at the time of entry into force of the Convention, of eighteen and, after ratification of or accession to the Convention by the thirty-fifth State Party, of twenty-three experts of high moral standing and competence in the field covered by the Convention. The experts shall be elected by States Parties from among their nationals and shall serve in their personal capacity, consideration being given to equitable geographical distribution and to the representation of the different forms of civilization as well as the principal legal systems.

2. The members of the Committee shall be elected by secret ballot from a list of persons nominated by States Parties. Each State Party may nominate one person from among its own nationals.

3. The initial election shall be held six months after the date of the entry into force of the present Convention. At least three months before the date of each election the Secretary-General of the United Nations shall address a letter to the States Parties inviting them to submit their nominations within two months. The Secretary-General shall prepare a

list in alphabetical order of all persons thus nominated, indicating the States Parties which have nominated them, and shall submit it to the States Parties.

4. Elections of the members of the Committee shall be held at a meeting of States Parties convened by the Secretary-General at United Nations Headquarters. At that meeting, for which two thirds of the States Parties shall constitute a quorum, the persons elected to the Committee shall be those nominees who obtain the largest number of votes and an absolute majority of the votes of the representatives of States Parties present and voting.

5. The members of the Committee shall be elected for a term of four years. However, the terms of nine of the members elected at the first election shall expire at the end of two years; immediately after the first election the names of these nine members shall be chosen by lot by the Chairman of the Committee.

6. The election of the five additional members of the Committee shall be held in accordance with the provisions of paragraphs 2, 3 and 4 of this article, following the thirty-fifth ratification or accession. The terms of two of the additional members elected on this occasion shall expire at the end of two years, the names of these two members having been chosen by lot by the Chairman of the Committee.

7. For the filling of casual vacancies, the State Party whose expert has ceased to function as a member of the Committee shall appoint another expert from among its nationals, subject to the approval of the Committee.

8. The members of the Committee shall, with the approval of the General Assembly, receive emoluments from United Nations resources on such terms and conditions as the Assembly may decide, having regard to the importance of the Committee's responsibilities.

9. The Secretary-General of the United Nations shall provide the necessary staff and facilities for the effective performance of the functions of the Committee under the present Convention.

Article 18
1. States Parties undertake to submit to the Secretary-General of the United Nations, for consideration by the Committee, a report on the legislative, judicial, administrative or other measures which they have adopted to give effect to the provisions of the present Convention and on the progress made in this respect:
(a) Within one year after the entry into force for the State concerned;

(b) Thereafter at least every four years and further whenever the Committee so requests.
2. Reports may indicate factors and difficulties affecting the degree of fulfilment of obligations under the present Convention.

Article 19
1. The Committee shall adopt its own rules of procedure.

2. The Committee shall elect its officers for a term of two years.

Article 20
1. The Committee shall normally meet for a period of not more than two weeks annually in order to consider the reports submitted in accordance with article 18 of the present Convention.

2. The meetings of the Committee shall normally be held at United Nations Headquarters or at any other convenient place as determined by the Committee.

Article 21
1. The Committee shall, through the Economic and Social Council, report annually to the General Assembly of the United Nations on its activities and may make suggestions and general recommendations based on the examination of reports and information received from the States Parties. Such suggestions and general recommendations shall be included in the report of the Committee together with comments, if any, from States Parties.

2. The Secretary-General of the United Nations shall transmit the reports of the Committee to the Commission on the Status of Women for its information.

Article 22
The specialized agencies shall be entitled to be represented at the consideration of the implementation of such provisions of the present Convention as fall within the scope of their activities. The Committee may invite the specialized agencies to submit reports on the implementation of the Convention in areas falling within the scope of their activities.

PART VI

Article 23

Nothing in the present Convention shall affect any provisions that are more conducive to the achievement of equality between men and women which may be contained:

(a) In the legislation of a State Party; or

(b) In any other international convention, treaty or agreement in force for that State.

Article 24

States Parties undertake to adopt all necessary measures at the national level aimed at achieving the full realization of the rights recognized in the present Convention.

Article 25

1. The present Convention shall be open for signature by all States.

2. The Secretary-General of the United Nations is designated as the depositary of the present Convention.

3. The present Convention is subject to ratification. Instruments of ratification shall be deposited with the Secretary-General of the United Nations.

4. The present Convention shall be open to accession by all States. Accession shall be effected by the deposit of an instrument of accession with the Secretary-General of the United Nations.

Article 26

1. A request for the revision of the present Convention may be made at any time by any State Party by means of a notification in writing addressed to the Secretary-General of the United Nations.

2. The General Assembly of the United Nations shall decide upon the steps, if any, to be taken in respect of such a request.

Article 27

1. The present Convention shall enter into force on the thirtieth day after the date of deposit with the Secretary-General of the United Nations of the twentieth instrument of ratification or accession.

2. For each State ratifying the present Convention or acceding to it after the deposit of the twentieth instrument of ratification or accession, the Convention shall enter into force on the thirtieth day after the date of the deposit of its own instrument of ratification or accession.

Article 28

1. The Secretary-General of the United Nations shall receive and circulate to all States the text of reservations made by States at the time of ratification or accession.

2. A reservation incompatible with the object and purpose of the present Convention shall not be permitted.

3. Reservations may be withdrawn at any time by notification to this effect addressed to the Secretary-General of the United Nations, who shall then inform all States thereof. Such notification shall take effect on the date on which it is received.

Article 29

1. Any dispute between two or more States Parties concerning the interpretation or application of the present Convention which is not settled by negotiation shall, at the request of one of them, be submitted to arbitration. If within six months from the date of the request for arbitration the parties are unable to agree on the organization of the arbitration, any one of those parties may refer the dispute to the International Court of Justice by request in conformity with the Statute of the Court.

2. Each State Party may at the time of signature or ratification of the present Convention or accession thereto declare that it does not consider itself bound by paragraph I of this article. The other States Parties shall not be bound by that paragraph with respect to any State Party which has made such a reservation.

3. Any State Party which has made a reservation in accordance with paragraph 2 of this article may at any time withdraw that reservation by notification to the Secretary-General of the United Nations.

Article 30

The present Convention, the Arabic, Chinese, English, French, Russian and Spanish texts of which are equally authentic, shall be deposited with the Secretary-General of the United Nations.

IN WITNESS WHEREOF the undersigned, duly authorized, have signed the present Convention.

Some tools for a gender-sensitive analysis of budgets

A variety of different 'tools' can be utilized for a gender-sensitive analysis of budgets. This list identifies some tools that have been widely used in gender analysis of budgets. It is neither prescriptive, nor exhaustive. The tools to be used must be chosen in the light of specific circumstances and be adapted to meet the requirements of those circumstances. New tools are continually being developed by GBIs, and updates can be found on www.gender-budgets.org

1 Gender-aware policy appraisal

This is an analytical approach which involves scrutinizing the policies of different portfolios and programmes by paying attention to the implicit and explicit gender issues involved. It questions the assumption that policies are 'gender-neutral' in their effects and asks instead: In what ways are the policies and their associated resource allocations likely to reduce or increase gender inequalities?

2 Gender-disaggregated beneficiary assessments

This research technique is used to ask actual or potential beneficiaries the extent to which government policies and programmes match these people's priorities.

3 Gender-disaggregated public expenditure incidence analysis

This research technique compares public expenditure for a given programme, usually with data from household surveys, to reveal the distribution of expenditure between women and men, girls and boys.

4 Gender-disaggregated tax incidence analysis

This research technique examines both direct and indirect taxes in order to calculate how much taxation is paid by different individuals or households.

5 Gender-disaggregated analysis of the impact of the budget on time use

This looks at the relationship between the national budget and the way time is used in households. This ensures that the time spent by women in unpaid work is accounted for in policy analysis.

6 Gender-aware medium-term economic policy framework

This attempts to incorporate gender into the economic models on which medium-term economic frameworks are based.

7 Gender-aware budget statement

This involves an accountability process which may utilize any of the above tools. It requires a high degree of commitment and coordination throughout the public sector as ministries or departments undertake an assessment of the gender impact of their line budgets.

Source: Adapted from Diane Elson (1997b), 'Tools for gender integration into macroeconomic policy', *Link in to Gender and Development*, 2, Summer, p. 13.